Politics, Power and Policy
The Governing of Local School Districts

LAURENCE IANNACCONE

Ontario Institute for Studies
in Education

FRANK W. LUTZ

Pennsylvania State University

CHARLES E. MERRILL PUBLISHING COMPANY
Columbus, Ohio
A Bell & Howell Company

MERRILL'S SERIES FOR
EDUCATIONAL ADMINISTRATION
Under the Editorship of
DR. LUVERN L. CUNNINGHAM, Dean
College of Education   The Ohio State University

DR. H. THOMAS JAMES, Dean
School of Education   Stanford University

Standard Book Number: 675-09386-4

Library of Congress Catalog Card Number: 70-101582

1 2 3 4 5 6 7 8 9 10–75 74 73 72 71 70 69

PRINTED IN THE UNITED STATES OF AMERICA

With gratitude for their enduring support and patient understanding, this book is dedicated to our wives,

Faye and Susan.

Foreword

There has been a temptation throughout the American educational experience to deny that anything labeled "politics" is involved in educational decision-making. Part of the denial has been a tendency to ignore or deliberately to suppress the realities. How can one study a political phenomenon which is not intended to exist? Schools, as the key to the nation's as well as to children's futures, were written into the political lexicon under the terms "bipartisan" and "impartial" and "apolitical." If the terms were wrong, aberration and deliberate calculation made it so.

Attitudes do change. Enough concrete research has now been done to confer legitimacy on the old reality. The educational structure at every level—local, state and federal—is regarded as a fundamental part of the American political system. From the city school board to the congressional committee, education is politics. The relationship between those who teach, when they teach, and politics is recognized as probably the single most important question in determining the course, present and future, of American education.

The change has come about for several reasons. First, as local property taxes and state levies have proved distressingly inadequate to support the mounting costs of educational systems, the educational establishment has entered wholeheartedly into the competition for increased state and federal funds. To do so, local school decision-making has become intricately involved with federal decision-making and with national political pressures. Those comfortable days, still sought after, are gone. Then local school decisions were made quietly, the yells and howls, pressures and conflicts were set aside as sort of a private preserve open only to the insiders, namely the members of the board, and perhaps a few administrators. This too was political, but it wasn't talked about, seldom if ever admitted, and certainly not studied. But today, education has become at least somewhat more easily seen as a national *political* phenomenon. As almost every school district in the nation copes in its own fashion with centrally shaped programs and guidelines, researchers are more and more able to find among them common patterns of action and reaction within the local political-educational framework.

The second major change as well as a reason for the increasing number of scholars seriously concerned with the politics of education, is that education is more and more a *crucial* political issue. Since 1954 school desegregation for example has been a major source of political conflict. The implications of integration here have undergone a vast expansion and represent now a general, rather than a narrow, single-issue oriented political conflict. It has become one of the central testing grounds of the present American political scene.

Schools figure in almost every aspect of today's urban-racial crisis. Inadequate schools in big city slums have come to be regarded as the breeding grounds of frustration, unemployment, and violence—as a key to what is popularly regarded as the "poverty cycle." At the same time, rising community and racial consciousness in inner city areas has transmitted such formerly local issues as school board representation, student discipline, and parental responsibility into wholesale political crisis. Concepts such as "Community Control" and "the neighborhood school," are rallying cries all across the country, a convenient short hand for a revolution in local decision-making and political participation of service recipients in every area of social service. The Ocean Hill-Brownsville crisis of Fall 1968 which shook New York City *and* state politics is only one example of an increasingly common phenomenon.

Beyond the inner city, local school boards have problems of their own. Under heavy pressure to conform to high uniform standards of academic achievement, they must at the same time cope with equally serious pressures to avoid uniformity and tailor each program to the specifically designed needs of the individual. Both goals take more funds than most school districts have available. Each is the motivating cause of some strong lobby group. School boards, like most of our institutions, are being forced to pick a middle way which often suits no one. The finding of that way is unquestionably a political problem.

The clients of local educational decision-making structures—parents, students, and community—are not the only ones who are bringing school issues into the urban political framework. The educational structure itself is becoming increasingly politicized. Teachers are no longer restricted from exercising the traditional weapons of organized labor. They are definitely becoming an important factor in the politics of local school board decision-making. In the past six years, the American Federation of Teachers has become the sole collective bargaining agent with school boards in New York, Detroit, Boston, Chicago, Cleveland, and Philadelphia.

The National Education Association, to counter Union inroads into its membership has radically reformed its internal structures and urged its teachers to include demands for professional negotiation—NEA's substitute phase for collective bargaining. This development has stripped any notion that teachers are "not involved in politics."

In summary, all of these factors have made us aware of the increasingly political nature of the educational structure.

The contemporary school system, despite its unique openness, despite its enormous need for public support, despite its alleged passion for the truth and presentation of the facts, despite its increasing demands for scarce resources, is still a peculiarly elusive subject matter. In the age of *opinion* polls, biographies, digests, investigations, and reports, few analyses have come to grips with public school problems. There are virtually no biographies of outstanding school administrators. State and Federal legislative inquiries and investigations were virtually non-existent until the Brown decision calling for desegregation in the public schools prompted demands for information about compliance and non-compliance. The pioneering works of a "self-appointed critic" James Bryant Conant, stand out not only for what he reported, but for the fact that he reported anything at all. That in itself *attracted national attention among scholars.*

Why has this been so? Why do we know so little about a system this vital to our well-being—and one which consumes financial resources at paces rivaled only by the Defense Department. Thomas H. Eliot, the first political scientist to question our lack of understanding, explains it this way, "Perhaps political scientists, like educators, have been lulled by the myth that public education is a 'non-political' subject by which educators mean, I think, that education *should not be* (whether it is or not) a partisan issue or an area of political patronage."

Yet I believe we delude ourselves to think that educators themselves were lulled by this myth. The people involved in public education, at least those at the very top, were too busy playing politics to study it objectively. More than one observer has noted how colleges of education emerged and flourished through the use of state requirements for teachers, requirements that had the force of law. When one is using political power to maintain a "non-political" structure, hopefully immune from outside interference, it would be folly to launch simultaneously full-fledged political inquiries.

Moreover, in the thirties, when a professor at Columbia Teachers College, took a close look at the social composition of school boards and discovered that self-interest played a part in school decisions, he was quickly denounced as a left-wing communist or worse. Only an alien ideology could motivate one to touch a sacred cow. Unquestionably, the experience of this professor affected the direction of school inquiries for a number of years.

But this has all changed. A few generations from now, hardly anyone will remember exactly what the old myths were about, or even why they were so jealously guarded. That particular battle for understanding has been won; it was won not only by men like Conant and Eliot, but by the press, and as a result of the ever increasing concern of the public itself with the quality of education and how decisions were made to determine that quality.

Today another battle, equally important, is in progress, the battle for a higher quality of understanding. There are those who still resist inquiry, perhaps out of fear or even a desire to conceal. Others, while agreeing that education and politics are intertwined, think that too much study is not altogether healthy and believe that we should leave "well enough alone." Fortunately—for all of us Frank Lutz and Laurence Iannaccone have not listened to those who leave "well enough alone." Whatever the series of events that combined or conspired to focus the attention of these two well-known scholars on this vast and intriguing subject, we all should be grateful that they embarked on this effort. For they have attempted—and I think succeeded—in developing an explanation of district school politics at a time when district school decisions are still the basic ones in our public education system. This study, which to be sure builds on earlier ones, comes to grips with what hitherto were subjects only for speculation and unsupported generalization.

Nicholas Masters

Professor of Political Science
Southern Illinois University of Edwardsville

Preface

Politics, Power, and Policy has a central theme. It is chiefly concerned with a particular sort of historical period in local school districts: that period through which a district moves when the heightened political nature of educational affairs leads to a sequence of (1) division at the polls over school board elections; (2) the defeat of incumbent school board members and their replacement by new men; (3) the developing conflict between new and old educational values; (4) the firing, euphemistically in the jargon, the involuntary turnover, of those superintendents too set in their ways to change or too slow to see the need for change and (5) their replacement by an outside successor superintendent, an alien to the old school district, who will implement the policies of the new power structure. This is the most common sequence through which communities move as educational policy changes.

The story told by this book and the aspects of governing local school districts that are explored are not exhaustive. There are longer, quieter periods of political maintenance in the history of every school district. We do not particularly address ourselves to these. They are the ground on which our figure is drawn; they precede and succeed the conflict periods about which we write. Some aspects of school governance are ignored. They have deliberately been subordinated or sacrificed to the central thrust of the book, the mobilization of power through political action to change educational policy, which has been the key to the governing of local school districts in our era more than any other since before World War I.

Politics, Power, and Policy could not have been written ten years ago, let alone twenty or more. There was too little recognition of the politics of education and too much complacency about school governance in the midst of controversy over school curricula. Recently the arena of conflict has begun to change and, we predict, battles will be increasingly fought for control of the school board as the policy center of the local school district's government. This is a costly and drawn out process.

We focus on it because it is what our research extending over more than half a decade showed us. But we focus on it hoping that a better understanding of the dynamics of policy change by those actively concerned with governing school districts whether in the roles of professional educators, board members, or active citizens will make the future process of educational policy change quicker and less costly to the human beings involved.

This book is written for four groups of readers: (1) students and professors interested in the political relations between school and society, especially those in schools of education which have turned away from courses in the manipulation of communities through public relations and have adopted instead a public policy-making orientation; (2) practicing school administrators and other professionals in education; (3) school board members; (4) the citizen who, with or without children in the schools and whether or not he pays the taxes to support schools, wishes to influence the decisions of his school board.

Politics, Power, and Policy begins with a three chapter examination of political theory about local school districts and the peculiar metamorphosis by which the nineteenth century rural school district became the suburban school district of today dominating our concept of educational good government. Chapters four, five, and six are primarily empirical in orientation. They pay detailed attention to the story of Robertsdale, a district undergoing abrupt political shifts in power and educational policy.

Hypotheses about the process are introduced along with the Robertsdale story. The last chapters turn more to analysis as the Robertsdale story is extended and generalized through the development of theory and the reports of additional verificational studies of educational policy. Finally, while there are few heroes and fewer villians in our story, there are some victims of the process not the least of whom are the hundreds of school superintendents quietly and honorably discharged because they moved too slowly or not at all.

Introduction

This book is partly the product of our teaching graduate courses in education concerned with school community relations and local school district politics. Consequently, it is designed to fit the needs we have uncovered after approximately a decade of teaching. *Politics, Power, and Policy* is also partly the product of research conducted by both the authors during that time. It therefore reflects our research and teaching experiences from both coasts and mid-western U.S.A.

The book is not concerned with traditional school community relations which is an area for school administrator manipulation or technical expertness. It is, instead, addressed to the modern view in educational administration and social foundations, and it seeks to understand the causes, processes, and difficulties in local school district politics which need to be taken into account by school people and concerned laymen if they are to influence future developments in the governing of local school districts. Specifically, it explores in depth those crucial periods in a school district's development when major policy changes take place.

Politics, Power, and Policy consists of three parts. The first three chapters are concerned with the belief systems of Americans and the context within which the governing of local school districts really operates. Chapter 1 is primarily addressed to the contrast between what we believe about educational politics and the way they actually operate. Chaptel 2 describes the most salient patterns of local school district power structures using the sacred-secular community typology as its chief conceptual tool of discussion. Chapter 3 examines briefly the historical genesis of present local school district politics.

The second part beginning with Chapter 4 explores in detail one case of a school district undergoing the tense experiences of the eclipse of an established power system and the beginning of a new one. The details of conflicts on the board and of changes in policies and personnel are similarly explored especially in Chapters 5 and 6. A dozen hypotheses concerning these changes are first presented in Chapter 4 and then woven through this section.

A single case, the Robertsdale School District, is used to provide depth in reality and detail. The richness of detail around school board meetings in Chapters 5 and 6 illustrates, perhaps too vividly, the tedium of boardsmanship. However, we have found the detailed diary of Prentice, the new board member in Robertsdale, invaluable to our students as they wrestle with the problems of developing their own explanitory statements, theory, if you will, of school board operations.

Robertsdale is, however, a fictitious name as, indeed, are all the other names in the case. Footnote references in these chapters to the board minutes for example are accurate but cannot be found because all names and other traces which would identify the people involved have been changed or illiminated. This was done to provide faithfulness of record for the reader, student, instructor or others; without the possibility of embarrassment for the individuals involved.

The third part is primarily concerned with the school district's local government after the conflict, incumbent defeat, and the change of power. Verification studies which extend and allow us to generalize the lessons of the Robertsdale story, while introduced in the second part of the book, are central to the last two chapters of *Politics, Power, and Policy.* These studies and the last chapter link our knowledge of the adaption of educational innovations to our new understanding of the governing of local school districts especially at those periods when their politics, power elements, and policies undergo rapid change.

It is, perhaps, unnecessary but a pleasant task to point out that for much of our thought we are deeply indebted to others. Our students who over the years have in various ways analysed the Robertsdale story have helped us see it more clearly. Some of these undertook research tasks testing generalizations emerging from these analyses. To all of these persons we are grateful.

Table of Contents

Politics, Power, and Policy
The Governing of Local School Districts

1

Myth and Reality

There is a myth in America that education and politics exist separate from each other. If the world of politics means something more than the choice between political parties and if public education includes policy making and school administration, then the myth hardly describes reality in American local school districts. It describes reality at state and federal levels even less adequately. The myth is a political one which functions as an element in the politics of education, especially as a tool useful to educationists. This may be one reason it has persisted so long. However, the myth of the separateness of politics and education is also supported by the shadow of a reality. Because the politics of education is unique, different from the customary Anglo-American two-party politics of democracy and divorced from the multifactional (usually called non-partisan) politics of local government, the myth gains a semblance of fact. Despite this appearance and the American habit of restricting the word "politics" to its two-party connotations, the politics of local school district elections lies at the heart of policy making in public education at the local level.

1

A School District Votes[1]

It was school board election day, just after eight thirty in the evening on the second Tuesday of May. The telephone was ringing in the board room of the Suburbantown School District Education Center where the five members of the local school board, the district superintendent of schools, a handful of school employees, and a dozen or so friends and other interested persons had gathered to await news of the fate of Mrs. Adams and Mr. Benson, incumbent board members seeking reelection. The polls had been closed for more than an hour and a half, but as yet there had been no report from any of the precincts. The first report, however, had not been expected any earlier as the voter turnout had been heavy, and final results were not expected for two or three hours.

Miss Ross, the superintendent's secretary answered the first of many telephone calls from the schools which had been designated as polling places. As she took the calls, she recorded figures on a ruled sheet of paper. Mr. Steel, the superintendent, and Mr. Benson watched over her shoulder. This year they were prepared to keep abreast of the reports from the polls. Last year's school board election had been for only one board position, but the turnout had been heavier than expected. It had been difficult to keep an accurate running record of the votes for the incumbent, Mr. Carter. He had barely won over six opponents. This year the election involved two board positions. The first telephone report accounted for only a few votes at the one precinct; it indicated that Mrs. Adams and Mr. Benson were running third and fourth respectively in a field of four candidates.

Leaving the telephone, Miss Ross announced the early tally together with the report from the precinct that the voting had been particularly heavy just before the seven o'clock closing time. All the voters who were in line to vote when the polls closed had not been able to get to a voting booth until seven thirty. The ballots had now been unfolded, and the counting was under way. A quick succession of calls from other precincts reinforced the report from the first.

At all school board elections before the one last year, the news of the victory of the incumbent candidates had been received by this hour. But this news had not really been necessary. It was a foregone conclusion that the incumbent would win. These last two elections had been very different. They were like no previous school

---

[1] The following incident was adapted from Richard S. Kirkendall, "Discriminating Social, Economic and Political Characteristics of Changing versus Stable Policy-Making Systems in School Districts" (Unpublished Ph.D. dissertation, Claremont Graduate School, Claremont, California, 1966).

board elections in the district. Ordinarily incumbent candidates ran unopposed, and the resulting voter turnout was usually very light. When an opponent to the incumbent entered the race, he received only a token number of votes.

Just as the events of election day had been different these last two years, so had the campaigns which had preceded them. Two years ago each candidate's campaign, if it could even be called that, had usually amounted to an announcement of candidacy accompanied by a picture in the local newspaper. Opponents, when they existed, were usually not critical of the incumbents.

Last year, however, four of the six candidates running against incumbent Mr. Carter were very critical of the existing school board, the superintendent, and their policies. The criticisms were not too specific, although two of the candidates did single out individual schools in their criticisms. The viewpoints of all seven candidates received extensive coverage in the local newspaper. Four of the seven, including Mr. Carter, devoted much time to speaking at PTA meetings and appearing at coffee klatches held on their behalf. Although the opposition to the incumbent candidate was strong, it seemed to be diffuse and without organization.

This year the field of candidates was more limited and the battle lines were discretely drawn. The two opponents, Mr. Peters and Mr. Quarrel, campaigned together as did the two incumbents, Mrs. Adams and Mr. Benson. Mr. Peters and Mr. Quarrel's criticisms of the existing board and superintendent were more specific, direct, and consistent than they had been the year before. Mrs. Adams and Mr. Benson's defense of the board and its record was equally direct and consistent. All of the campaign techniques which had been used the year before were used again this year but even more extensively and by both sides. To these techniques were added campaign handbills, signs, and automobile bumper stickers. Most people in the community belonged to one of the two camps.

Anxieties continued to run high in the board room of the district office as final voting reports came from the individual precincts. When all reports were in, Mr. Peters and Mr. Quarrel had unseated Mrs. Adams and Mr. Benson on the board of education.

The superintendent now found himself in the position of working with a board of education whose membership had changed and now represented educational goals and purposes which were not previously represented and which he did not share. Mr. Steel had been very closely identified with the old board and with the educational values and purposes which it represented. Were the superintendent and his policies as much on trial at this election as were the incumbent school board members and their policies? Was the rejection by the voters of Mrs. Adams and Mr. Benson also a rejection of Mr. Steel?

Although the superintendency is not an office directly subject to the ballot box, in a very real sense Mr. Steel's own tenure had been affected. A majority of the board members' beliefs were in harmony with his own, but the division promised a much more difficult road for the future than had been the case in the past. The kinds of information and the types of alternative proposals that would be acceptable to the new board would now be different. The official record of future board actions would probably indicate unanimity of purpose, but conflicts would occur in the board deliberations. If the board's actions were inconsistent with the values held by a majority of the community, the next school board election could very well mean that the new value orientation would gain a majority representation on the board.

What took place in this election did not happen by chance. It was evidence of a change in community values and interests as they relate to education. It was the product of conflict between the old and new values, and it was precipitated by competition between people representing both limits of these values. Such conflict and competition would probably not end with the victory of the two new board members.

For a long time this community like many others had proceeded without change in its formal educational power structure. Incumbent school board members ran, were reelected, or if they chose not to run, others who supported the same value system ran and were elected without competition. Obvious indications of the emergence of a new set of educational goals, different from those of the past, had occurred only recently. The resulting change in the formal power structure (the school board) had been abrupt. It seems logical that the changes in the community which preceded and which precipitated such a change in the power structure of the community would give some evidence of their existence prior to the actual change in board membership.

LOCAL SCHOOL DISTRICT POLITICS

Two Party Pattern

Much of the political life of the United States, particularly in larger governmental units, converges and finds its focus in the political party system. The two-party system specifically involves combinations of interests expressed by groups linked together within party organizations. The existence of coalitions of interest groups within a political party requires a series of compromises in which divergent and sometimes conflicting interests are brought together in order to produce a victory at the polls. Through elections these coalitions seek to capture the offices of government and the right to make authoritative decisions. Each party in the two-party system is the result of compromise among component interests, and each coalition tends to differ only slightly from the other as it searches for a larger percentage of voter support. The more skillfully the parties devise such coalitions, the closer each party approaches the opposition and the smaller the difference between them. In this typical process of the two-party system, interest groups are forced, even if only temporarily, to modify and limit their agendas within the party organization. The political party, especially on the eve of elections, acts as a mediating agency among its component interests, including the political professional's interest in acquiring the office *per se.* Thus, a partial consensus among interests is produced.

In this process issues are discussed, positions taken and modified, concerns expressed, ideas advanced and withdrawn. Strengths and weaknesses are displayed and revealed, bargains are struck, and programs emerge. Not only do conflicts of interest become resolved, sometimes for long periods, but ideas are also tested in the process. According to the late Ernest Barker, it is the open discussion of ideas and the evolution of programs from such discussion more than the existence of universal adult voting rights which characterizes the strength of Anglo-American democracy and which is central to the meaning of liberty.[2] With all its weaknesses, party politics in the United States is still a politics of discussion.

The political life in local units of government, which comprise the vast majority of suburban and rural school districts as well as some urban units, is usually quite different. Here the number of different organized interests that need to be brought together in order to win local elections are fewer. Consequently, fewer compromises are needed to develop a position that will appeal to enough voters to secure election.[3] The differences among local interests whether great or small are seldom compromised before the election and are carried into the offices of local government. Differences over local educational policy

---

[2] Ernest Barker, *Reflections on Government* (New York: Oxford University Press, 1958), *passim,* but especially pp. 30-72.

[3] The large urban unit is often an exception to this rule, as is seen on pp. 49-51.

are often presented at school board meetings by spokesmen of community groups or by board members. Particularly at the local school
district level, the politics of education tends not to be the politics of
the two-party system. The party does not exist as a means for mediating differences among interest groups. Without the political party
mechanism to absorb the multiple aspects of conflicting interests, the
multifactional politics of education must achieve its consensus through
informal community structures, the superintendent's office, or direct
confrontation at the central agency of school district government,
the school board meeting.

The politics of education in some localities and states, however, *is*
imbedded in the politics of party. This situation can be seen in some
larger cities and particularly in states undergoing political realignment such as Michigan in the 1950's and California in the 1960's.
Here, educational issues have played a significant part in the public's
concern for the offices of government. Educational issues are significantly included in the public positions taken by the speaker in
the lower house, the governor, and the majority leader in the state's
upper house. Until the last moments of the 1969 legislative session,
New York state's central offices of government and legislative leaders
found themselves beset by problems of educational legislation with
serious implications for the two parties. It is probable that the role of
the political party in the politics of education will grow larger as
educational issues gain in public importance, especially at the federal
level. The prevailing pattern at the local district level, however, is
likely to continue to be more typically that of the politics of interest
groups.

A Recurring Dilemma

The politics of interest groups lacking the mediation of the political parties is faced with a recurring dilemma. Interest groups in the
local district must either achieve some consensus based upon educational issues and policies prior to board meetings or risk continuous
conflict and stalemate at meetings. In the absence of the party system,
school superintendents and their staffs have developed social mechanisms to avoid continuous stalemate by achieving a measure of consensus among conflicting groups prior to official board action. These
mechanisms range from nominating caucuses for board office (sometimes influenced by the superintendent) to a wide variety of citizen
advisory groups. The webwork of citizen groups working with school

personnel may extend from *ad hoc* committees created to advise on specific policies, such as school building needs, to permanent organizational units like the Parent Teachers' Association. However permanent or transitory, whether operating centrally or peripherally to board activities, these groups are characterized by a common element. They confer a special advantage upon the insiders, the professionals of a district who are usually school administrators. Characteristically, suburban and small school districts display a network of citizen groups surrounding many, perhaps most, of the school's activities. School administrators and teachers (often selected by the administration), working in cooperation with citizen groups, provide one kind of machinery for building partial consensus around specific educational policy issues. Thus, they fill part of the vacuum produced by the absence of the two-party system in the local school district. This social structure also constitutes a local establishment in education, usually a professionally led influence structure in the school district.

A second alternative to the two-party system may be found in rural districts or in districts with high social stability where there is little social and geographic mobility. This alternative pattern for achieving partial consensus on educational issues prior to board action is older, historically preceding the professional influence structure cited above. In small-town America of the nineteenth and early twentieth centuries, an extralegal power pyramid most often stood behind the school board. Such informal social structures influenced much of town and village life, including the schools. An informal social structure reflecting the socioeconomic class structure of relatively homogeneous and stable communities often developed a consensus on educational policy issues prior to school board meetings. In these local districts, the school board tended to reflect the community power structure, the classical monolithic power pyramid of many small communities. The vacuum left by the absence of the two-party system in this case is filled by the informal community traditions.

Special Constitutional Arrangements

The traditional community power pyramid has been discussed too much and blamed too often by educationists for the weaknesses in American schools. Conversely, too little attention and too much credit for the good things in American schools has been attributed to the typical social structure developed by the local educational establishment. Neither alternative is all bad or all good. However, each of these systems depends, for its existence, on the special constitutional arrangements for governing education through local school districts. Both "establishments" tend to give insiders special advantages. Both have the effect of reducing public conflict over education and open discussion and consideration of alternative educational policies and programs. Both of them also require political upsets and power structure reorganizations in order for the school district to redirect its educational policies.

Constitutional arrangements exist in most states for local school districts and their goverance. These provisions may be found in legal statute and often in the written constitutions of the states. When arrangements governing education are imbedded in written state constitutions, they are most difficult to change. The existence of special governmental provisions for the public function of education strangely affects the politics of education, especially at the local district level. One effect is to increase the extent to which the governing of education appears to be unique among the public functions of American governments. It is but a single step from this notion to the myth that education and politics are separate in America, although the significance of that step is great.

For most of its history, education in the United States has been a state function administered through local school districts. Intermingled with the myth of the separation of politics and education is the belief, often encouraged by schoolmen, that the local school districts cohabit the territory of the states in a manner analogous to the relationship between the states and the federal government. Were this analogy well drawn, the local school district would be an agency of government not dependent on the state for its legal existence. In America the constitutional concept of sovereignty over education is lodged exclusively in the states; hence this statement: *Education is a state function.* Unlike the federal system, any state may eliminate local school districts by state action. In New York State, to cite an extreme instance, action by the Commissioner of Education is legally sufficient. The local school district is not constitutionally independent or in any legal sense equal to the state. School people and local citizens frequently complain about state encroachment on the presumed prerogatives of the local district, but the fact that education is administered through local school districts in forty-nine states does not reduce the state's sovereign power over education.[4] Such an arrangement has, however, fostered public awareness of the uniqueness

---

[4] Hawaii's educational system has no local districts.

of educational governing and the myth of separateness between politics and education. From the point of view of the political life style, this traditional arrangement has also influenced the nature of the ground rules in the politics of education without eliminating political activity in school districts. The effect of special governmental arrangements for education and the school district structure in particular has been to create an issue area in which political behavior and activities are narrowly focused to the exclusion of other local and community public affairs. It has contributed to the separateness of educational politics but has not produced an area of public life free of politics. Indeed, the separateness of educational politics may be more imagined than real, since public office in education (e.g., school board membership) may be a step on the political ladder.

The special constitutional arrangement which characterizes educational governance in general and school districts in particular is mainly a relationship between a sovereign state and delegated local powers. This is a carryover from the eighteenth and nineteenth centuries in the United States. Chartered cities and incorporated local governments have largely become free from state control for many of their public services such as police, fire, or sanitation. Education constitutes a major exception to this change and continues its nineteenth century character into the second half of the twentieth century. This presents a paradox. School districts are nearer to local control than any other major public service, yet they are legally less free from state control.

Education's Unique Government

School districts are governed by their own elected representatives within the limits of state law. These representatives are generally elected by the citizens of the school district and constitute a local school board. Board members have no power to act for the district except when sitting as the school board. They have the legal power and the obligation to provide for the public education of the children of the school district. To that end the school district and its board are empowered to make policies governing the schools, to borrow monies within the legal limits specified by the State, to spend, and to tax. The existence of the local school districts with such powers creates a set of local governments with powers and obligations in the area of education which are woven into and overlap the local governments of counties, cities, towns, and villages. Then the power to tax is given to local school districts and boards within legal limits without the intervention of city or town governments. Most school districts are said to be fiscally independent. Conversely, when a school district must submit its proposed budget to another governmental agency such as a city board of estimate or the mayor, it is said to be fiscally dependent. Viewed in terms of their fiscal taxing power, independent districts may be seen as presenting education with a special advantage in raising local funds for its operations. The fiscal independence of local school districts from other local governments constitutes one special arrangement for the governing of education that tends to set education's governance apart from other local government. This financial independence of school districts obscures the fact that they are legal creatures of the state without sovereignty of their own. It tends to produce a different political life in the educational area with its own political arena, the school board, apart from the rest of local government. This separation often contributes to a condition of stress, establishing a shaky coexistence between school districts and other local governments, particularly as they draw upon a common citizenry and the same wealth as bases for taxation.

Geographic Separateness

Local school districts often overlap the territory of other local governments without being coterminous with any. There are school districts which have territorial boundaries identical with some other local government. These may be found more often in New England than in other regions of the nation. When found in other regions, they include the large cities more often than smaller suburbs or rural areas. However, most local school districts are not coterminous with other local governments. Many school districts exist which encompass the territory of more than one other local government. Not a few school districts encompass parts of several other local governments. Without attempting to detail all the combinations which exist, it may be enough to emphasize that the territorial boundaries of school districts are usually different from the local governments that they overlap. As a result, such school districts will each display unique territoriality, having some residents from different towns and villages. Thus, the electorate of a given school district will be unique. Voters of one school district will not all share concerns about local governmental affairs except that of the school. The simple fact that unique territoriality most often characterizes the school district once again tends to produce a separation between the local school district with its political life and other local governments with their political lives. As a result, education in the United States has been viewed apart from other public services and their government and politics to such an extent that education is usually thought of as non-political.

Special Elections

Consistent with the pattern of separateness which emerges from an examination of the typical school district's territorial limits and its fiscal powers is the fact that the elections in most school districts are held apart from other elections. From the voter's point of view, it is inefficient to go to the polls twice during the year instead of once. Separate elections—one for voting as citizens of the school district and one as citizens of the city, state, and nation—often result in a poorer voter turnout in school district elections than in those for governor, mayor, or congressional representatives. It might be argued that holding separate elections on educational matters allows the voter to concentrate exclusively on school affairs, avoiding the confounding of educational issues with other public issues and, hence, resulting in a clearer expression of the public will on educational matters. Were this argument as good a reflection of reality as it appears on the surface, school boards would know what their constituents wanted better than their political counterparts in other local government bodies, such as village boards and city councils. School boards would be most in tune with their communities, the school district's voter would seldom feel frustrated, and education in the United States would seldom fail to receive the solid support of the local citizenry. The facts hardly support this argument. Special elections for school districts are one more element of separation between the general governmental life of the country with its politics and the government of education with its own politics. This contributes to the development of unique ground rules, behaviors, and beliefs that tend to set the governance and politics of education apart from the rest of American government and politics.

The basic fact of constitutional law governing education and local school districts is summarized in the statement, *Education is a state function locally administered.* The local district is characteristically the state's arm for local administration of education and exists as an agency of the state with delegated powers. A number of special arrangements for the local school district exists resulting in a high degree of separateness from the rest of local American government and tending to produce its own brand of politics. As was pointed out, these arrangements include the school district's fiscal independence, its characteristic lack of coterminality with other local governments, and its separate elections. Together these tend to produce a separate school district citizenry with its own political ground rules.

The beliefs and emotional attachments which cluster around educational government in the local school district provide another sort of influence on the politics of education. These beliefs, along with the special constitutional arrangements, play a large part in producing political advantages for insiders in the short run and in establishing long run penalties in the politics of local school districts. The constitutional and legal structure of school districts and the beliefs and emotional attachments of Americans concerning education have produced a peculiar life style in the politics of local school districts.

BELIEFS AND EMOTIONS

Functions of School Government

Modern governments and governmental subunits such as school districts serve two functions, according to Banfield and Wilson.[5] One is an economic function, the supply of goods and services not supplied by private agencies; the other is a political function, the management of conflict in matters of public concern. School districts through their boards perform these two types of functions. In the case of school districts, it would appear that so long as they perform their service function in such a way as to retain a large measure of public support and approval, they would seldom become seriously involved in the management of conflict. It becomes clearer that their decisions and the school's activities have implications for the values of the society in which they exist. Though less obvious, the educational services performed by school districts have value implications, especially since curricula, teacher behavior, the school's system of rewards and penalties, and textbooks all influence the value development of pupils. As Childs points out, planned education as incorporated in schools is "an enterprise of purpose."[6] The fact of planning in

---

[5] Edward C. Banfield and James Q. Wilson, *City Politics* (Cambridge, Mass.: Harvard University Press and The M.I.T. Press, 1963), pp. 18-22.

[6] John L. Childs, *Education and Morals* (New York: Appleton-Century-Crofts, Educational Division, Meredith Corporation, 1950), p. 100.

the educational enterprise itself dictates that "education is a value-conditioned activity. The school seeks to cultivate selected values in the young by means of both the subject-matters and the methods that it employs in its program."[7] School board decisions concerning teaching methods, administrative arrangements, guidance processes, and curricular patterns, for instance, rest on value premises, unintentional or quite deliberate. Such decisions carry value implications no less serious for individuals or groups and their cherished beliefs than those implied by the title of Moreno's classic work, *Who Shall Survive?*[8] Perhaps it is the very basic and deadly serious importance of education that underpins the development of highly romanticized and unrealistic views of the schools, teaching the politics of education. But school districts do not only influence values through their decisions and the services they perform, they also depend on value commitments of people in schools to make their decisions effective and on the district's citizens for support, both financial and moral. The government of school districts rests on more than force and the sanctions of law. Beyond these there is the power of emotional ties and beliefs. Here indeed, error believed becomes truth in effect. People behave on the basis of their political beliefs and emotions.

Emotional Involvement

Few areas of life in America generate as much emotional appeal as education. The local school district continues to appear in professional literature and common language with the halo of the sacred nineteenth century rural community. American value commitments to education have historically been akin to and, in fact, linked with religious activities. The current disputes involving such matters as religious education, Bible reading, released time, and the observance of religious holidays offer continuing evidence of that relationship. The very origins of public education in New England—"The religious care of posteritie" cited in the Roxbury agreement of 1645 and the subsequent "Old Deluder Act"—testify to the religious motive behind them. Perhaps more important in instilling a "mystical" flavor in American education has been the emotional pull of the children who are the school's clientele. Schooling in America has often been viewed as a panacea for social ills and the chief vehicle for individual upward mobility. Too often the disillusionment one generation ex-

---

[7] *Ibid.*
[8] J. L. Moreno, *Who Shall Survive?* (New York: Beacon House, Inc., 1958).

periences in its struggle with stubborn reality becomes displaced by its unrealistic hope for the next generation. It is hardly surprising that schools, particularly in America, carry strong emotional tones of hope and idealism—appearing as a Wonderland in which children are all good, needing only to be understood to become "motivated—" a place of learning where teachers are underpaid, dedicated, and warm-hearted persons to be admired if not taken too seriously. Here the curriculum prepares children for a better role than that of their parents without engaging in the study of controversial matters or sordid social realities. The sweet but all too often saccharin emotional overtone extends to the public view of school administration and policymaking. While school administrators may be perceived as the "heavies" when they are engaged in conflicts with teachers, they too benefit and sometimes pay the price of being seen as well-meaning, warm-hearted, dedicated educationists, albeit somewhat unrealistic in their financial requests for schools.

In contrast stands the readiness to consider politicians as self-serving and corrupt. It should not be surprising then to find that one of the cardinal beliefs shaping the educational professional, the politics of education, and the ground rules by which it is conducted is the belief that education stands apart from political life.

A Romantic View

The nineteenth century's rural romanticism died slowly in the twentieth century. The sacred rural community was beheld in all its virtues, expurgated from its weaknesses and petty cruelties. The American founding fathers shared this rural bias. They looked to the yeoman farmer as the repository of old Roman civic virtue and popular government; they saw in the city not only the squalor of ignorance and poverty, but also the mob ready to be controlled by boss-ridden political machines. The fact that the demagogue has more often found his success among rural populations in states such as Louisiana has seldom disturbed the unfavorable American myth of the political unreliability of the city mob. Few areas of American public life have succeeded in resisting the twentieth century process of urbanization as well as public education, especially the local school district.

The educational profession's view of school government and school districts has tended to reinforce the picture of the local school district as akin to the romanticized rural community. In part, this may have resulted from the fact that the establishment of graduate programs in school administration and the advent of the professional school administrator took place in the first quarter of the twentieth century before the mature development of secular urban values. The individuals who left their mark on the new profession in its formative days were rural in origin and, more important, continued to display these origins in their language and writings throughout their influential careers. Perhaps most important, the educational professions, despite their revolt against nineteenth century rote learning and even in their most radical search for pupil-centered learning, continued to display a commitment to a romanticized notion of community— whether their referent was the "community of scholars" in the university or the euphemistically labeled "school district community." Indeed, long after successful leadership in school district consolidation has resulted in the elimination of coterminality between school district and natural communities, educationists persist in using the language and concepts of rural communities when talking and thinking about school districts. Similarly, the American public tends to think nostalgically of school districts as if they were small town centers of "true" democracy in contrast to the rest of American governmental life.

A corollary of the romantic view of the American school district is the implication that the school district is atomistically composed of individual citizens endowed with equal political power, each one acting on his own. On the romantic side of the coin lies the unified egalitarian community with the obverse side presenting the equally unreal rabble hypothesis. Both of these views have served the key professionals in school districts. School administrators beset by conflicting factions in the district have denied the existence of organized political power in school districts. School people are often unconscious of the fact that the school organization with committees of teachers, its citizens' advisory councils, its nominating caucuses, and parent-teachers' associations constitutes an organized power subsystem within the school district.

Direct Democracy

Less emotionally loaded but no less politically significant is the view that the local school district is the last stronghold of direct democracy in American public affairs. This view tends to rest on the belief that the local school district "belongs" to its citizens, ignoring, in effect, the fact that the local school district is legally an agency of the state. This belief in the local school district as a stronghold of

democracy constitutes a formidable reality of political life. It gains
in political importance as other levels of governmental decisioning
become further and further removed from the voter. Thus, it appears that some negative reactions to increases in taxation at state
and federal levels of government may find an outlet in voting on
financial issues at the local school district elections. Despite the constitutional view of school district existence, as long as citizens believe that school districts are and should be independent local
governments separate from other governments, they will tend to
exist this way. Equally important, the belief that the local school
district is and should be separate from the rest of government carries
with it the belief that politics and education should be separate. In
fact, one interesting tribute to the strength of this belief may be found
in the language people customarily use when speaking of school
districts, school boards, and their decisions. Seldom is a school district
spoken of as a governmental unit, let alone as a branch of state
government. Similarly, the word "government" is seldom connected
with the school board or its activities, even though many school
board decisions have the force of law.

A Realistic View

A governmental unit with an elected governing board making
policies cannot exist in a democracy without politics. Hence, the
belief that politics and education are or should be separate either
expresses an unworkable article of faith that exists as do preambles to
constitutions without being intended as operational statements, or the
word "politics" is used in a special, invidious way. Both of these statements are true to some extent. The prescription of separation constitutes a kind of ritual statement of belief concerning an emotion-
loaded public service area. To the extent that the statement refers to
the stereotype of "dirty" politics and the "evils" of party politics it is
more realistically grounded. This latter view still assumes that educational policy can be developed through "objective" expert advice in
some sort of antiseptic vacuum. Decisions affect people and individuals as well as groups that have varying needs and interests. They
also have differing conceptions of the general public interest. Out of
these different conceptions arises the desire, even the need, to exert
influence on behalf of their conceptions. Thus public decisions in
education at local district as well as other levels of government will
not be made in a social vacuum but in a political arena with varying

forces competing for advantage and public interest, *as each sees it.*
On the other hand, the assumption that party politics are evil seems
incongruous, to say the least, when found in the dominant ideology of
the school people in a democratic nation characteristically displaying
and championing the two-party system in much of the world. It becomes more comprehensible when it is placed in the context of early
nineteenth century political beliefs in America. Contempt for political
parties and a muckraker's view of local city governments and politics
is appropriate to the ideology of American school district governance.

The belief that politics and education can and should be separated,
however unrealistic a view, does constitute an additional barrier between the political activities of other local governments and the school
district. Nor is this separation universally opposed by the professional
politician. One effect of the characteristic of the separation is to re-
lieve the political professionals of the responsibility for education.
At the same time the belief in separateness between politics and
education presents a political hazard that most officeholders and professional politicians are perfectly willing to ignore. For the local
governmental official of a village or city to become embroiled in educational issues in conflict with the cherished beliefs of many citizens
could well be political suicide. It is thus highly probable that the extensive involvement in educational issues of politicians and elected
officeholders (other than school board members) will only be found
when school boards have not successfully resolved the conflicts in
their districts or provided educational services acceptable to enough
voters. Generally the professional politician avoids areas of involvement which violate the customary beliefs of voters. In general, there
is little political gain in such areas and much political risk. Education
has historically been such an area. Masters and others conclude their
study of the politics of education in three states with the statement:
*"With few exceptions political officials feel that efforts in behalf of
education offer few of the traditional prizes; therefore they avoid
direct involvement."*[9] They concluded that public school causes did
not ". . . contain much political currency (voter appeal, patronage)."[10]
These conclusions stand in sharp contrast to the political developments
in California in the late 1960's. The key to the differences may be
found in the political conditions of education which produced the two.
The states studied by the Masters team displayed relatively less

---

[9] Nicholas A. Masters, Robert H. Salisbury, and Thomas H. Eliot, *State Politics
and the Public Schools* (New York: Alfred A. Knopf, Inc., 1964), p. 275.
[10] *Ibid.*

public discontent about educational services and were better able to contain and manage public conflict over educational matters than was true in California. More often than not, the statement that political officials avoid direct involvement in educational matters is demonstrably true. Exceptions to this pattern, such as California or New York in 1968, will usually follow unsuccessful efforts to change education within the traditional school board and local district patterns of education and separate itself from other governments and officials. Further, it can be expected that citizens will seek to replace local school officials before turning to the other agencies of local government or other levels of government. Dangerous though the politics of education may be for the professional politician, and regardless of how infrequent may be the moments when there is political coinage in education, nevertheless such moments do exist. Then the traditional quiet politics of education gives way to a more vigorous and, for some, more painful brand of politics.

A POLITICS OF INSIDERS

Focus on the Board

Perhaps the most visible effect of the special governmental arrangements for education with its peculiar emotional appeals and beliefs is the almost complete elimination of overt political party activity in school district affairs. Consequently, the politics of education has resembled the politics of multiple interest groups within a somewhat unified and sometimes monolithic pyramid of power at the local level. Yet the absence of the two-party mechanisms has not resulted in the elimination of politics in educational decisioning or policy making. In school districts the politics of education finds its chief legal focus in school board deliberations and decisions. Here the absence of the political party mechanism is felt. School board policy making does not operate in a social or political vacuum. As one of the present authors pointed out:

> School systems with their legal structure of boards, administrators, and teaching staffs increasingly tend to be encased in a network of extra-governmental friends and allies. A civic cocoon of advisory groups, lay committees, parent-teacher organizations, grade mothers, Girl Scout Brownies, and athletic boosters surround,

politically protect, and nurture the local educational leaders in school district matters.[11]

The creation of such a webwork of semiformal social organizations provides the machinery for the mediation of differences among interests seeking to influence school district policy. Here the discussion and debate of proposed solutions for school district problems takes place before these solutions are put before the school board. The school district and especially the board thus have the benefit of the discussion and the give-and-take among interests which in the two-party system normally goes on first within each of the political parties and later between parties before action by the agencies of governments, legislatures, and city councils.

Semiformal Mechanisms

The analysis of the operation of the semiformal mediating organizations that clustered around the formal decision-making organization of the Jefferson School District indicated that the parents and teachers of Jefferson had developed mechanisms through which they simultaneously resolved their differences and attempted to influence school policies. The machinery had a healthy effect on the school district because the Jefferson Teachers' Association and the Jefferson Parent Teachers' Association "fought out" their differences in joint committees. Within their organizations, these differences had no direct effect on the school.

> Therefore, the flames of issues not yet resolved between the groups never had a chance to spread in the direction of the formal institution and thus cause school policy to shift temporarily in one direction or another. Agreement between both semi-formal institutions on an issue before it was presented to the board helped the formal institution in its task of ratification of that issue into policy.[12]

If such alternatives to the two-party structure were better than equal to that characteristic structure of the Anglo-American democracies, these nations would long ago have abandoned the costly

---

[11] Laurence Iannaccone, *Politics in Education* (New York: The Center for Applied Research in Education, Inc., 1967), p. 10.

[12] Daniel E. Griffiths *et al.*, *Organizing Schools for Effective Education* (Danville, Ill.: The Interstate Printers & Publishers, Inc., 1962), p. 259.

and inefficient two-party system. In the long run, the price paid by schools for their complex one-party and multifactional webwork of semiformal organizations may be costlier than the benefits gained by standing apart from the two-party system. The die is now cast, however, and it is unlikely that school districts with the history of educational politics will, can, or should enter the two-party system in spite of the cost incurred by their present political operation.

Debate Discouraged

The direct democracy implied by the focus of the school board's politics of education places a premium on achieving a consensus among interested parties prior to official and public confrontations at school board meetings. As a result, the politics of education has traditionally been a politics of low visibility and informal agreement. School district-wide discussion and debate of educational issues, especially discussion on the values to be emphasized or de-emphasized by the schools, are discouraged because of the characteristic consensus politics of education.

Initiation of policy has generally fallen to school superintendents. Historically, superintendents and their staffs have held an effective monopoly of technical information on educational matters concerning their schools. Bringing such information to bear on board discussions often determines the outcome. Faced with a knowledge explosion and a technological revolution in teaching, the professional educationist finds it increasingly difficult to pose with integrity in the role of sole educational expert before his board or his community. The schoolman's new technological dilemmas are confounded by the political history of education as it has produced a tradition of minority control with low visibility politics. This tradition may no longer be viable in many areas of the county.

Although most school board meetings are open to the public, usually few observers are present. It is unfair to blame this light attendance on lack of citizen interest. Instead, school board meetings have developed a tendency toward meaninglessness which discourages observer attendance. For example, in the case of the Jefferson School District, meetings of the "Committee of the Whole" were closed to the public. These preceded the legal board meetings and determined the board members' feelings on given issues. In turn, this knowledge influenced the manner in which the agenda was handled; professional recommendations were made and matters settled or tabled for future modification.[13] Thus the official school board minutes displayed almost complete unanimity of voting by board members. This is not unusual. Differences in positions taken by board members on educational issues exist. Some ultimately break open into severe political battles. Most differences, however, are concealed from the public and may only be seen in closed subcommittee meetings and executive sessions. Such privacy is probably more necessary in the absence of a party structure and to some extent controls debate on the floor of legal board meetings. The closed meeting results in open meetings which are largely ceremonial in nature. This arrangement provides the observer with a flat, stale experience as a substitute for the heady wine of partisan debate. In an effort to avoid the appearance of conflict, discussion and debate throughout the school district is discouraged.

Little Loyal Dissent

There are few if any effective political mechanisms for loyal dissent in the typical American local school district. The absence of the two-party mechanisms blunts the sharp edges of different positions on educational issues through the privacy of closed meetings. Lacking a tradition of vigorous discussion within established ground rules of equality in debate, the politics of education has produced a political system devoid of a loyal opposition, a minority pro-public school but opposed to the local educational establishment. Without the development of viable political mechanisms for provoking district-wide discussion and debate and without provisions for legitimate public dissent with confrontation between opposing views on educational matters, the school administrator is usually reduced to manipulating his board by posing as more of an expert than any one man or single group of professionals can ever be. Thus, the board is faced with the extreme alternatives of accepting staff recommendations *in toto* or rejecting its professional staff. The public is most often confronted at the polls with a choice between electing candidates supporting the local educational establishment, or individuals representing extreme factions of the community hostile to the basic goals of American education. This dilemma is even more apparent when the voter faces a similarly polarized choice in school referenda. He must vote for the entire program proposed by the local established leadership of

---

[13] Griffiths *et al., Organizing Schools for Effective Education,* **pp.** 228-34.

the school district or totally deny the public schools the resources necessary for a decent program. His only other means for registering his will is by making a lone protest at board meetings or, perhaps even less satisfying, talking with the superintendent, whose "door is always open."

Invisible Politics

The absence of mechanisms and traditions for expressing dissent honestly and loyally without threatening the entire educational enterprise has tended to produce a life-style of low pressure, invisible politics of the initiated rather than the high pressure, colorful politics of the marketplace. As described by B. Dean Bowles:

> The two genre of politics are different in kind. The politics of the market-place is visible and thrives on the resolution of conflict. The politics of the priesthood is hidden and shrouded in mystery and subsists on the development of a consensus.[14]

The politics of the polite priesthood—seeking consensus rather than facing and resolving conflict—is rooted, nurtured, and hedged about with sacred values expressed by educationists. It places a premium upon low visibility politics and informal agreement among its internal groups, conferring special advantages on "the insider."

> It is a politics of the sacred rural rather than secular urban community . . . The politics of the hustings are visible and thrive on conflict and its resolution. The colorful kaleidoscope and cacaphonic calliope of the campaign is its milieu. The politics of the priesthood are hidden and shrouded in mystery.[15]

The low visibility politics of education can hardly be expected to produce a high level of voter turnout. Rather, the vote is composed of a small portion of the community who, because their children are currently in the schools, feel a direct sense of involvement in the school district's political activity. In contrast to the nineteenth-century sacred rural mythology, voter turnout in education is related to organized efforts to turn out the vote of a particular group and the saliency of the issues involved in the given election. The average

---

[14] B. Dean Bowles, "Educational Pressure Groups and the Legislative Process in California, 1945-1966" (Ph.D. dissertation, Claremont Graduate School, Claremont, California, 1966), p. vii.

[15] Laurence Iannaccone and Frank W. Lutz, "The Changing Politics of Education," *AAUW Journal,* May, 1967, p. 161.

voter can hardly be expected to pay more attention to local issues than he does to national issues in this era. The absence of the political party machinery for turning out the vote is also felt in local school district elections. Except in times of crises for the local school district, low voter turnout in school elections has become a normal fact of educational political life. Only when controversy erupts publicly does the voter turnout rise above the minimal proportions. This usually results in the defeat of a referendum or an incumbent board member. This is one of the prices Americans pay for the traditional local district system of control of public education separated from other governments and operating without the two-party system.

Control of Nominations

One other function served by the political party is that of nominating candidates for elected office. In many districts the professional staff, especially the superintendent of schools, plays a key role in the nomination of school board members. The superintendent's personal stake in the nominations is clear. Probably more important than this is the superintendent's concern with the school district as a whole, its children, their educational program, and their needs as he sees them. Few individuals are as concerned with the entire school district as most school superintendents are. Hence, *in the absence* of other political mechanisms, it may well be that the school superintendent is more able than anyone else to take the total needs of the school district into consideration when influencing the election of board members. But is it possible for any individual or group actively engaged in providing a public service to be as objective about their work as others? The substitution of the superintendent's influence on nominations in place of the party mechanism is hardly a recommended solution. In the Jefferson School there had developed over a time a citizen's nominating committee, extralegal in nature, but successful in gaining and retaining political support for their nominees from the communities which composed the Jefferson School District.[16] The superintendent of schools had been an influential figure in creating this nomination pattern and was called on regularily to help select candidates for school board elections.

Less extralegal in nature but to some extent similar are the nominating caucuses of Illinois and Nebraska. These are formal legal elements

---

[16] Griffiths *et al.*, *Organizing Schools for Effective Education*, pp. 236-38.

in the school district structure and are open to all qualified voters in the district. A caucus committee, according to Muns, is a "body of representatives of a school district chosen for the purpose of canvassing, screening, and nominating the best available candidates for school board membership."[17] Whatever the particular local school district's system of nomination, it becomes increasingly necessary to find some method of fulfilling this function normally met by the party in American politics, particularly as reorganizations and the geographic mobility of people produce school districts that less and less approximate single communities. As the school district has become a convenient geographic entity of educational government to a greater degree and less of a community in the classic sociological sense, it has also become more susceptible to capture and control by well organized minorities.

Crisis Government

The history of educational government at the local level is replete with crises. The typical local school district may be viewed as moving from one educational crisis to another with periods of dullness between. The fact of low voter turnout results in minority control of most school districts. Often politically active minorities have been friends of the schools, proponents of public education, and supporters of the local school district's traditional leadership. Increasingly these are the professionals of the district and other leaders of educational interest coalitions brought together around the school. Still the dominance of a well organized minority opposed to the school or their leadership is not infrequent.

During the McCarthy era of the early 1950's, a number of plush suburban school districts were faced with book-burning threats. Ultra-patriotic groups have found in the schools a meaningful goal. The fact that most school districts are normally governed by officials representing a minority of their community's citizens makes them easy prizes for other well organized minorities. Extremist groups from the right or left who continue for years as small minorities unable to extend their values into the mainstream of the society find the capture of the major political parties and their offices beyond their capacity.

---

[17] Arthur C. Muns, "A Study of Caucus Committee Procedure for Nominating Candidates for Boards of Education in Cook, DuPage and Lake Counties, Illinois" (Ed.D. dissertation, School of Education, Northwestern University, 1961), p. 2.

Small local communities where a pattern of minority control already exists provide easier pickings in the absence of the two-party mechanisms. Such groups easily turn to the school to gain control of its operations as a defense against the spread of opposing values and as a means of extending their own values. In rapidly growing suburbs, particularly of southern California and Long Island, a number of board take-overs for at least one election have occurred.

On the other hand, countless *ad hoc* community groups representing groups of citizens disturbed by a particular school board decision or educational practice may spring into existence and offer a challenge for control of the school board. The Levittown, New York, story serves as an example. Built on a basic economic concern and fear of rising taxes, a rapidly growing community turned against the school leadership, and the school board was overthrown at the election.[18] In this case, the incident that triggered the political explosion was a concert that was regarded as leftist. The Pasadena story of the early fifties shows a similar local reaction to what some viewed as a too liberal or left-of-center position. This incident was used as the occasion for upsetting the traditional leadership of the district. So it goes and so it has gone for years with insurgent groups replacing old-timers on the boards, either liberal or conservative.

Most often each policy conflict represents different minorities of the eligible voters in a system characterized by having a majority of the potential voters on the sidelines. Often the particular event around which the *ad hoc* group rallies the vote tends to be trivial. Underneath, however, the issues of Reds, race, religion, and real estate taxes continue to divide the local district and to give consistency to these otherwise unique educational policy battles. A second consistency of such policy conflicts appears in the frequency with which political struggles in the local district are struggles of minorities. In America, because of its characteristic pattern of minority control and the moralistic aspects of education, the local school district becomes an area of ideological warfare when it moves into action out of its more customary political dullness and inaction.

Small voter turnout and the value implications of education are, perhaps, the main reasons for the frequency with which ideological struggles blossom into school district politics. The importance of value choices about education should result in a higher voter turnout than is

---

[18] Joseph F. Maloney, *"The Lonesome Train" in Levittown* (Indianapolis, Indiana: The Bobbs-Merrill Co., Inc., 1958), I.C.P. Case Series 39.

customarily seen. Such is the case when board decisions are clearly perceived as involved in determining the value choices of the community.

The low visibility, consensus style of politics is that advocated by most textbooks and teaching in school administration. Almost any text concerned with community relations will urge the use of lay advisory committees, avoidance of closed board meetings, frequent communication with the public, and participation of lay leaders in studies for program development. The language schoolmen use suggests they have heard this advice and believe it. The cynicism shared by teachers concerning the genuineness of the school administrator's efforts to include others is nevertheless constantly heard. Education needs independent critics friendly to the schools but not controlled by them. This is, in part, what the "loyal opposition" does for the party in office when the two-party system operates. Both parties share a major commitment to the ground rules of the political game that rests on voter approval. Each struggles to be more representative of the voters than the opposition. If either party moves too far away from the mainstream of the society, it can only expect defeat. Hence, the party must in part surrender its own predilections if it wishes to win majority support. But if there were no second party, no loyal opposition to the team in office, then to what degree could the party's leaders be expected to include voices opposing their ideas? To what extent would they avoid "educating" these opponents to their point of view and so lose the virtue of that opposing voice?

A Closed System

One concludes that when the locus of the accommodation of differences among diverse interests takes place in a single, noncompetitive social system, the opportunities for criticism producing change are less than in competitive social systems. When, in addition, the single social system providing a locus of accommodation among various interests and groups is able to choose its own representatives, then the chances against openness to criticism and change become small. When the locus of accommodation lies within a single social structure, selecting the interests for inclusion and accommodation, and that single, self-selecting social system is itself controlled by its own operational group, the system becomes almost closed. Such a social system is almost certain to label any continuing opposition as irresponsible, not to be taken seriously, and certainly not representative of any serious segment of the community. This kind of social system has a closed political operation.

As a social system becomes increasingly closed, it decreases its exchanges with its environment. This is true of political as well as other social systems. The movement towards becoming more closed results in an increased internal stability of the social system. In the case of school districts, for example, internal relationships among board members, subgroups of the board, and the superintendent will become more stabilized. Similarly, board policies, procedures, habits of behavior, and value orientations will become less flexible and less easily changed. Viewed externally, fewer exchanges of ideas, people, group desires, and information go on between the board and its community.

The cost of this process of closed system politics may be seen best as a gap opens and increases between the board and the community. The process producing this widening gap may be viewed theoretically in terms of a predictable relationship of ebb and flow between the complex social systems of two gross dimensions which may be thought of as the governmental and societal.[19]

The governmental dimension, in the case of school districts centering in the board, may be thought of as existing with long periods of stability and shorter periods of abrupt change. The periods of stability result from the fashioning of successful coalitions of influence which then continue to influence. Normally, it takes the development of a different coalition to change governmental directions. The new coalition of political forces must win offices or significant influence in order to redirect or modify governmental policy. This is seldom accomplished easily. It takes time and experience to develop a political coalition and win a school board election. In the meantime, the operations and policy directions of government are not likely to change much. When victory at the polls takes place, the new coalitions are likely to make as full a use of their political power as they can. Thus it can be predicted that the governmental dimension will be characterized by rather long periods of social stability with relatively abrupt moments of change.

The societal dimension may be viewed as more fluid than the governmental since it lacks the formal structures of offices with regular calendars of elections and meetings. Because the societal dimension is more fluid, it tends to be characterized by a more continuous and constant rate of change than the governmental. The social and eco-

---

[19] Laurence Iannaccone, *Politics in Education*, pp. 14-18.

nomic mobility of people and their geographic mobility into and out of communities are likely to produce changes in the community's social composition. Such changes will often be reflected in changes in the attitudes of the community toward the school and its programs. This is a simple reflection of the well-known phenomenon that differences in educational values and commitments concerning the value of education are related to differences in social and economic status. Thus it can be predicted that the societal dimension will be characterized by a relatively constant rate of change.

The interaction between society and government depends on how closely matched each is to the other. Specifically, when the government displays an extended period of stability, the character of constant and progressive change in society will produce a widening gap between the two. The gap between the two is almost always closed as a result of political action that changes the schools' policies.

In summary, it is natural that governmental bodies and the society they govern should move closer together and further apart within a reasonable range of time. The politics of school districts, influenced by their special governmental arrangements and the emotional commitments of American society in the absence of the two-party system, have developed an unusual degree of autonomy. This has resulted in an amazing capacity among school districts for rejecting changes that would modify their usual processes and their internal status structure. The rejection of new inputs, people, ideas, activities, and technologies is hardly surprising when those who have the most to lose by this innovation constitute the internal power structure of the existing system. The absence of the characteristic two-party system leaves education's political pattern without a loyal opposition. To develop and institutionalize a loyal opposition within a public service area, e.g., education, seems a difficult task without this two-party device!

School districts in the American political milieu—relatively closed political systems—will continue to display convergence and divergence between their governmental and social dimensions. As stated elsewhere:

> Something of the flavor of a revolution—without bloodshed but with many destroyed careers—is likely to characterize the shifts in the closed political systems of education.[20]

---

20 Iannaccone, *Politics in Education,* p. 18.

2

Sacred and Secular
Communities

School district politics tends to maximize the search for consensus and avoid open conflict, creating opportunities for the manipulation and control of school boards and educational policies by relatively small and narrowly based cliques. Suburban school districts, especially ones not contiguous with a single community, tend to display considerable control of the school district's leadership by the education specialists, especially the superintendent. The chief school administrator is often not only the leader of his board's deliberations but is also involved in the selection of school board members. Avoiding open conflict and maximizing a consensus in decision making provides him with the most favorable conditions for enhancing his influence over school matters and strengthening his position in the school system. The concepts used by sociologists to describe the sacred community in contrast to the secular community offer one way of describing the most commonly found pattern of policy making for the school district. This sacred community type is the traditional school district with its strong tendency toward consensus politics. This is the most commonly found pattern of local school district politics.

Sometimes the sacred community is led and influenced

by community leaders, persons who tend to be at the top of relatively monolithic community power structures. Their leadership and dominance, whether resulting from apathy on the part of others or from their own capacity to deal with community problems, are generalized as the power pyramid which they lead and influences various discrete decision areas. Often the school district is apart from the rest of local government. Its top organizational leadership displays greater technical and specialized knowledge and skill than in the case in which the generalized top leadership pattern predominates. Here the specialist is not merely a hired expert, a servant, of the community's top leadership. This second pattern does not imply, however, either an unstructured social world or the absence of a power system. It suggests that the school district's power system is sufficiently detached from other local power systems to be considered independent. This arrangement need not mean the complete separation one from the other any more than the legal separateness of school districts from other local governments is so complete that no interaction occurs between the taxing arrangements of one and the fiscal base of the others. Nevertheless, a majority of suburban school districts and their boards are separate enough from other local governments to be led by different leadership groups.

Equality of influence among participants is nonexistent. It is found neither where a single leadership group exists, which has general influence in various decision-making areas, nor where multiple leadership groups exist, each with specialized leadership in the appropriate decision-making areas. Instead there is a pyramid of social power. In single leadership groups there is a single pyramid across the range of community life. In pluralist structures each area of community decisions displays its own pyramid with its own specialized leadership.

THE SACRED COMMUNITY

The image of the sacred community is useful for understanding the traditional consensus politics of American local school districts. The concepts of the sacred community are taken largely from the work of Howard Becker. He characterized societies along a continuum of sacred to secular types with the theory that changes in given societies, communities, organizations, or social movements can be viewed as proceeding along the sacred-secular continuum. Change may be in either direction. Since the central device is constructed or "ideal," change may be seen in the relatively increased secularity or sacredness of the social universe being studied without the expectation that any society or organization will fit perfectly either of the extreme types at each end of the continuum. Becker defined his polar type societies as a sacred society that is unwilling to accept the new as the new. In contrast, a secular society is willing to accept the new as the new.

Reaction to Change

The sacred community is seen first of all in its evaluation of change. For the sacred community, old ways are better than new. Fads and new notions are inherently dangerous and even small differences from customary patterns of behavior may be the start of a road away from virtue from which there is no turning back. The old days are safer and preferred to the new age. The tried is thereby the true and that which has not been experienced is probably false. Conversely, the secular community is one which places a high positive value on change itself. Modern modes are better than old fashioned modes. Being up-to-date is prized; retaining something no longer "in," leaves one "out." Old virtues are more often seen as hypocrisy or blind conformity depriving one of freedom. The future—or the present thrilling moment, the extreme polar instance of the secular type—is preferred to the past. The tried is always imperfect and found wanting and that which has not been experienced is most sought after. As one moves from the sacred toward the secular, the test of a new idea becomes its rationality. Finally, at the extreme of secularity the acceptability of an idea depends on its bizarreness and whether or not it is "in."

The sacred community may display sentiments which are consistent with its central character—the tendency toward avoiding or resisting change. These include high evaluations of the holy and of loyalty, allegiance, and patriotism. With these the values of social intimacy, friendship, and good faith *within one's own society* are cherished. There tends to be strong, positive emotional responses to the familiar domestic environment and to the place of one's birth. Anxiety, distress, fear, and strain accompany change or the suggestion of change and provide an emotional base for resistance to it. The secular community also expresses sentiments consistent with its central character, the tendency to welcome or seek change. As communities move toward the secular, they display emotional neutrality toward the holy, and toward loyalty, allegiance, and patriotism. At the secular pole is the zeal of the true believer,[1] the emotional recklessness of fanaticism, exhilaration with positive values toward the high "change," and thrill.

Differences of Behavior

The sacred community's customary behavior displays the usual small town patterns of "small talk," and accepted ways of "breaking the ice." A high proportion of the social behavior of sacred societies has the function of enhancing or maintaining group and community solidarity. Hence, the "etiquette of gossip"[2] tends to be well developed and provides a non-public outlet for the criticism of others in lieu of public attack, formal confrontation, and open debate. Sacred societies place a high value on activities devoted to security. In them, specialization of tasks with high esteem for specialized expertise is relatively low. Activities directed toward provoking a response of social recognition are nonrational and accord to a traditionally ascribed status and a behavior consistent with the status which produces recognition for the actor instead of measurement of his specific achievements in competition with others. The converse is seen in the extreme secular type. Small talk is scorned, and the big social questions, the deeply felt things, are openly discussed, sometimes shouted out publicly. Social formalities and formulae of behavior are rejected as a fetish of nonconformity is imposed on the society. A high proportion of the social behavior of secular societies, which at one stage subjects behavioral patterns enhancing solidarity to the acid criticism of logic and evidence, becomes at its extreme stage disruptive behavior with intransigent positions characterizing different groups in the society. Hence, public attacks on the ideas and decisions of officials are accepted behavior; disrespect for office holders and traditionally respected leaders become the norm. Risk-taking activities are valued, and specialization of tasks with commensurate high esteem for specialized expertise is greater in the secular society. Activities directed toward social recognition are rational and less traditional with achieved status, and the behavior of actors is measured competitively. Performance rather than the ascribed status of officee insures merit.

---

[1] Eric Hoffer, *The True Believer: Thoughts on the Nature of Mass Movements* (New York: Harper & Row, Publishers, 1951).

[2] Arthur J. Vidich and Joseph Bensman, *Small Town in Mass Society* (Garden City, N.Y.: Doubleday & Company, Inc., Anchor Books, 1960), p. 43.

Patterns of interaction in the sacred community tend to take place among clearly delineated groups, and relationships among these tend to be well established. Communication across group and class boundaries exists but follows established formulae, taking place at traditionally determined and limited linkage points among community social systems. The sentiments which foster parochialism are reflected in the in-group patterns of interaction and the suspicion of strangers, especially cosmopolitans. This situation tends to produce monolithic social structures and community power pyramids. The secular community's systems of social relationships are more fluid. Interaction across groups is greater than in the sacred community and the boundaries of groups are less sharply evident. Communication across groups and classes exists and follows established formulae but also develops new ways as old groups break up and reform. Sentiments which support cosmopolitan attitudes are reflected in the patterns of interaction outside the community and cosmopolites become opinion leaders. This tends toward pluralistic social structures, and community power is dispersed, though unequally.

The Introduction of Innovations

Finally, the successful introduction of changes and innovations takes different and to some extent opposite methods in the sacred as opposed to the secular community. It seems that the sacred is a static society displaying a condition of virtual equilibrium while the secular lacks stability and is in constant flux. The sacred–secular continuum, especially at its polar types, is an abstract construction designed as a tool for understanding reality. It is not intended to be a photograph but a painting which says more than a photograph to the student of school administration. Hence, the community most classifiable at the sacred pole does accept some changes, and its opposite extreme does retain, unchanged, some of its old elements in the face of alternative offerings. Inventions can be more easily introduced in the sacred community as slight modifications of accepted techniques than as new methods for doing things. An invention or innovation defined by a sacred society as "what we've been doing all along" will be accepted. The same invention or innovation defined by a sacred society as new and different will be rejected. For the sacred community, experience is the best teacher and the adoption of perceived innovation takes place, if at all, only as one's intimates report successful experiences with the innovation under consideration. The agricultural model of adoption of innovation evidences the sacred society nature typical of rural communities. The test of a new idea is personalistic in the sacred society, especially influenced by whether it is held by one's respected intimates. Finally, a sacred community is more likely to adopt an innovation it sees as symbolizing its sentiment and supporting its social structure as a defense against change perceived as forced on it from outside.

The secular community nearest the polar type is in continuous flux. In the secular community, the expert's testimonial, rather than experience, is valuable as leverage for the adoption of a perceived innovation. The written word rather than exclusive reliance on face-to-face communication with intimates can provide the basis for the diffusion of an innovation. The use of an innovation by other communities which are viewed competitively increases its chances of adoption in the secular society. A secular community, as it approaches the extreme type, runs the risk not only of change for its own sake but also of the phoniness which results when the redefinition of old activities as "innovations" suffices to protect them long after they should be abandoned.

The Orientation in Schools

American school districts with their peculiar social organizations, traditional behavior, and particular ethos tend to resemble the sacred rural community even in suburban metroplexes. Not withstanding the secular urban context of New York City, the governmental process and decision-making patterns of that city's school district tend to reproduce the sacred rural community values for educational policy and for political behavior in the city's school government. Nor does New York City stand alone in this, for Los Angeles, Chicago, San Francisco, Atlanta, and St. Louis seem, at least at the school board level, to have found greater success in displaying the sacred nineteenth century small town American orientations toward education and its government than a secular twentieth century urban outlook. Not a few of the unresolved problems of urban education remain unresolved, becoming increasingly unmanageable partly because of this curious development of the ground rules and flavor of the sacred society in the politics of urban education. However, many local school districts are governmental units which represent sacred rural American communities. The boundaries of these communities are virtually coterminous with other local governmental and social units. Such rural districts epitomize the sacred society aspects of educational governance. A brief examination of one of these reported in the literature of community studies may serve to illustrate the operations of the customary consensus politics of local school districts which often seem to survive twin processes of urbanization and secularization.

THE SCHOOL DISTRICT IN THE SACRED COMMUNITY[3]

The political system of Springdale may be described as monolithic, rurally dominated by prosperous farmers, and coordinated by Jones, one of the wealthy feed mill owners. Jones acted as the political broker and link between the various interests and the political subsystems of town, village, and school district. Coterminous with town government, the school district displayed the active engagement of a constituency different from the town. Roads and related issues characterized the center of town government, whereas the school curriculum, purchasing, and personnel issues characterized the district and school board decisions. However different in some ways, all governments in Springdale had the ethos of the sacred rural community. Thus, they were characterized by (1) a minimization of decision making, (2) unanimity of decision making, and (3) a low tax ideology. The dominance of prosperous farmers, expressed through an invisible government centering on the feed mill owners who best combined the rural and village interests, was an additional element of commonality linking each of the Springdale governments. This produced an extralegal, somewhat informal, *common* government for Springdale. The common leadership, shared by each local government resulted in a generalized leadership, and hence generalist leadership type. This is in contrast to the specialized leadership and specialist leadership type which tends to emerge where each major issue area of policy and government is led by different leaders with specialized knowledge and skills. The pattern of leadership in Springdale was the sacred society type.

The Rural School Board

The Springdale school board was a five member board elected, one each year, for a five-year term. Hence, a relatively high degree of

---

[3] Vidich and Bensman, *Small Town in Mass Society*, especially pp. 175-275, as the source for this section.

stability was built into the school district's structure. A serious redirection of the school district's policies would conceivably require three years of successive incumbent school board member defeats. The importance of the school becomes evident when it is seen that the major community events of Springdale's social, cultural, and athletic interests took place in the school. Its budget made it the major industry in the village. Springdale was a fairly typical rural school district offering an excellent illustration of the sacred rural community in its school politics as well as village and town politics. In fact, the school board was the political area in which most of Springdale's community issues and discussions were found. School board decisions had implications for many aspects of life in Springdale. The decisions of the school board were highly visible. In contrast, Vidich and Bensman suggest because of this visibility of outcomes the *process* by which decisions were made involved the low pressure politics of consensus, efforts at secrecy in decision processes, the use of executive sessions to conceal differences of opinion among board members from the public, and a strict adherence to the principle of unanimity of decision.[4] School board minutes recording final votes indicated a formal unanimity despite many real disagreements.

The significance of school board decisions in Springdale, coupled with the tradition of concealment of differences in public and the accent on the positive public posture with its etiquette of gossip, tended to produce periodic crises which for brief periods involved a larger number of citizens than usual in school board decisions. A series of crises with mass protest increased school board efforts at concealing the locus and process of decision making from the public. In general, these efforts were successful for "in spite of these crises, the decisions of the board stand and the social composition of the board remains the same from year to year."[5] Then tendency of the sacred community to avoid or resist change is illustrated here as are its correlates of behavior and values stressing social solidarity and unanimity even in the face of periodic protest.

The Springdale Board's power structure reflected the interests of prosperous farmers.[6] It displayed the characteristic monolithic power pyramid described by Floyd Hunter.[7] The local institutionalized but informal leadership in Springdale's village and town governments

---

[4] Vidich and Bensman, *Small Town in Mass Society,* pp. 175ff.
[5] *Ibid.,* p. 178.
[6] *Ibid.,* pp. 178-88.
[7] Floyd Hunter, *Community Power Structure: A Study of Decision-Makers* (Chapel Hill, N.C.: University of North Carolina Press, 1953).

found its counterpart in the school district. The Jones and Hilton feed mill and the interests of the prosperous farmers were represented overwhelmingly on the school board. The monolithic power structure was manifest in Springdale's nomination system for school board members as well as for village and town government. "The most invisible act of local politics is the process of selecting nominees for school board membership," say Vidich and Bensman. Behind a legally open nomination system, "the members of the board, the legal counsel and, without doubt, Howard Jones have selected the nominee. . ."[8]

Among the consequences of rural dominance and invisible government linkages of the school board were the support for the characteristic sacred rural values of slowness to change and parochialism, as for example a demand for hometown purchasing. Moreover, the rationale offered for innovation in the Springdale schools typically avoided discussion of the advantages of newness or the value of change itself. Instead, the rationale for innovation emphasized how new programs would support the same traditional, rural values. In effect, school people seeking support for innovations sought to sell these not as new, different, or future-oriented changes but as elaborations of the traditional "as defined in that society." This, perhaps more than anything else, says that Springdale lies at the sacred rather than the secular end of Becker's continuum.

The Superintendent's Role

The self-selection or cooptative political structure of the school board had implications for defining the school superintendent's role.[9] His role and political influence rested on his degree of success as a perceived alien expert. His influence on school policy and activities depended on the extent to which the board and community viewed him as a technical expert and how appropriate his putative expertise was on various issues, especially those involving the budget. In Springdale one reason Peabody, the superintendent, was successful was because of his painstaking care in having the facts about issues presented to the board, thus validating his expert role.[10] Peabody also proved adept at recognizing differences of power in his community and avoid-

---

8 Vidich and Bensman, *Small Town in Mass Society*, pp. 180-81.

9 The term "supervising principal" in its unique meaning for Central districts in New York State is used in Vidich and Bensman's report, *Small Town in Mass Society*.

10 Vidich and Bensman, *Small Town in Mass Society*, pp. 196-99.

ing confrontations beyond his own power. This resulted in his not
being able to receive concessions for his teachers. In addition, he had
developed a power base of his own in the P.T.A. partly dependent on
his expertise. His high vulnerability before the local power pyramid
made it necessary for him to abandon his P.T.A. allies at times and
thus risked losing their support. As Vidich and Bensman point out,

> While giving due weight to these various interests he must at the
> same time try not to alienate any of them. As a result he publicly
> tends to agree with everyone . . . But, in order to accomplish
> his program, he must constantly make concessions to the domi-
> nant interests behind school policy and attempt to implement his
> program through more indirect and subtle means.[11]

The typical rural school district's government is likely to be tightly
linked to the dominant political structure of the community. The
elements of the sacred community are present to a high degree in such
school districts. The low pressure politics of consensus rather than
the high pressure and open conflicts of the secular society are probably present. Unless the school superintendent is a local power holder
for some reason other than his office, he is most likely to be an alien,
technical expert. As such, he is a bridge to the increasingly secularized
mass culture within which the rural school district exists. Vidich and
Bensman point out that such experts are hired by the community and
as such they can be and are readily removable. However, as a linkage
to the larger society, such a school superintendent is also supported
by his outside professional groups and institutions, such as schools of
education. His role is characterized by a high degree of vulnerability,
and because of its importance in the small town, he is watched by
those at the top of the local power pyramid.[12] On the other hand, as
the case of Springdale suggests, there are a number of ways by which
a superintendent can reduce the vulnerability of his office. These require indirectness and subtlety. He must believe in conforming with
the sacred community values. So Peabody tended to agree with everyone. He must know the social power differentials in his district and
avoid confrontations. He needs to use his expertise to acquire control
of the administrative structure and processes of his district and the
leadership of the P.T.A. without in turn becoming too closely tied
to it. This may mean occasionally pulling back from his allies and
standing against his own programs. He must exercise caution and
avoid demanding large increases in expenditure. This is probably

---

11 *Ibid.*, pp. 199-200.
12 *Ibid.*, pp. 274-75.

impossible if concessions are made to teacher requests.[13] He must sell his program as an elaboration of traditional operations, in terms of the old values as the sacred rural district defines it. In short, he needs to avoid conflict, rest heavily on his putative expertise, and where possible, develop the support of local lay citizen groups such as the P.T.A. Thus he cautiously develops his own school-connected power base for the future. The school superintendent in such a community can never become more than a respected second echelon power holder, a leader of the school district's infrastructures of social power such as the P.T.A.

His Base of Influence

The conclusion above appears implicit in the description of Springdale's leadership group and fits the sacred community's leadership type. This type is generalist rather than specialist in nature. The generalist leadership type is necessary to the existence of a single power pyramid interlocking with town, village, and school governments as these deal with their several relatively specialized concerns. While superintendents exist who are reported to be members of the apex of such top policy-making groups in monolithic power pyramids, they occupy this role not as specialist experts but as holders of wealth and patronage.[14] The sacred society norms for leadership are generalist, emphasizing folk wisdom, experience, seniority, and localism, but the "alien expert" role of the professional school man rests on technical knowledge, up-to-date training, and cosmopolitanism. Hence, our conclusion is that, if his base of political power is to a significant extent different from his expert role, or if the school district's population varies from the sacred type of society, the school superintendent can be a top political power figure even in the educational policy making of his community when this policy implies changes in taxation, treads on core values, or has economic implications for the community. The necessary though nonsufficient conditions for achieving such status as a professional requires the secular society with regard for the specialist's technical expertise. Power structures tending to reflect specialized interests also help the specialist.

---

[13] Salary demands in particular, but most teacher requests in general cost more; e.g., smaller classes. Here may be one reason for the increased militancy of N.E.A. affiliates in sacred type states.

[14] Peter Schragg, "Appalachia: Again the Forgotten Land," *Saturday Review* (Jan. 27, 1968), pp. 14-18.

Despite the differences in the potential status open to the school-man or superintendent in each type of society, as long as his official role is under discussion, it must be said that his base for effective influence is the same. He must validate his right to be respected in both sacred and secular type school districts with evidence of expertise. Success at this in the sacred community such as Springdale leads to becoming well established in the alien expert role necessary to, if not completely trusted by, the community. In the secular society his base more often leading to top leadership in educational matters is again the evidence of expertise not generally available in the society. His mode of communication, the particular tactics he uses, his style of introducing change, and the peculiar mechanisms he employs to influence decisions will vary between secular and sacred communities. It may be that a superintendent will function effectively in one type of district but quite poorly in the other. Nevertheless, his base of influence, his fundamental power resource, will, as in Springdale, remain his perceived expertise. Similarly, whatever the legal variations concerning the superintendent's tenure in office, the office of superintendent remains fundamentally the same as that of Peabody—politically vulnerable in both sacred and secular types of communities.

School Districts in the Southeast[15]

The research of professor Ralph B. Kimbrough in the south-eastern portions of the United States supports the thesis concerning the school superintendent's legal vulnerability and the means by which it may be reduced. Stated briefly, Kimbrough's research indicates political linkages between the local school district and the community power holders. This has led him to the conclusion that too much time is spent by students of administration on the formal institutional mode of educational government at the local school district level. Instead, Kimbrough found that local school districts tended to be one element of community government which is greatly influenced, if not dominated, by informal power structures common to the communities displaying generalist leadership. Kimbrough's studies demonstrated that power was largely monopolistic and pyramidal in nature. The monopolistic power pyramids, as seen in Vidich

---

[15] Ralph B. Kimbrough, *Political Power and Educational Decision-Making* (Chicago: Rand McNally & Co., 1964).

and Bensman's report on Springdale, governed most local school districts. Since these pyramids displayed various structural forms without losing their monopolistic character, we may infer that they were of the generalist leadership type. A second pattern Kimbrough listed was described as essentially competitive rather than monopolistic. Nevertheless, the competition for power was usually between established traditional pyramids and emerging newer ones. Each displayed the power pyramid pattern with a generalized leadership type at the top of both of the competing groups.

Alternating Patterns

Following the research of Gladys M. Kammerer, and her colleagues,[16] Kimbrough offers a third pattern of community power structure. This suggests the hypothesis that the monopolistic and competitive patterns of control over local jurisdictions alternate, each giving way to the other as an older pyramid of power weakens and faces the challenge of newer pyramids. Sometimes these newer pyramids consist primarily of the sons of the old guardsmen, while on other occasions the influx of new and different residents creates emerging competitive power pyramids. This view suggests that the monopolistic–competitive distinction used by Kimbrough refers to opposite sides of a single coin with important consequences especially for the student concerned with social or educational change. Implicit in this view is the possibility that the competitive pattern is but a transitional phase between longer periods of more stable, monopolistic control. Thus a period of competitive power structures might be expected as the transition of control of the local administrative unit takes place between power systems led by different generations or different social classes. Such an historical pattern may have been present in the 1938 and 1960 events in the Robertsdale school district.[17] As long as more than one arena of political decisioning exists, the transfer of power from one leadership group to another—even within a single issue area—is likely to display a pattern of power exchanges between monopolistic and competitive structures. Otherwise, political monopolies in school districts would end through abnegation, through the social suicide of surrendering their political advantages without a struggle.

---

[16] Gladys M. Kammerer *et al., City Managers in Politics* (Gainesville, Fla.: University of Florida Press, 1962).

[17] See Chapter 4.

Informal Power

In addition to the discovery of the generalized leadership pattern in the southern school districts they studied, the Kimbrough group's research led to a series of conclusions concerning informal power and educational policy making.[18] Consistent with virtually all other studies of community influence patterns, he concluded that there are inequalities of influence among citizens. Thus, educational policy decisions reflect differences in power resources and the effective use of these among citizens in school districts. Kimbrough stressed the importance of informal groups with the disproportionate resources of private institutions at their disposal as being more influential than public officials, such as school board members, in determining public policies at the local unit level of government. In fact, Kimbrough concluded: "Decisive power is exercised in most local school districts by relatively few persons who hold top positions of influence in the informal power structure of the school district."[19] Moreover, he found that businessmen formed the largest occupational segment of the society found at the decision-making centers of the informal power in many school districts. These findings are consistent with the results of studies concerning the social composition of school boards and the influence of the business ideology on educational administration.[20,21] The pattern noted by Kimbrough, through which informal groups of a few leaders influenced policy, was the use of informal agreement on issues prior to the formal action by official boards. The formal action thus became a public, legal ratification of decisions and accommodations arrived at earlier. In addition, the extension of the influence of leaders through their interaction with other influential leaders tended to produce systematically linked networks of power and probable influence on educational decisions. Finally, Kimbrough noted, similar linkages were established through regular interaction with individuals holding important state and federal positions.

Kimbrough's research has implications for the superintendent's role in the Springdale case. It is not surprising that Kimbrough notes tactics that are similar to those discussed earlier in connection with Superintendent Peabody of Springdale. The sacred community pat-

---

18 Kimbrough, *Political Power and Educational Decision-Making,* pp. 195 ff.
19 *Ibid.,* p. 200.
20 Raymond E. Callahan, *Education and the Cult of Efficiency* (Chicago: University of Chicago Press, 1962).
21 For example, George S. Counts, *The Social Composition of Boards of Education* (Chicago: University of Chicago Press, 1927).

tern, whether found in rural New York State or in the South, places the same requirements on its specialist officials. Specifically, Kimbrough notes the importance of the superintendent identifying the informal or invisible government in his community.[22] The recognition of differences of political power among citizens and the use of that knowledge to obtain the cooperation of leaders in the informal power structure is cited.[23] Kimbrough noted that this tactic of using knowledge of the informal power structure to gain support for the superintendent's policies before public announcement allowed the superintendents he studied to successfully influence policy. The classic element of low pressure secret politics of the sacred community appears. Kimbrough does not use the exact language of Vidich and Bensman when discussing the superintendent's problem of leadership, but he takes substantially the same position. Thus, after pointing out the superintendent's vulnerability in Springdale, they say of his style that ". . . in order to accomplish his program he must constantly make concessions to the dominant interests behind school policy and attempt to implement his program through more indirect and subtle means."[24] Kimbrough says of one superintendent, "Lacking the personal power resources necessary to put over projects, he effectively used the resources of others."[25] Similarly, both authors stress the superintendent's need to understand the local power system and take this into account in order to accomplish his goals for the school district.[26,27] As to the power base of the superintendent, both authors are again in agreement. Men in the private sector have more control than those who rely on public office.[28] Expertise and knowledge are basic to the power of the superintendent. Further, the superintendent needs a command of facts and manipulative skills to deal with power wielders, especially in the sacred community.

Kimbrough's work has contributed to the understanding of educational policy making in the local school district. The evidence shows that the pattern of the sacred rural community, as reported in a rural New York State school district, is neither unique to Springdale nor confined to highly rural districts. In the Southeast too, local school districts including those in cities reveal patterns of control in determining policy similar to Springdale's government and politics.

---

[22] Kimbrough, *Political Power* . . . , pp. 221-36.
[23] *Ibid.*, especially pp. 228-9.
[24] Vidich and Bensman, *Small Town in Mass Society*, pp. 199-200.
[25] Kimbrough, *Political Power* . . . , pp. 227-8.
[26] *Ibid.*, p. 275.
[27] Vidich and Bensman, *Small Town in Mass Society*, p. 199.
[28] *Ibid.*, pp. 197-9; Kimbrough, *Political Power* . . . , pp. 277-8.

The same type of generalized community leadership and invisible government influence the school district's decision making. Kimbrough's research also indicates that schoolmen probably need to take the changing power structures into consideration when examining their districts in order to understand them and work in them. His stress on informal group leadership and its virtual dominance of policy making, even if overstated, offers a useful correction to the naive formal, institutional emphasis commonly taught to school administrators. His emphasis, however, tends to merge two distinct concepts into a single one. Often, the informal aspects of leadership appear to be identical with the monolithic power pyramid structure. This description characterizes the communities he studied. The local units which he studied revealed that a large measure of influence was wielded by informal groups held together more by personal than institutional relationships. These generally were unified power pyramids, essentially monolithic in structure. There is no reason to believe that the existence of informal leadership groups or the accommodation of contending groups prior to formal meetings implies the existence of monolithic or unified structures. In fact, the present writers know of no formal decision-making operation with any serious responsibility which operates in a completely public and formal pattern without informal, social linkages.

In summary, recent research on school district politics in the Southeast turned up a number of local school districts with power systems similar to that of Springdale. They displayed a high degree of informal political activity in decision making, generally with a pattern of accommodation of interests in a single leadership group. Formal governmental agencies, such as school boards, were likely to act in accordance with the decisions arrived at by leadership groups. Similar informal patterns seemed to exist whether the community's power structure pattern was monopolistic or competitive. This suggested that a alternative pattern of monopolistic to competitive to monopolistic existed in these communities.

Community leaders' regard for expertise and need for information produced support for specialist experts such as the superintendents. But such experts were not part of the inner groups of such leaders. This indicated that the leadership types were generalist, as in Springdale, the status of expert specialists being that of second-level hired leaders. Further, representatives of the institutions of the private sector, linked to community leaders through personal ties, tended to appear most frequently in the top policy-making groups. Public officials in various decision arenas tended to be controlled in their decisions by these leadership groups. The wide range of issues that such leadership groups took up also indicated that the generalist type of leadership governed the communities on which Kimbrough reported. The existence of two types of community power structures, monopolistic and competitive, whether alternating forms of the same *genre* or polar extremes of a single continuum, did not alter the characteristic generalist type of leadership reported by Kimbrough, which is characteristic of the sacred community.

Pluralistic Communities

Noticeably absent in the communities studied in the Southeast is the pluralist pattern of power structure reported in larger northeastern cities such as New Haven and New York. The politics of urban school districts may be considered as a proper subcategory of the politics of education; however, it will not be discussed extensively in this book. The urban district may best illustrate the politics of pluralism and the secular society, neither of which is confined to the urban center.

New Haven

The first case of the pluralistic power pattern to be briefly examined is New Haven, a northeastern city with a history of alternating monopolistic to competitive, as described by Kimbrough. By the beginning of the second half of this century New Haven had developed the third political pattern with which we are concerned—*pluralism.* New Haven has accordingly come to resemble New York City more than Springdale—or Atlanta, as described by Floyd Hunter.[29] Dahl attributed the pluralist pattern in New Haven to the intervention of industrialism during the shift from agrarianism to the modern secular American society.[30] Various elites which had governed New Haven prior to its pluralism began with the commercial patricians in a largely agricultural universe still displaying the major elements of the sacred society. He viewed industrialization as producing a pattern of dispersal of the universal political inequalities present in the previous monolithic and monopolistic concentrations of political power in the successive

[29] Floyd Hunter, *Community Power Structure.*

[30]Robert A. Dahl, *Who Governs?* (New Haven, Conn.: Yale University Press, 1961), pp. 1-86.

political elites governing New Haven. Thus, one characteristic of the New Haven pluralist power system was a set of dispersed inequalities. The absence of a single elite governing New Haven did not result in an equalization of political power among all citizens but instead in a multifactional distribution of political power in which specialist leadership could flourish because of the lack of a single center of decisioning. Hence, there was no overriding need for the generalist leadership type.

Dahl refers to those much more highly involved in political thought and activities than the rest of the population as the *political stratum* (but this term does not connote that these are a single natural group). The political stratum for Dahl is a statistically identifiable category of persons. It is not a social group or class formed by a common pattern of interaction. Dahl's concept of the political stratum as found in New Haven stands in direct contrast with Gaetano Mosca's political class concept which connotes a pyramid of interaction focusing in a small group.[31] Thus, both monolithic and pluralistic concepts agree on the basic universal of political inequalities, especially when they focus on the question of who initiates authoritative decisions for the community. They do differ, however, on the question of unity or diversity of policy-making leadership—on whether a single interacting group tends to initiate policies in a number of different aspects of public life, or a number of different top policy groups tend to initiate policies in their own areas of public life. In turn, each of the top leadership groups publicly confronts and openly conflicts with one another. Eventually, they enter into bargains resulting from the politics of conflict resolution. In classical Aristotelian terms the question could be posed as to whether there exists a polity or several polities in New Haven, New York, Atlanta, or whatever local governmental unit is being considered.

Political Leadership

In his study of New Haven government Dahl undertook to answer for that city the question posed above by examining three issue areas. For him the central issue was whether New Haven displayed one, two, or three leadership groups in these issue areas. If the answer were one, then the monolithic power system which Floyd Hunter described in his study of Atlanta would also best describe

---

31 Dahl, *Who Governs?*, pp. 90-94; Gaetano Mosca, *The Ruling Class* (New York: McGraw-Hill Book Company, 1939), pp. 50-69.

New Haven. If each issue area instead displayed a different leadership group, then a plural pattern of political power holding would better describe the New Haven governmental system. The assumption that the pluralistic political system better fulfills the democratic belief system need not concern us here.[32]

The nomination of party standard bearers fails to live up to the legal theory and democratic myths of political parties in three ways.[33] Party members are only a small part of those usually voting with the party. The party members who play an active part in caucuses and primaries are the smaller portion. The machinery of nominations is generally used to ratify the decisions of leaders rather than give control of the party to the rank and file. Dahl indicates that not only does the nomination subsystem of New Haven government usually select party nominees prior to formal nomination conventions but the negotiations for selecting such candidates have for years taken place among at most, a half dozen party leaders. Others may exert an indirect influence on these men but this is not demonstrated by Dahl's data. The conclusion of indirect influence of potential voters or power holders on the observed behavior of key influentials is common in research reports involving community studies. Though appearing reasonable, such conclusions too readily support the biases of their users. In any case, Dahl's evidence supports his statement that "except for the rare instance of the subleader who seeks to challenge the top leadership, most subleaders are content to permit a few top leaders . . . [to] decide on nominations."[34] Further, he points out that, even if an insurgent faction led by a subleader were to win, it would only mean the replacement of one small group by another. Thus viewed in isolation, apart from the other decisional organizations and issue areas, the nomination system displays the typical social oligarchy of social organizations.

Urban redevelopment reportedly displays the characteristic pyramid of top leadership, subleaders, the political stratum, and the apolitical mass.[35] Preferring to avoid the more common analogy of the monolithic school, Dahl characterizes this distribution of influence as triangular in shape. In any event, the analysis of fifty-seven decisions reveals that half are attributed to Mayor Lee and his development administrator. Similarly, the interview evidence reported by Dahl indicates that, while a large set of committees involving a wide range of

---

[32] For a discussion of this issue, see pp. 50-51.
[33] Dahl, *Who Governs?*, p. 104.
[34] *Ibid.*, p. 108.
[35] *Ibid.*, pp. 115ff.

individuals and organizations participated in urban redevelopment efforts, they did not make the decisions. Their involvement and support were necessary but decisions concerning redevelopment came from the Mayor's office. There is evidence that specialist subleaders played a more significant role than the economic notables and other political "muscles" represented on the Citizen Action Commission.[36] Thus, the issue area of urban redevelopment, central to New Haven governmental life during the period studied by Dahl, saw the sub-leadership of a very small group of specialists focused toward the top leadership of the Mayor, an elected public official. The arrangement stands in contrast to the informal power of a group of private individuals frequently reported in monolithic community power structures.

The issue area of public education in New Haven displayed the same consistencies in nomination and urban redevelopment areas.[37] With a more routinized, lower pressure and a more bureaucratized decisional pattern than the other issue areas, the school maintained the nonpartisan stance and insulation from party electoral politics customary to urban school districts. Because of New Haven's adoption of the educational doctrine of separation between politics and education, the mayor's attempts to influence the decisions of the board and superintendent would be resisted by the political stratum interested in schools. The appointment of board members by the mayor is an indirect influence, but the seven-man board is appointed for four-year, staggered terms. By tradition, reappointment is the rule. A balance of religious interests is also maintained on the board, though not as rigidly as New York's pattern of three Catholics, three Jews, and three Protestants. Within these traditional restrictions mayors can appoint men whom they think will most likely act as they would. Similarly, the superintendent of schools once appointed is difficult to remove, as Dahl points out, "because he can invoke the support of national professional groups if his removal does not appear to be based on considerations of professional adequacy."[38] He concludes that a superintendent may "acquire a major, perhaps decisive, influence on policies relating to essentially internal school matters."

Examination of educational issues and decisions in New Haven led to the conclusion that only a small number of citizens participated in important decisions bearing on the schools. Further, it was public

---

36 *Ibid.*, pp. 130-7.
37 *Ibid.*, pp. 141-62.
38 *Ibid.*, p. 151.

officials who exercised direct influence over decisions. Finally, the mayor's office had seemed to become the key center of influence instead of the superintendent of schools. Nevertheless, the school administrators and teachers with their traditional P.T.A. followings constituted a force of specialized leadership. However, the school administrators were reported as an elite within the eystem. Teachers and the Parent Teachers' Association were viewed as supportive troops. In fact, the P.T.A. was indispensable to an administrator's success. Once again, the leadership of a small group of specialist leaders—in this case, educational professionals—directly controlled their issue area.

Comparative examinations of the three issue areas reveal that New Haven was characterized by a high degree of separate—or to use Dahl's term, specialized—subleadership.[39] The top leadership level was characterized by individuals who displayed a high degree of concentration on a single issue area rather than two or all three. Further, the most central leadership was not found in an invisible government of economic notables but in elected public offices, especially the mayor's.

Characteristics of Pluralism

One characteristic of the pluralistic system found in New Haven and pointed out by Dahl is the difference between the power resources available to most citizens and their actual use of these. There is thus a large amount of political slack in the system. Leaders can call upon this slack, mobilizing it for or against given policies. It provides a reserve fund of political power leading either to stability or change. It is, however, the professionals in party work, in urban renewal offices, in the schools, and in other public policy areas who have the time and enough at stake to invest in acquiring the skills to exploit more fully their power resources to influence decisions.[40] Hence, there is a greater likelihood that the pluralist pattern will display a higher degree of specialist leadership whether this is found at the very top or mainly in subleadership groups.

The pattern described has a number of significant outcomes, some similar to the monolithic structure and some markedly different. The secular city governmental system lacks the high level of integration

---

[39] The term as Dahl in *Who Governs?* uses it need not imply particular expertise or professional knowledge and skill. It does, however, imply that the individual subleaders concentrate their participation on one issue area.

[40] Dahl, *Who Governs?*, pp. 305-10.

found in Springdale and other sacred rural communities. However, the central agencies of city government ratify the accommodations which the specialist experts and other interested satellite groups in each issue area arrive at. Low visibility politics and informal accommodation characterize the process within the various decisional issue areas including education. Internally, the school system of a pluralist city pattern exhibits many aspects of the monopolistic small town of rural America, as described in the Kimbrough studies. Externally, the whole system for local government is different.

In New Haven, unlike Springdale, the struggles among decision centers are not characterized by low visibility politics of consensus and the etiquette of gossip but by a search for a good press and the politics of conflict resolution. Here the open confrontation of specialist experts, most often *of different expertise*, is an everyday occurrence. In the secular society not only is this open confrontation possible at the formal governmental boards but the status of the expert is consequently different from what it is in the sacred society. In New York, for example, the specialist is not necessarily an employed alien expert forced to influence through indirection. Not only is open conflict possible at the formal governmental level but the status of the expert is significantly different from hired help. He openly plays an active leadership role where his expertise is itself a respected power resource rather than merely the basis from which he may approach the real community leaders.

Another element which the pluralist and monolithic systems share is that most decisions are molded by a small segment of the population. Inequality of power and political influence tend to be cumulative in the monopolistic system. The lack of influence which one has in a given public policy area correlates with and reinforces a similar power deprivation in other areas. Inequalities of political influence and power tend to be dispersed in the pluralistic system. The lack of influence in one public policy area may be offset by much larger holdings of influence in another area. Nevertheless, relatively small groups dispose of any significant political power in both systems. Hence, neither system can be offered as a model of egalitarian democracy.

The special consequences of the pluralistic political system includes the existence of a multicentered decision-making structure which, like a complex maze of risky hurdles, is inherently conservative, with frequent delays and stalemates. Unlike the monolithic, single community power structure, the multicentered decisional pattern lacks a community-wide outlook. Similarly, the multicentered pattern makes it difficult for voters to ascribe blame to anyone, the political slack noted by Robert A. Dahl.

The pluralist system is open to a variety of groups. Opportunities for the origination of action are many. Here are its virtues: The system, inherently filled with vetoes, protects groups from attack and tolerates diversity. It is a system of checks which in some cities increasingly appears to be losing effective balance.

The ideological predilections of monopolistic or pluralistic advocates are not our present concern. Much of the discussion and conflict between these schools of political thought is less illuminating than it is friction-generating. Too often community power research tends to reflect conflicting assumptions, conceptual systems, and empirical results. Sociologists typically have found elite leadership structures, while political scientists have more often found pluralistic systems. There has also been a tendency for pluralism to be associated more often with larger, more complex northern urban governments. The issues of political ideology, however, deserve some attention.

Recent political writings that are ideologically committed to pluralism as a democratic institution rest on the argument that the combination of the absence of a single elite and the presence of a number of elites with different power bases provides an open system. The individual's power is no greater in this system than in the monolithic system. It is when a single elite comes into being in the community that the increasingly closed social development takes place. In an issue area such as education, if the sphere of policy decisions displays a dominant elite even though other elites exist for other issue areas, the educational decisioning system becomes relatively closed. It is then subject to all the weaknesses and strengths of the monolithic power pyramid. From the viewpoint of a democratic theory concerned with the individual's rights and his capacity to escape the demands of an elite by moving into another interest area, there may be much to be said for the value of pluralism. But from the viewpoint of those inescapably caught in a given issue area, such as education, the existence of other elites in different walks of public life offers cold comfort, indeed. The teacher who is too heavily invested to change his profession, the pupil under compulsory education, and the parents without the realistic option of private schools are all trapped in their educational aspirations by a closed elite's control of educational policy making.

3

The Leadership of
Educational Administration

Central to the monolithic power pyramid is generalized
leadership, a group of leaders at the apex of the community's social system who share the oversight of the major
public decision-making arenas and services. The sacred
community with its relatively low esteem for the alien
expert is much more likely to display this type of a power
structure than is the secular society. Other probable correlates of the monolithic power pyramid include (1) the
size of the school district, (2) its degree of urbanization,
(3) the relative amount of geographic mobility found in it,
(4) the extent to which the school district and other local
governmental units are coterminous, (5) the cosmopolitan
vs. local character of its residents, and (6) its political associations and whether they display primarily neighborhood
and kinship bases or reflect occupational and other specialized interests. These factors are likely to be influenced
by regional culture. So, for instance, one would expect to
find more sacred communities in the southeastern portion of
the United States than in the Northeast.

The six factors cited above are not truly discrete categories but are likely to overlap. For example, the amount
of geographic mobility and the extent to which political

associations reflect neighborhoods are likely to be highly related. Nevertheless, these six variables may be used to examine local school districts and to assess the probable existence of generalized leadership and invisible government, such as Kimbrough noted was found in Springdale.[1]

It is reasonable to expect that the larger a school district is, the greater its population's heterogeneity as to values and aspirations held for education; further, the less likely there is to be a single dominant power structure, an invisible government with generalized leadership. The more urbanized the school district, the less it is likely to resemble the sacred community. The larger the amount of geographic mobility —of movement into and out of the district—the greater are the chances that the district's government will utilize formal machinery for policy making and the less likely it is to depend on informal networks and linkages of traditional local actors. The generalized leadership of invisible government in Springdale existed in a school district roughly coterminous with the town. This is not surprising. A moment's reflection indicates that it would be easier for a monolithic, generalized leadership group to link together educational and other governments when these include a common set of citizens, social systems, and territory. This coordination would be much more difficult if the boundaries of each governmental unit which they tried to hold together were quite different, involving different participants and subsystems. The more cosmopolitan the character of a school district's residents, the more toward the secular end of the continuum will be that district's social and political patterns. Finally, rural communities tend to display neighborhood organizations of considerable political significance, and even in the United States these are not infrequently seen to display some elements of kinship linkages.

Communities that display a wealth of political subsystems reflecting occupational or other special interests are more likely to value technical expertise and develop expert leadership groups along special interest and occupational lines rather than to defer to a generalized leadership group. These communities are likely to display the characteristics of secular rather than sacred societies. School districts like these are more likely to display the pluralist patterns. Elected officeholders and specialists are more likely to be found in leadership roles in the pluralist secular societies, while economic notables are more likely to occupy such roles in the monopolistic sacred ones.

---

[1] Ralph B. Kimbrough, *Political Power and Educational Decision-Making* (Chicago: Rand McNally & Co., 1964).

Where dominance of the typical economic notable occurs with its generalist leadership, the role of the specialist leader such as the school superintendent is best viewed as that of alien expert. In the secular type the specialist may have his greatest opportunity for top leadership.[2] With the increasing secularity of American society, and particularly since the turn of this century, educational professionals have had increasing opportunities for political leadership.

EFFECTS ON THE POLITICS OF SCHOOL DISTRICTS

The sacred–secular continuum provides insight into educational policy development not only in local school districts but also in the teaching profession. As Robert K. Merton points out, individuals who occupy positions in a bureaucracy run the risk of developing the bureaucratic personality. In particular, a tendency may be found toward less risk-taking behavior, especially organizational defensibility of decisions, searching for security with a concern for seniority rights, and consequent rigidity in behavior and procedures. In short, elements of the sacred community may develop in a bureaucracy or formal organization. Apparently rational bureaucracies have, over a time, become highly traditional organizations virtually impervious to demands for change.[3] Similarly, as Merton points out, ". . . there may ensue, in particular vocations and in particular types of organizations, *The Process of Sanctification* (viewed as the counterpart of the process of secularization)."[4]

The Process of Sanctification

The teaching profession, especially given its client population of students and their emotional appeal, is likely to develop the process of sanctification to a high degree. Every profession seeks to surround its practitioners with elements of mystery with the imputation of specialized knowledge apart from that held by others. Given the fact

---

[2] Robert Presthus, *Men at The Top* (New York: Oxford University Press, 1964), pp. 138-203.

[3] Laurence Iannaccone, *Politics in Education* (New York: The Center for Applied Research in Education, 1967), pp. 25-29.

[4] Robert K. Merton, *Social Theory and Social Structure* (New York: The Free Press, 1957), p. 282. *See also* E. C. Hughes, "Personality Types and the Division of Labor," *American Journal of Sociology*, 33 (1928), 754-68.

that professionals engage in the less than certain diagnostic and re-medial application of scientific knowledge to problems, they cannot be certain of their judgments. The cloak of the professional mystique helps protect both the professional's self image and his public rela-tionships. It also gives the client faith in the professional. The use of the term "layman," for a person outside the profession reveals the un-conscious sacred point of view of the professional towards his pro-fession. The teaching profession may be even more subject to this tendency toward sanctification than most other professions because it deals in values, is engaged in a moral enterprise, and appears to hold in pawn the lives of children. Perhaps, too, the teaching pro-fession may be among those professions least sure of their techniques and hence most in need of its mystique. Teaching displays the ten-dency toward the process of sanctification. The influence of the educa-tional professions on the local school district, its standards, its policy development, its systems of approval and disapproval, and its poli-tics inclines these districts toward the sacred rather than the secular society—even within a secular world.

Thus, for example, the teaching profession places a higher value on experience than on training. More significant is the reliance placed on experience and seniority by informal adult social systems in schools. Student teaching, the key point of entrance into the profession, the "narrows" through which almost all teachers pass, is characterized by the apprentice-master relationship in which it is openly seen that the cooperating teacher's right to respect is based not on recentness of training or advanced study but experience. Until very recently, experience rather than specialization or amount of training had been used as the chief basis for respect by the profession and the general public.

Emphasis on Security

As the sacred community's valuing of experience is reflected in the education profession, so the emphasis is on security rather than risk-taking. The heavy dependence on tenure, the long standing resistance to overt distinction between average, below average, or outstanding teachers, and the successful struggle of the profession against signifi-cant merit salary systems substantiate the commitment to security rather than risk-taking. The noncompetitive recognition of ascribed status rather than specific achievement may also be seen in the continuous resistance to many forms of teacher evaluation, the rejection of product measures, and the resistance to regional or national assessment programs.

Finally, the profession's unwillingness to openly criticize any of its members, its lack of self-policing, and the absence of a teacher's term comparable to "quack" or "shyster" are reflected on the obverse side of the coin by its etiquette of gossip. In the experience of these authors, educational grapevines—whether within a particular building, district, state, or throughout the country—carry evaluations of individuals and schools remarkably similar to Springdale, as described by Vidich and Bensman.

> The etiquette of gossip which makes possible the public suppression of the negative and competitive aspects of life has its counterpart in the etiquette of public conversation which always emphasizes the positive . . . More than this, the level of public conversation always focuses on the collective success of the community and the individual successes of its members. . . . At the public level all types of successes are given public recognition while failure is treated with silence.[5]

Finally, education displays the sacred community's high regard for office and appointed officeholders. Only recently—since the society around schools has begun to display more and more of the hippie subculture, a secular extreme—have school administrators begun to take on the appearance of the villain in educationist discussions and writings. Nevertheless, school people continue to display a strong upward orientation toward public school administrators. If superintendents are no longer the highly respected figures they once were, they are still at least the occupants of offices to which "good" teachers aspire.

Perhaps no better illustration of the sacred community aspects of education may be offered than the well established educationist tradition of greeting each new educational innovation first with rejection and then with the appraisal that "it's not so different from what good teachers have been doing all along." When the road to the adoption of innovation is best smoothed by the identification of the new as really not so new, one is dealing with a sacred rather than secular type of social organization. It is hardly surprising if such a group offers resistance to change much of the time.

---

[5] Arthur J. Vidich and Joseph Bensman, *Small Town in Mass Society* (Garden City, N.Y.: Doubleday & Company, Inc., 1960), pp. 43-46.

The profession's preferred politics tends to reflect the sacred community's life style both internally in professional association politics and externally in school districts and states. However, these patterns of behavior and the local school district itself tend toward the sacred end of the sacred–secular continuum for many reasons, in addition to the profession's influence. As may be seen in the work of Solon T. Kimball and James E. McClellan, Jr., the American local school district of this century was shaped in the last century, especially by midwest agrarianism and main street towns.[6] Even education's prophets of progressivism displayed a rural rejection of the secular revolution produced by the modern industrial and urban developments. Hence, the local school district continues to "remain as the governmental operation most like a midwestern adaptation of the New England Town Meeting or like the operations of the Music Man set in Peyton Place."[7]

HISTORICAL ROOTS

The period of American history in which educational administration had its formative stage saw the rise of the narrow efficiency values of Taylorism applied to schools. The close relationship between this and the efforts to rid education of politics has recently been studied by Raymond E. Callahan. His studies of the development of the superintendency as the key policy office in the local school district show this arrangement came about during a period of high stress on the schools. Severe public pressures were generated by the rapid expansion of the school population near the turn of the century. These included restructuring the control of local schools resulting from the development of the high school and exposing the poor conditions and excessive use of corporal punishment in schools. In addition, a series of articles in national magazines told of political corruption and influence, especially in the city schools which were part of the spoils system. Such were the conditions on the eve of the critical period Callahan called, "the struggle for power between school board and superintendents." The role of the superintendent was, even in larger cities, highly vulnerable; superintendents' hands were often tied. Key decisions in the late nineteenth century were often retained by

---

[6] Solon T. Kimball and James E. McClellan, Jr., *Education and the New America* (New York: Random House, Inc., 1962), pp. 64ff.

[7] Iannaccone, *Politics in Education,* p. 9.

the school boards. As Callahan stated, "The problem, of course, was to convince school boards, who had the legal power to make decisions, to turn this power over to superintendents."[8] In other words, what was needed was a transfer of leadership from generalist leaders to specialist leaders. It was precisely the argument of expertise in contrast to political corruption used by the national leaders in education. The effects of the progressive movement after 1900 were noteworthy because they purged schools of political corruption. In this process the nature of the superintendency underwent significant modification.

The Struggle for Leadership

As early as 1880 the National Education Association—led by men such as Nicholas Murry Butler of Columbia, Charles Elliot of Harvard, William Maxwell, the highly educated and respected Superintendent of New York, and William T. Harris, United States Commissioner of Education—initiated studies and then action to solve the many educational problems of the era. Among these were the problems of the organization of the larger schools and the office of superintendent. In 1890 superintendents considered their situation so vulnerable (they actually used this term) that they were *afraid* to advocate that the boards turn over the selection of teachers to them because they felt that the board would refuse to do so. They thought this would lead to more attacks on superintendents. These educational leaders felt that schools were behind other institutions in progress "toward differentiation and specialization of function,"[9] characteristics of the secular type of society. Callahan states that the boards appointed teachers, ignoring the expertise of the administrators. Political patronage was present in these appointments, and superintendents were aware of their legal and political vulnerability. Recommendations to strengthen the superintendency offered by its own association's committee failed to gain sufficient support from the National Council of the National Education Association. Only the attacks on the weaknesses of the schools by nonprofessionals from outside—especially Joseph Mayer Rice, according to Callahan—gave the superintendents the necessary

---

8 Raymond E. Callahan, *The Superintendent of Schools: An Historical Analysis* (Washington, D.C.: Co-operative Research Branch, U.S. Office of Education, Department of Health, Education and Welfare, 1967), p. 67.
    9 *Ibid.*, p. 73.

push to engage the school boards in a battle for recognition of their specialist role. Rice urged the schools be taken out of politics.

The basic goals sought by the proponents of strengthening the superintendent's legal power included control over appointments of personnel and control over details of expenditure within a budget established by the board. Following the traditional American governmental model, they suggested that the superintendent be considered the executive of the school district, having a veto power in relation to his legislature, the board. In addition, their agenda called for his appointment by the board for a long term. Some advocates for achieving this strengthening of the office turned to state legislation as a means of reducing its vulnerability.[10] Callahan concludes that toward the turn of the century "the drive for power which the leaders in educational administration launched in 1890 was paying dividends toward the end of the decade."[11] Naturally, this drive and the proposed changes in the legal structure of the board's relationship to the superintendent provoked opposition from school board members. William Bruce, the publisher and editor of the *American School Board Journal,* widely read among school board members and superintendents, led the fight against the proposed changes. Even the general reform trends which were to reorganize many cities failed to help the advocates of a stronger superintendency carry the issue.

Uneasy Command

The war for legal protection and role specification of superintendent leadership was lost, but a few major battles were won. The conflict and airing of the issues increased the number of boards which without legislation delegated power to superintendents. Callahan states: "Year after year in the twentieth century they have been making more of the major educational decisions—they have been in command. But it has been an uneasy command."[12] The tactics by which they succeeded in making these gains had already been used by some of the superintendents who managed to survive the long years when the battle was fought. The conservative superintendents of the 1890's had urged everyone to avoid the direct confrontation of the political

---

[10] *Ibid.*, pp. 124ff.
[11] *Ibid.*, p. 131.
[12] *Ibid.*, p. 143.

issue. They not only predicted the failure of the struggle but also
provided the models of future success. They operated by indirection
to educate and persuade boards but also to manipulate a public
opinion favorable to their leadership.[13] They were, in this way, the
prototype of the professionally educated school administrators of most
suburban, rural, and small city schools of today. The success of superintendents advocating the utilization of the sacred community behavioral patterns, including slowness to change, stood in contrast to
those advocating open political confrontation. The victory of this
group at the very time that educational administration was to begin
its professional training placed its stamp on that training and future
programs of school administration. Finally, the efficiency movement
with its defense mechanisms and popular appeal helped schoolmen to
acquire recognition as specialist leaders. Although subject to local
financial limits, the combination of public credit as a specialist with
the norms and traditions of the sacred community inside the profession has resulted in considerable influence for the school superintendent of today.

THE SECULAR SUBURB

The Jefferson School District is familiar to students of educational
administration and has been described elsewhere.[14] Jefferson was a
suburban school district outside of a large metropolitan center. The
district included a village and portions of two other local governments.
Hence, it was not coterminous with any other local government.
Jefferson was studied in the late 1950's in detail. It included six
schools—four elementary schools, one high school, and one junior
high school. Measured by pupil expenditure, Jefferson was one of the
wealthiest school districts in America, its citizens among the most
cosmopolitan, its children among the more academically able, its
environment more advantageous for education, and its undistinguished
educational program better than average. In a cosmopolitan, secular
suburban society, this school district existed with the customary
semiautonomous governance of education. This governing pattern
displayed many of the sacred community patterns under the pruden-
tial influence of a school superintendent trained in the "democratic"
manipulative tradition of his profession and committed to the ideol-

---

[13] *Ibid.,* pp. 142-3, 170-1, and 176.
[14] Daniel E. Griffiths *et al., Organizing Schools for Effective Education* (Danville, Ill.: The Interstate Printers & Publishers, Inc., 1962), pp. 225-93.

ogy of keeping education and politics separate. Hardly democratic in its internal relationships, it had the virtue of freedom from political corruption.

The Board

The schools were administered by their six principals and a central office staff headed by Superintendent Donnelly under a six-member board of education. The board met monthly for regular meetings; additional "adjourned" meetings were also generally held each month.

Central to the school board operations was the figure of Dr. Donnelly, the superintendent. Dr. Donnelly had previously been the high school principal in the district. His concern that the Jefferson Village politicians, who had been dominant in the school district prior to 1940, be replaced had been shared particularly by the wealthier upper middle-class residents of the district in areas outside of the village. Thus, an element of class values entered into the change. Further, the approaching retirement of the old superintendent made the early 1940's particularly significant both for the Jefferson School District and Dr. Donnelly.

A citizens' Committee for the Selection of School Board Nominees was brought into existence in the late 1930's to screen names proposed for school board membership and act as a caucus for their selection. Partly because board members representing the village politicians had served repeatedly and partly under the leadership of Dr. Donnelly, the committee decided to limit its support of board members for only two three-year terms of office. The committee's political success and Dr. Donnelly's elevation to the superintendency coincided. Consequently, his impact on the committee was significant. He was always consulted concerning potential nominees for board membership, and while he declined to take a position on particular candidates, he did customarily suggest criteria for board membership. These tended to fit residents outside of the village center who had higher incomes and a personal history of working well with the educational professionals of the district, especially the school administrators. For more than twenty years the committee succeeded in winning the elections for its nominees, selected with the criteria and friendly help of Dr. Donnelly.

The selection committee's own mode of appointment, its composition, and procedures revealed the extent to which Jefferson had developed into a monolithic political type. It expressed the sacred community pattern of educational politics even though it developed in a secular suburban milieu. In April of each year an open meeting was held, usually at the home of some prestigious citizen of the school district, attended by about fifty people. At this meeting, twelve representatives were elected to the selection committee, which reflected three geographic sections of the district. Twelve others were appointed from the old committee to represent a link with the past. The committee thereupon invited proposals for candidates and screened these using a six-member subcommittee and frequent help from Dr. Donnelly. This process resulted in committee-supported candidates only for each position open in the election. The selection committee always supported incumbents for reelection in a second three-year term, but never more. Once, the committee managed to avoid an open conflict and test of two-term tradition when an incumbent running for a third term withdrew on the eve of election. This threat to the nomination system and its leadership was avoided by informal pressure and friendly persuasion of the incumbent candidate.

Thus, the committee's traditions, composition, and political behavior revealed the type of political system which controlled the crucial element of school board nomination successfully in Jefferson for most of twenty years. That system was essentially of the sacred community type. The active participation of a small proportion of the people of Jefferson resulting in their successfully controlling school board nominations for most of two decades is similar to Springdale's control of all local elections. The use of cooptation as a regular device to produce each new nomination committee resulted in stability and resistance to change. The pattern of supporting only one candidate for each available office indicates that the committee did more than screen and determine the qualifications of candidates. It is an effective means of political support. There seldom is a better opportunity for understanding the heart of a social system than when it is subjected to stress such as presented by the threat of the violation of the third-term rule. The use of persuasion operating informally through friendship groups which avoid open political confrontation supports the sacred community pattern. The history of the selection committee's development and Dr. Donnelly's role in it strongly suggests that he fits the pattern of professional leadership by indirect political manipulation advocated by the conservatives of the 1890's.[15]

---

[15] See p. 59.

Board and Superintendent

The Jefferson School Board's procedures and traditional practices further stabilized the district's leadership pattern. There were no standing committees. When committees were needed, they were *ad hoc* in nature and disbanded when their specific tasks were completed. A published set of policy statements existed and were rigidly followed by Dr. Donnelly and the administration. The policies might change slowly but they were always enforced, even in cases where all agreed that they worked unfairly. In general, Dr. Donnelly did not favor policy or rule changes. He supported such changes only after considerable delay allowing for study and the development of professional and public support of the changes. School board meetings were open to the public, and while there were no closed executive sessions, "Committee of the Whole" meetings were held prior to each board meeting. The public was excluded from these meetings, and the agenda for the coming meeting was discussed so that the board members could determine their public behavior after discovering the line-up of forces on the issues. This agenda was prepared in advance by Dr. Donnelly and his staff. Items on which there was substantial agreement were easily identified, as were those on which there was little agreement. In contrast to his role in open sessions, Dr. Donnelly acted as chairman as well as chief initiator of agenda items in these closed sessions. Thus, the public meeting was conducted with the benefit of the closed "Committee of the Whole" meeting.

Dr. Donnelly often stated that his position was that of servant to the Jefferson board and community. He displayed this definition of his role in muted language by sitting at the foot of the board table. The board president, who traditionally was a member in his last year of office, chaired the board meeting using Donnelly's agenda. As each item was introduced, the chairman turned to Dr. Donnelly for his recommendation before asking the board to discuss it. Donnelly's recommendations tended to take one of two forms. Sometimes he would take a strong position on an issue, offering information and evidence for his position, occasionally appearing to be willing to stand alone on the issue. The second was the statement that he had not placed the item on the agenda for immediate action but had felt it necessary for the board to think about the issue before they were called on to act. He would then recommend that the particular problem or issue be studied and would offer preliminary suggestions for its resolution. These suggestions usually included the use of central office staff members, committees of teachers, citizen advisory groups, *ad hoc* committees of the school board, or a combination of these.

The discussions of board members tended to indicate the two specialized interests represented on the board. One was expertise on matters of finance, law, or real estate. The second was an interest or commitment on specific educational issues. For example, the traditional lone woman board member tended to be more concerned with curricular issues in the elementary schools than was any other member. Less visible at board meetings, but present as a function of the geographic distribution of the Jefferson Board's composition, was a representation of the elementary school attendance areas of the district. Finally, the three major religions were represented on the board by at least one Catholic, one Jew, and one Protestant.

Often the board spent most of its time during public meetings on those items which had required little discussion in the private sessions and where there had been substantial agreement. Agenda items which had revealed serious disagreement in the closed meetings were often handled expeditiously during the public board meetings. Such issues had been discussed enough in private so that the superintendent and the board members could reveal their concerns about the issues without becoming publicly committed to a particular solution. This allowed the public, mainly P.T.A. observers, to see their representatives validate their right to office without producing internal board conflict. It further indicated the positions that needed to be taken into account in order to achieve concensus without conflict. Dr. Donnelly was able to offer his criteria for a solution to the problem, avoiding a confrontation between his office and any board member but still beginning the search for alternatives without jeopardizing his position. The extensive discussion of matters where agreement had been revealed in their closed sessions could hardly have been informative to board members or Donnelly. These discussions of previously found agreements had the social function of emphasizing and reinforcing the established solidarity of the board. These discussions also further validated Donnelly's and the board's rights to continued political leadership of the Jefferson School District.

The prevalence of sacred community elements is clear but with some aspects of the secular society. The careful avoidance of the language of executive session—a practice condemned by university-based professors of education—with its retention in fact under a different title illustrates the mixture. The language meets the secular society's ethos but the operations reflect the sacred. In contrast, the true sacred community such as Springdale would not be so influenced by the external, university-based specialist opinion. The sacred community may even prize the university specialist's disapproval. Hence, the Jefferson Board pattern retained the substance of the monopolistic community power structure without its traditional form.

The Superintendent's Power

Dr. Donnelly's key role in the school system's politics was supported by the board's pattern of operations and the system of nominations for school board members. Even without the knowledge that Donnelly had played the central role in establishing the board's policies and procedures, it would have been clear that his office was strengthened by most of these. A high degree of bureaucratization is apparent in the norm of rigid adherence to policy statements regardless of the situation involved. His position at the top of the bureaucracy together with his having initiated board discussions both speak eloquently of his power in Jefferson. The avoidance of board standing committees further reduced the possibility of the development of board groups opposing his traditional leadership. This practice increased the chances that Dr. Donnelly would be the Jefferson District's top specialist leader. His preparation and control of the agenda also supported him in this role. The language of self-abnegation, which he used in his frequent references to himself as the servant of the board and community, provided protective coloration for his true political role. This role was more clearly seen at the "Committee of the Whole" sessions where Dr. Donnelly, with the same agenda used later at the board meeting, privately led "his" board more overtly than he did an hour later in public.

Dr. Donnelly did not always have his way. He was often forced to compromise, as all top leaders must. Donnelly, however, managed to avoid the appearance of loss of power even when forced to yield. His resistance to change never reached the point of intransigence which would have resulted in the demise of his political system. Instead, when Donnelly disagreed with groups of parents or teachers, he maintained his own point of view unless the other position was supported by some board members in "Committee of the Whole" discussions. If the opposing view received board support, Donnelly would then soften his position in the public meeting.

The opportunity to size up the strength of the opposing forces without public conflict was invaluable. It allowed Dr. Donnelly to

open avenues for a future convergence of opposing positions without
appearing to suggest compromise. It also gained time, allowing
him to develop his own tactics of opposition or compromise. Keeping
the issue open but at a low priority level made it impossible for
one to accuse Dr. Donnelly of avoiding the issue or deliberately opposing anyone. At the same time, such issues were never given an
immediacy likely to provoke political activity in opposition to Dr.
Donnelly and the board. Further, Donnelly reversed the usual liability
of financial limitations. He generally appeared and sometimes was
more financially responsible than his board, always insisting that the
cost of innovation be clarified to the community. His estimates of
the cost of proposals which he did not support tended to be higher
than the estimates of others. Thus, it took a strong combination of
interests to win in the face of Dr. Donnelly's opposition.

Only twice in sixteen years did it appear that Dr. Donnelly had
suffered serious defeat. On other occasions when he was forced to
concede, the appearance of leadership was preserved. On such occasions, the movement from his initial position toward a compromise
with others allowed Donnelly to become the initiator of the final decisions at the board meeting as well as in Committee of the Whole sessions. He and his staff were thus the architects of the compromises
when needed, without engaging in the negotiations and bargaining
found in secular patterns. Dr. Donnelly's style was as flexible as that
advocated by the conservative superintendents of the 1890's who used
manipulative and informal cooptation, and avoided political confrontation. Donnelly never lost sight of his legal vulnerability. Instead, he used it publicly as protective clothing for his political role
and power base. Through the selection committee which he helped
make effective when he was still high school principal, Donnelly used
Jefferson's informal political system to his advantage.

Summary

The Jefferson School District indicates a third alternative to the
monopolistic politics of the sacred community and the pluralistic
politics of the urban community, having elements of each. This
suburban pattern is influenced in its development by the secular,
highly mobile society of the suburbs. The relatively autonomous
nature of suburban school district governments produces a monopolistic, largely sacred brand of educational politics. At its center, as the
key political figure, is the superintendent of schools, whose putative

expertise supports his specialist leadership image. The use of various citizens groups provides him with a unique political base in the school districts' local establishment.

Thus, the historic battle for legal power lost by superintendents at the turn of the century has been resolved extralegally in favor of many superintendents. These superintendents have their best opportunity for acquiring top leadership in school districts having a high regard for specialized expertise. Such districts are likely to have boundaries different from those of other local governments, hence maximizing the district's opportunities for political autonomy. Parents in such districts, operating through the P.T.A., often comprise the largest portion of active voters in school district elections. Such associations are likely to be greatly influenced, if not controlled, by local school administrators. The chief school officer in such cases often sits at the peak of an internal political power pyramid, one which is similar to the traditional sacred community's monolithic political structure but different in its pluralistic acceptance of expertise in educational governance.

Roscoe C. Martin's conclusions from his studies of suburban school government suggest that the Jefferson story is far from unique.[16] He argues that the power system of the suburban school district is closed, producing only limited access to boards of education with an electorate dominated by school patrons. The domination of the political process by a small percentage of citizens is common to all the types discussed.[17] The essential feature in Jefferson and the sacred pattern in the secular suburb is the domination by school patrons led by the professional. Such districts display a pattern of leaving decisions and school affairs to their boards of education.[18] In Jefferson the board was also largely coopted and controlled by the professionals of the school district.[19]

Where top power and leadership will be located in a school district varies from one community to another. In some, especially smaller rural ones in the Southeast, it will most often be found at the top of a monolithic community power structure composed of generalist leaders controlling other local units of government as well. In urban cen-

---

[16] Roscoe C. Martin, *Government and the Suburban School* (Syracuse, N.Y.: Syracuse University Press, 1962).

[17] Walter Bloomberg, Jr. and Morris Sunshine, *Suburban Power Structures and Public Education* (Syracuse, N.Y.: Syracuse University Press, 1963), pp. 70-71.

[18] Martin, *Government and the Suburban School,* pp. 57-58.

[19] Bloomberg *et al., Suburban Power Structures and Public Education,* pp. 240-59.

ters it will more often be found in a pluralistic, multi-centered decisional system with educational policy most influenced by specialist
schoolmen or elected city officials. Often in modern suburbs, the
specialist leadership of the superintendent rests on the esteem that
a modern technological and secular society confers on professional
training in connection with the political skills of the sacred community. David W. Minar makes a similar point as a result of his research.
He suggests that a distinction be made between communities where
rank authority (sacred) is most influential and where technical authority (secular) predominates.[20] Where technical authority characterizes the community, the superintendent is likely to be the key to
power. Here the school board becomes an agency legitimizing the
superintendent's initiative.[21] Minar concludes, ". . . if anyone lurks
behind anyone else, making 'real' decisions, it is the superintendent
lurking behind the board."[22]

---

[20] David W. Minar, "Community Characteristics, Conflict and Power Structure," in *The Politics of Education in the Local Community,* eds. Robert S. Cahill
and Stephen P. Hencley (Danville, Ill.: The Interstate Printers & Publishers, Inc.,
1964), pp. 132-3.

[21] Norman D. Kerr, "The School Board as an Agency of Legitimation," *Sociology of Education,* XXXVIII, No. 1 (Fall, 1964), 34-59.

[22] David W. Minar, "Community Characteristics, Conflict and Power Structure," p. 132.

4

The Road to
Incumbent Defeat

Every governmental or constitutional system has a tendency to develop its own equilibrium. Those governmental systems that come closest to eliminating effective dissent, thus avoiding public controversy, come nearest to achieving equilibrium and maintaining the *status quo*. One price paid for this equilibrium is what Michels[1] has described as "The Iron Law of Oligarchy," the tendency of self perpetuation by leadership groups at the expense of the goal achievement of the social organization. Another price is found in the widening gap between the particular organization and its larger social universe. This gap widens more rapidly when the social composition of the environment undergoes relatively rapid change. The Robertsdale School District illustrated this condition. The defeat of the incumbent school board members was brought about by developing an internal equilibrium and a widening gap between the board and the district, its larger social sphere.

The story of the Robertsdale School District illustrates the syndrome of political events we have come to recognize

---

[1] Robert Michels, *Political Parties* (New York: The Free Press, 1962).

as characteristic of the process by which the widening gap between the school and its community is abruptly closed. These events may be seen in a sequence beginning with the voters behavior at an election which defeats an incumbent schoolboard member. They· continue through the struggles for control of the school board and educational policy and end with the replacement of the superintendent of schools by a successor, usually from outside the district.

The Robertsdale story begins with brief reference to the period roughly twenty-five years preceding the main story when conflict around district policy had resulted in the failure to renew a school superintendent's contract. This conflict and the selection of his successor almost prophetically pointed to the day roughly a quarter of a century later when that successor, in turn, was faced by a board which was learning to mistrust his leadership. A cycle in the normal history of a school district is circumscribed by these events. But our concern is with the events surrounding the periods of conflict in Robertsdale at the beginning and end of the cycle rather than the longer period between.

Chapter Four first looks at the conflicts of the late thirties which began a long, relatively peaceful, cycle of school district government in Robertsdale. Next, it turns to the end of that period and the social and economic changes leading to the crucial upset election of 1960. The events of Robertsdale are then used in developing an explanatory model of cyclical change in the governing of local school districts. This consists of twelve sequential hypotheses. Finally, the discussion of changing school district policies through political action is extended beyond the illustrative case of Robertsdale through subsequent verificational research.

HISTORICAL PERSPECTIVES OF ROBERTSDALE

Robertsdale is a school district in the midwestern section of the United States. The state and county in which Robertsdale is situated shall be referred to as Midwest. While Robertsdale is over one hundred years old, this study is concerned with its history since 1938. At that time Robertsdale faced a series of conflicts which resulted in the selection of a new superintendent who was still in office almost twenty-five years later. The first official record of conflict was the report of a special school board meeting on April 2, 1936.[2]

---

2 "Official Minutes of the Board of Education of Robertsdale," April 2, 1936.

At that meeting the board considered the question of giving the incumbent superintendent a three-year contract. The matter was tabled and not brought up again until a special meeting on April 21, 1938, two years later. The board minutes for April 21, 1938 contain the following:

> . . . there being a delegation of about twenty people present, the office in which meetings are usually held could not accommodate them. Dr. Bunch suggested that we pass to the next room—a classroom. . . . Dr. Bunch took the chair, asking if anyone had anything they wished to say. There was silence. Finally Mrs. Jane Cook arose and said that it was her understanding that a taxpayer could attend any meeting without special reason. The six board members then retired to the office for a conference.
>
> Upon the return of the board members, the special meeting was called to order by the president, Dr. L. A. Bunch. Purpose of the meeting was to retain or reject Superintendent Holt and Principal Webster.
>
> Dr. Bunch gave anyone having anything to say an opportunity to do so. He then said that Mr. Holt and Mr. Webster could be excused from the room during the balloting. Both men left the room. Dr. Bunch then instructed the secretary to pass the ballots . . . There were six votes for dismissal [of Holt].
>
> Dr. Bunch then instructed secretary to pass ballots to board members in order to vote upon retention or dismissal of Mr. Webster. At this point Mr. McGraw interrupted and started speaking. Mr. Rose said, "This man is out of order," and Dr. Bunch sustained his objection. Then Mr. Bering of the Midwest Baptist Orphans' Home arose and said that Mr. McGraw should be given an opportunity to speak. Having previously given everyone an opportunity to speak, Dr. Bunch asked the board if he as their president was sustained in his ruling that the man was out of order. The board unanimously upheld their president. There were six votes against retention of Mr. Webster.[3]

This meeting gives some insight into the Board of Education's operation in 1938. The fact that there were visitors at this meeting was unusual. The board had to move from their usual meeting room which was not large enough to accommodate the "delegation of about twenty" to another room in the building. The president opened the meeting by asking if the delegation wanted to speak. The board's reaction to the group's reply that "a taxpayer could attend any meeting without special reason" indicates that this was a right seldom used.

---

[3] *Ibid.*, April 21, 1938.

The board retired to the office for a closed conference. In passing, it may be interesting to note that in 1960 the board was once more reacting in the same way to the presence of visitors at school board meetings.

After the executive session, the board returned to its regular open meeting of April 21, 1938. The purpose of this meeting was made explicit. The board was to determine whether to "retain or reject" the superintendent and the principal. Again the "delegation" was given the opportunity to speak but remained silent. A vote was taken that was unanimously in favor of dismissing the superintendent. When the president directed that a vote be taken on the retention or dismissal of the principal, someone from the "delegation" rose to speak. This spokesman was ruled out of order. The director of the Midwest Baptist Orphans' Home rose to ask that the "delegation" be allowed to speak. The president's ruling was sustained by the board, and the principal was dismissed by unanimous vote.

Even with no more detailed information about Robertsdale, it can be seen that many of the elements of the sacred community's political life style were present in Robertsdale in the late 1930's. The Robertsdale School Board displayed the characteristics of slow change, the parochial outlook, and the low expenditure ideology seen in Springdale. Although the school board minutes did not reveal it, the pattern of self-selection and cooperative nominating of school board members had resulted in an increasingly closed social system with the board at its center. Finally, if Springdale's superintendent serves as the model of alien expert leadership, then one would expect that by 1960 Mr. Joyce (the outside Superintendent chosen in 1938) would have overcome the legal vulnerability of his office and would have developed a more secure role resting on his putative expertise.

The board meeting indicates that there were interested parties in the community in 1938 who supported Principal Webster but failed to support Superintendent Holt. One of these parties is identified in the minutes by his institutional role, director of the Midwest Baptist Orphan's Home. The minutes of the next meeting give additional support to these conclusions:

> The special meeting of the Board of Education of the School District of Robertsdale having visitors, passed to the next room, a class room, in order to accommodate everyone.
>
> Prior to calling meeting, Dr. Bunch, president of the Board, asked those present, namely Mr. Bering of the Midwest Baptist Orphans' Home, Mrs. Herbert Little, Mr. & Mrs. McGraw, and Mr. and Mrs. Sharp, if they had anything to say. The spokesman,

Mr. Bering, upon presentation of the petition said as speaker for the committee, "We are not here because we object to your failure to reelect Mr. C. C. Holt as superintendent but to present a petition to rehire Mr. Webster, and inasmuch as there is a vacancy for superintendency, that he be considered for superintendent." Mr. McGraw also made a few remarks in furtherance of Mr. Bering's mission. There being no further remarks, the Board retired to office for closed meeting.[4]

It is now clear that there were some segments of the community supporting the principal but not the superintendent. Leaders of these segments can be identified in the minutes. One segment was the Baptist organization in Robertsdale; the other, a section of the community represented by the Little family. Both of these groups were still active in Robertsdale more than twenty years later. It is also possible that these groups supported the dismissal of the superintendent.

Selecting the New Superintendent

The board meeting continued in executive session without the public. The minutes follow:

Special meeting called by Dr. L. A. Bunch, president of Board of Education of School District of Robertsdale.

All members present.

First order of business was to consider petition presented by above-named committee. Matter was discussed at length, all members expressing themselves. A vote was taken on whether or not to compromise by electing a new superintendent and to permit him to make a recommendation.

Dr. Bunch then announced that they would carry out the purpose of meeting, to elect a superintendent.

The names of a number of men were presented by members of the board—men they had previously interviewed. Those having made sufficient impression to be of consideration were presented. After Board had interviewed all candidates to their satisfaction a vote was taken, and Mr. F. W. Joyce elected upon the second ballot.

Mr. Joyce was then called into the room. After his acceptance of the superintendency, Mr. Joyce entered into an agreement with the board that he would interview the teachers and principals before making recommendation for their reemployment.[5]

---

[4] *Ibid.,* April 28, 1938.
[5] *Ibid.,* April 28, 1938.

During the executive session, the board split 3–3 on whether or not to rehire Mr. Webster, the principal. It would appear that those citizens who petitioned for Webster's rehiring were represented on the board. A compromise was reached which passed the decision to a new superintendent. In fact, the three men who had voted to rehire Webster could have blocked any other appointment. The meeting closed with the appointment of F. W. Joyce as new superintendent. He was still serving in this capacity at the time of this case study.

On May 19, 1938 the board met, and Joyce recommended Mr. Chod for the principal's position instead of Mr. Webster. Joyce's recommendation was accepted by the board by a vote of four "yes" and two "no" votes.

When Joyce recommended teachers, he failed to recommend one teacher who was known and liked by one board member.[6] There was a "no" vote cast against this recommendation, but the recommendation was approved five to one. No indication was given in the minutes as to who cast either this "no" vote or the preceding two "no" votes. After one further order of business, the board president verbally tendered his resignation and left the meeting. The vice-president concluded the business.[7]

While we cannot indisputably state the nature of dissension on the board that caused this action, there is no doubt that serious conflict was present. A survey of the board's voting record between April 2, 1936, the first time conflict over the contract of Superintendent Holt occurred, and April 28, 1938, the date Joyce was appointed new superintendent, revealed no conflict. All votes of the school board during this two-year period were unanimous.

Even though three members of the board voted in executive session to retain Webster, all members voted before the public on April 21 not to rehire him. In appointing Chod, Joyce did not follow the position of either the Baptist organization or the Little family who appeared at the board meeting favoring the appointment of Webster. Joyce did some rapid fence-mending, however.

Data collected between 1960 and 1964 (the time of Joyce's final retirement) indicate that much of what was learned about the Robertsdale District from the 1938 minutes remained in Robertsdale as vestiges of the past. The Little family remained influential in school district decisions as members of the board of a local bank. Joyce was a prominent member of the Baptist community and was referred

---

6 Interview with F. W. Joyce, Superintendent of Schools of Robertsdale.
7 "Official Minutes. . . ," May 19, 1938.

to by one long-time community member with the comment, "He is the [Baptist] Church." Chod was still principal of the Robertsdale Elementary School and a strong supporter of Joyce. Although vestiges of the past, these linkages were still strong and important. They were important to district decision making and to the perceptions of influentials in the school district.

Growth of Robertsdale

The next point of significant Robertsdale history was a series of annexations that took place in the 1949-50 school year and a reorganization that occurred in 1950-51. At this time Robertsdale grew primarily in area. Next it was to increase in population. Perhaps one of the best pictures of the Robertsdale District can be obtained by viewing the city of Lakeside which is located in Robertsdale. In 1960 it was the largest single municipal area in Robertsdale.[8]

Lakeside was established on February 23, 1843 by the merger of two towns established under an old Spanish land grant. Thus, Lakeside was the oldest town in Midwest County. It was one of the most distant communities from the city of Midwest and was therefore late in starting its suburban growth. In 1953 a series of annexations took place and Lakeside began to grow into a large municipality. In 1966 it became the largest city (in square miles) in Midwest County, encompassing eleven and one-half square miles. Later annexation brought this total to seventeen square miles. Yet in 1958, Lakeside still had only one person on its municipal payroll. Until this point there seemed to be a lag between its physical growth and the growth of the municipal government. Then the shift began that established the new social and governmental organization of Lakeside. With over one hundred twenty miles of streets, Lakeside established a Department of Streets and Rabies Control. In 1959 a full-time police department was established which consisted of six full-time officers. The fire department changed from a volunteer department to a combination full-time plus volunteer system.

Until the middle 1950's there were no housing subdivisions. Much of the land was still being farmed. In the late 1950's a community known as Bluffview was begun. The homes in this community ranged from $16,000 to $25,000 in cost, and at the time of the study there

---

[8] Historical information concerning Lakeside from *Town of Lakeside Progress Report, 1960.*

were almost one thousand homes in Bluffview. (In 1967 there were 2500 homes in Bluffview.) There were four other subdivisions in Lakeside, by 1960, that ranged in size from eighty to seven hundred homes. All of the subdivisions lay largely or totally within the Robertsdale School District.

Industrial and commercial development had also shown signs of growth in the Robertsdale District. Two large shopping areas were built adjacent to the new residential areas. The one in Bluffview cost $1,500,000, and expansion was anticipated. Large sales locations were also developed, an example being a large auto auction center completed during 1961. Lakeside's location had the potential of attracting industry. Four major highways and a railroad ran through the area. Large portions of Lakeside were zoned industrial, and city government was expecting a heavy influx of industry between 1960 and 1965. The construction of a four-million-dollar flour plant began in Lakeside in 1960. In spite of the growth, Lakeside was ninety percent undeveloped. Lakeside had undergone considerable growth just prior to 1961, but its expansion was just beginning.[9]

A portion of the town of St. Quie that was in the Robertsdale District had three housing developments known as Elm Grove. Approximately 675 homes were in this area and 400 more were to be constructed. These homes were priced from $22,500. Elm Grove did not actually lie within the St. Quie corporate limits but was commonly thought of as such in as much as the residents' mail was directed through the St. Quie post office. In the western portion of this municipality, a large industrial park was being developed.[10]

The town of St. Joseph was a small, heavily populated area within the Robertsdale district. The average home in this area ranged from $9,000 to $12,000 when originally constructed, and there was a large concentration of commercial buildings in this area. A large Catholic population was centered here. This area developed between 1945 and 1950.

Bluffview, the Elm Grove area, and St. Joseph were the largest population centers in the Robertsdale District. Between Bluffview and Elm Grove was the portion of the district that was largely undeveloped at the time of the study. Many of the old residents of the Robertsdale District lived in this area. Most of this area was in the municipality of Lakeside. Although between twenty and forty per-

---

9 The largest suburban shopping center in Midwest State was completed in the Robertsdale District during 1965.
10 See Chart X, Chapter 5.

cent[11] of the population of the Robertsdale District lived in this area, it was not centered in any one development. Several farms were still operating in this area of Lakeside and St. Quie.

Background of the 1960 Election

Mr. Prentice[12] moved to Bluffview, the new subdivision in Lakeside, at the end of March, 1959. He had been a resident of another suburban community in the metropolitan area of Midwest. During his first two summers of residence in Bluffview, Prentice managed the Bluffview swimming pool and got to know many people. More important, people got to know him. In the summer of 1959, he was asked to write several educational articles for the "Bluffview Cider Jug," a monthly publication in Bluffview.

Prentice had taught for ten years in public and private schools and was a part-time student in the graduate school of the local university working toward a doctorate. He was probably among the best informed residents of Bluffview on issues concerning education. If Bluffview was in some way dissatisfied with its public schools, Prentice had the knowledge to help, and people knew this because of the articles he had written for the community paper.

In December, 1959 Mrs. Franz, a Bluffview resident and long-time resident of the Lakeside area, approached Prentice about a meeting that was being held to discuss the public schools. It was obvious that there were many things which people were unhappy about. The grading procedure used in the elementary school that the Bluffview children attended was one of the things causing discontent. The residents felt that grading was being done on a curve and that this practice was not appropriate for grading elementary school children.

Prentice indicated he would be happy to attend the meeting if the district's superintendent, Mr. Joyce, was also invited. Prentice asked if he might invite Joyce and request that he bring information on local policy related to the questions that were to be raised at the meeting. The procedure was approved, and Prentice called Joyce. Joyce declined the invitation but provided the information.

Joyce indicated that each school was somewhat on its own regarding grading standards. When asked a specific question regarding grading on a normal curve, he indicated that this procedure was not

---

[11] Estimate made by superintendent and high school principal.
[12] For a complete biographical sketch, see Chapter 5.

used. Several of the people present at this December meeting felt that this method was being used and that it was unfair, especially in a community such as Bluffview.

It was not until a year and a half after Prentice was elected to the board that he found that Bluffview children had been graded on a curve. Mr. Chod had been Joyce's recommendation to replace Webster in 1938 and had been in the district ever since. Chod was principal of the Robertsdale Elementary School which Bluffview children had attended until the Bluffview Elementary School was erected. He then served as part-time principal in the Bluffview building in addition to his duties as principal of Robertsdale Elementary. In 1961-62 a new full-time principal was hired for the Bluffview School. The new principal found that the normal curve had been used for grading purposes. Here again the superintendent attempted to prevent information from leaking to the new subsystems, a further indication that he wanted to keep the decision-making system closed.

Mrs. Code was the only supporter of the local school system present at this meeting. She was an active member of the Robertsdale P.T.A. and was later elected president of the new Bluffview School P.T.A. Prentice knew Mrs. Code. She had been in a life-saving class the summer before when Prentice had taught at the Bluffview pool.

Prentice took the position that he felt supported the public schools but tempered this notion with the philosophy that there was always room for improvement in any school system. He also took the position of supporting change within the present structure and operation of the school district. In this way he validated any assumption on the part of this group that he might be a man to support for election to the school board. Both citizens who were against the schools under the present administration and individuals who supported the administration but felt the schools had to change could support Prentice as long as he took this approach.[13]

At the conclusion of the meeting, Mr. and Mrs. Franz and Mr. and Mrs. Hartman (other Bluffview residents) approached Prentice with the idea of his running for the Robertsdale School Board the following April. Prentice replied that he would run if drafted. He said that he did not have the time or the desire to do much campaigning and that someone else would have to be willing to do this if they wanted him to run. No definite decision was made at this meeting.

---

[13] At this meeting Prentice's behavioral pattern was established by challenging the *status quo* in the district and yet generally supporting the district. This was a position supporting social reform rather than social revolution within the school district.

At the time of the April, 1960 election, two members of the school board had been on the board since before the reorganization. Scott[14] had been on the board for twenty-five years, and Mahan had been on the board for eleven years. Two of the members had been elected at the time of reorganization, Dyke and Wilke in November, 1951, and Clubb had been elected the following April. Each of these men had served for nine years. The sixth man, Jones, had served only three years, one elected term.[15]

Scott owned a small grocery store in the Robertsdale district. Mahan was a supervisor for a company specializing in moving and installing heavy equipment and machines. Wilke was a supervisor for a company that built storm sewers in subdivisions and commercial projects. Clubb was an intercity truck driver for a large oil company. Both Dyke and Jones were supervisors at a large plant in metropolitan Midwest. It should be noted that none of these men, unlike the Bluffview or Elm Grove residents, was a white-collar or professional worker. Bluffview and Elm Grove residents were not represented on the board.

Gaining Visibility

Before elections incumbents of the Robertsdale Board almost always spoke at P.T.A. meetings, but other men running for office were not permitted to speak. Incumbents' names appeared first on the ballot with all other candidates following in alphabetical order. Small turnouts at elections, which were to the advantage of the incumbents, were usual. Challengers were faced with not being able to secure pertinent information, not being able to speak before school parent-teacher units, and having to run in elections held separately from the regularly scheduled "political" elections.

As is the case on many school boards, once a man is elected to the board, he often stays until he decides to retire. There were several factors at work in the Robertsdale district that fostered this. Information concerning the schools was not easy to acquire.[16] While everyone was "welcome" at board meetings, very few people attended. The Robertsdale School Board took no action to change this situation.

---

[14] On the Robertsdale School Board at the time of Joyce's election to the superintendency.

[15] Chart X, p. 107, indicates the residences of school board members and candidates running in April, 1960.

[16] Note that this was one of the reasons for the meeting at the Franzes' in December, 1960.

They maintained a closed system defending their boundaries from encroachment by the new social subsystems developing in Elm Grove and Bluffview.

In January, 1959 Prentice filed as a candidate for election to the Board of Education of the Robertsdale School District. Since the time of the December meeting, he had been assured of considerable help. Soon after Prentice filed, Mr. Hartman, one of the Bluffview residents who had originally approached Prentice about running for the board, arranged a meeting with some residents from the Elm Grove area. The Elm Grove group was interested in electing a resident of Elm Grove, Mr. Holtzman. It was decided that the two newer housing areas would join in supporting Holtzman and Prentice.

Two other candidates filed in the election, Mr. O'Brian and Mr. Usher. Mr. O'Brian was a resident of Bluffview and a member of the Catholic Church. He did not campaign and had no support in Bluffview. The lack of organized support for him accounted for the very small number of votes he was able to poll in the April election. Mr. Usher had run for the board before. He was a resident of St. Joseph and an active member of the P.T.A. He ran only four votes behind Dyke, the winning incumbent.

During February, 1959, Prentice attempted to obtain invitations to speak before the various P.T.A. groups in the district. His first reply from P.T.A. leadership was that P.T.A.'s could not allow a candidate to speak as they were not a political organization. When Prentice pointed out that an incumbent was speaking, he was informed that the man was speaking as a school board member and not as a candidate for election. Prentice contacted Superintendent Joyce who said he saw nothing wrong with this procedure. Upon contacting the P.T.A. presidents by letter and phone, Prentice was informed that the P.T.A.'s had traditionally taken an inactive role in school affairs and they did not think they could allow Prentice to speak.

What Prentice could not accomplish by direct contact with P.T.A. leadership was in part accomplished indirectly. Mrs. Code who was active in the P.T.A. and had been at the Franzes' meeting spoke with Mrs. Howell, president of the Robertsdale Elementary School P.T.A. Due to conflicting dates, Prentice was unable to speak before this P.T.A. Mrs. Howell, however, read a statement written by Prentice regarding his qualifications for election to the school board. Subsequently the Elm Grove P.T.A. invited all candidates to speak; the St. Joseph and Mt. Olive P.T.A.'s soon followed this procedure.

In spite of all efforts, no school board can keep their system closed indefinitely. Prentice had now breached the boundaries which had been defended so vigorously. Now there was danger. Prentice had a way to communicate with a large and important subsystem of the school district. Whether or not the central subsystem (the board and the superintendent) realized the danger cannot be determined. Prentice recognized the value of contact with the P.T.A. He maximized it in the campaign and continued to use it as his major contact with the school district throughout the time he served on the board.

At the St. Joseph P.T.A., Prentice met Mr. Clubb, a member of the school board. Clubb was very friendly, and during the conversation with Prentice, Clubb said, "I probably cast more 'no' votes than any other man on the board." He went on to indicate that he did not like Dyke, pointing out that Dyke had switched his position regarding building permanent football bleachers, a question confronting voters. Clubb felt that Dyke would tell people whatever they wanted to hear. Clubb also indicated that he had little chance by himself of getting anything done, saying that he had once gotten through a motion refusing to renew Joyce's contract, which had two years to run. He said the only reason he got it through was that one member had been absent. The next meeting it had been brought up again and extended to a three-year contract.

The Blue Ridge P.T.A. invited all candidates to speak, but later had to cancel the invitation because of inclement weather. Neither the junior nor the senior high school P.T.A.'s communicated with Prentice. Nevertheless, Prentice attended their March meetings. No candidate spoke at the junior high school meeting, but Dyke spoke at the senior high school meeting. After the senior high school meeting, Prentice spoke to Mr. Tally, senior high school P.T.A. president. Tally was also on the Lakeside Town Council and was president of the Republican Club, an office formerly held by Dyke. Tally indicated he had no intention of allowing candidates other than incumbents to speak and that there was no point discussing it.

During the month before the election Jones, who worked the evening shift, did not appear at any of the meetings. Dyke, who came to all the meetings, often mentioned that Jones had done a very good job during the past three years. Dyke's platform emphasized that he had been on the board for nine years, knew the job, and "had never missed a meeting in nine years." Some citizens distributed circulars as a part of Prentice's and Holtzman's campaigns. Prentice ran on a platform described in this circular, which was distributed in Bluffview, the Elm Grove area, and St. Joseph. He also spoke at every P.T.A. meeting when he had the opportunity. Prentice's circular is shown in Chart I. Holtzman spoke at every P.T.A. meeting to which he had

Chart I*
YOUR CANDIDATE FOR THE SCHOOL BOARD
BIOGRAPHICAL SKETCH OF MARSHAL PRENTICE
RESIDENCE:

> Native of Midwest City; resident of Midwest County for six years; resident of Lakeside for one year; 31 years of age; married.

EDUCATION:

> B.S. 1950, Midwest University; M.S. 1954, Midwest University; presently engaged in work toward doctorate in educational administration at Midwest University.

EDUCATIONAL ACTIVITY:

> Served on joint P.T.A. committees; member of National Education and Affiliate Organizations; Phi Delta Kappa; member of House of Delegates of State and County Teachers' Association; member of Executive and Welfare Committees of Trail Teachers' Association; organizing member of Board of Directors of Field Junior Chamber of Commerce; Merit Badge Counselor of Boy Scouts; volunteer Red Cross Water Safety Instructor; taught in public and private schools for ten years.

The following outline taken from an article published in the February issue of the *National Education Journal* is the above candidate's views of what a school board member should be.

"What Makes An Effective School Board Member?"

First of all, an effective member has high moral values, courage, and integrity equal to the task as a leader in his community.

Next, he has practical wisdom and the time to devote himself unstintingly to his job as a school director. He realizes the importance of good public relations and is able to appreciate the points of view of all segments of society. He is able to distinguish between policy making and administration, and does not attempt to function in the area of policy execution.

He has the vision to see ahead, to plan ahead, as well as the ability to solve immediate problems.

He is in school work because he is interested in seeing his community achieve the highest educational standards possible, and not because he has an ax to grind, a pet theory which he intends to push at all costs, or resentment against a person or a group which causes him to use his position as a weapon.

He can vote independently upon issues, even when it means standing alone. But he also has the ability to work as a member of a team with other board members. He does not strive for self-glorification or use shock tactics to get his name in the headlines. He puts the school system first.

---

* Circular distributed during the April, 1960 campaign for school board.

been invited and distributed circulars similar to those of Prentice describing his qualifications. He was a college graduate, an insurance salesman, and had taught college business courses in insurance. Many felt that because he was Jewish he would lose votes in the St. Joseph area and older areas of the district. Neither O'Brian nor Usher campaigned much. Neither had literature distributed. O'Brian appeared at only one P.T.A. meeting and Usher at none.

During the last few weeks of March, Mr. Troy, a member of the Lakeside Council and resident of Bluffview, asked Prentice to contact Mr. Gram, the Democratic committeeman and representative from the district to the State House of Representatives. Troy indicated there was a possibility of running a candidate from St. Joseph who would be chosen by the Democratic Club.[17] Prentice said he would not run with such a candidate but would call Gram. When Prentice called Gram, he expressed the view that partisan politics did not belong in school elections. Gram said he was interested in Prentice's qualifications and would call him back. He never did, but Prentice received a call from Mrs. Brown, Gram's aunt. Mrs. Brown was a resident of Bluffview. She questioned Prentice about his candidacy but made no mention of Gram. A few days before the election Mrs. Hartman received a call from a member of the Democratic Club asking for some of Prentice's circulars to distribute. Prentice agreed to do nothing for Gram and received dubious help from his organization, if any at all.

The 1960 Election

The school election was held the day after the regular Lakeside city election. Since the city election had created a great deal of public interest, it was difficult to get out any large number of votes the following day. It is especially difficult to bring out more than the customary or traditional voters at such times. This arrangement works in favor of incumbents and against newcomers. Mr. Hartman and Mr. Troy spent the afternoon in a soundtruck campaigning for Prentice.

On the morning of the election twenty-four names of Bluffview residents were removed from the election books because it was claimed that they did not live in the Robertsdale district or the adjoining district. (The district's line cut through Bluffview.) These residents had been allowed to vote in the general election the day before but were not permitted to vote in the Robertsdale school election, even though some people produced tax receipts to the Robertsdale district.

---

[17] Such a candidate ran and won in the 1961 election.

Nor were they permitted to vote in the adjoining district. There was a transfer of names at the St. Joseph's polling place and six to ten people failed to get to the correct poll in time to vote. Both of these moves must have helped the incumbents and hurt Prentice and Usher. There is no doubt that there was nothing illegal about what was done, although one might question the timing. All Bluffview residents concerned were reinstated as residents of the Robertsdale School District two weeks after the election.

Prentice polled the largest vote in the election, and Dyke followed. Thus, these two men were elected. Usher ran only four votes behind Dyke, and when he was running in 1961 said, "I think I was robbed in last year's election."

The results are tabulated in Chart II. Several interesting facts are apparent in this chart. With only one exception, O'Brian, each candidate found his greatest strength in his home district. Finally and perhaps most important, Prentice made a consistently better showing in areas where he had spoken to P.T.A. groups. Only at Robertsdale,

Chart II

ELECTION RESULTS IN THE APRIL 4, 1960 ELECTION

ELEMENTARY SCHOOL POLLING PLACES	DYKE* (ELECTED)	JONES*	USHER	PRENTICE (ELECTED)	O'BRIAN	HOLTZMAN	FOR TEACHER'S FUND	AGAINST TEACHER'S FUND
Lakeside	93	75	38	195H	40H	129	175	101
Mt. Olive	48	41	76	57	6	11	69	51
Robertsdale**	187H	168H	118	70	6	47	178	136
St. Joseph	96	63	219H	89	22	12	157	125
Elm Grove	43	37	12	87	15	108H	114	42
Totals	467	384	463	498	89	307	693	455

* Incumbents
** Bluffview residents were voting at the Lakeside Elementary School.
H Home district for the candidate

because of a date conflict had he not made a personal appearance. At that meeting, the P.T.A. president had read Prentice's qualifications. In spite of this poor showing in the Robertsdale Elementary School, Prentice led in the total popular vote and was elected to the Robertsdale School Board.

The attempt to keep the central system closed continued throughout the campaign. The shifting of names in the polling books on the day of the election is at best an unusual procedure. Preventing members of new subsystems from voting is a form of boundary maintenance and an effective prevention of inputs potentially dangerous to the centralized subsystems. In spite of this, the closed central system was breached. In doing so, Prentice had done some things that could help him operate as a board member. He had established contact with an important subsystem of the school district. He had also interacted with Clubb and perceived him to be a potential ally.

Prentice refused to run as a candidate on a platform to overthrow the superintendent. He had refused to attend the original meeting unless the superintendent was invited. He refused to accept information from disgruntled parents about the district's grading practices. Instead, he had sought information from the superintendent which later proved to be false. He was not a revolutionary. If he was to change the system, Prentice believed he could change it without attacking the superintendent.

An Explanatory Model

The Robertsdale story, even the portion of it told in this chapter, stands as an isolated set of events with whatever interest a story holds for those who tell it or hear it. In order to be of more general worth, it must be understood through a conceptual and theoretical explanation. This is true of the Springdale and Jefferson cases discussed earlier and of other school districts as well. The events become vehicles for carrying forward a model of school district processes of change. This model rests on four statements of theory.

Statement 1. A school district and its decision-making subsystem, the school board, are social systems. The school board is referred to as the central subsystem.

Statement 2. Social systems can be placed on a continuum ranging from open systems to closed systems. Thus, a school district and its school board can be described as relatively open or relatively closed.

Statement 3. When the school board (the central subsystem) is relatively closed and the school district (the macrosystem) is relatively open, the school district will change its ideology and values about public education while the board will remain relatively constant. Under such conditions the differences and distance between the macrosystem and its central subsystem will become greater. Inputs and outputs between the central subsystem and the macrosystem will become relatively less frequent; thus, the school board will become progressively segregated from the total district.

Statement 4. Although the board can become progressively segregated from the school district, it cannot become completely segregated nor achieve independence from the district because of the legal and constitutional relationships between the board and the school district. Board members must be elected by members of the larger system, the school district. When a school board becomes closed to the inputs from its school district, and when it becomes increasingly segregated from that district, there is an institutionalized mechanism in most school districts to correct the situation—open the school board, and increase the input-output transmission between the macrosystem and its central subsystem, the school board. This mechanism is school board elections in most districts.

Hypotheses and predictions can be generated from these statements.

Hypothesis 1. When a school board remains constant in its membership, the school board (the decision-making central subsystem) of a school district will tend to develop stability (a steady state) between itself and the school district (the macrosystem).

Hypothesis 2. Such a school board will also tend to develop stability between itself and the superintendent (a microsystem of the decision-making subsystem).

Hypothesis 3. The development of unity and homogeneity within the school board results in a pattern of consensus rather than a pattern of resolution of conflict in determining policy. Such a decision-making system may be described as having a monolithic structure as opposed to a pluralistic structure.

Hypothesis 4. Since the board and the superintendent form a consensual decision-making system (a relatively closed central system), the superintendent is likely to become the "leader" of the board, the board responding to the superintendent's initiation.

Hypothesis 5. Under the conditions stated in Hypothesis 4, occasional changes in board membership will be represented by men "selected" by consensus of the board and superintendent. Those men so selected will tend to conform to the established norms of the decision-making group.

Hypothesis 6. Under the above conditions, when the school district is relatively open and changing (exchanging inputs and outputs with its environment), the gap between the school board and the school district develops and continues to widen, and the board becomes progressively segregated. This situation can develop through the following steps:

(*a*) The community changes through population increase or mobility; thus, there is a shift in the community's socioeconomic class.

(*b*) Meanwhile the school board remains relatively unchanged in composition and values. It becomes progressively segregated from the school district but not from the superintendent.

Hypothesis 7. When the school district (the macrosystem) perceives the progressive segregation of its school board (the central subsystem), it will attempt to prevent further segregation. The district will attempt to reverse the process by initiating messages to the board in the hope that these messages (outputs) will be received (become inputs of the board). Being basically a political system, these messages consist of political action.

Hypothesis 8. When the board becomes progressively segregated from the district, it decreases the linkage between itself and its changing macrosystem. Thus, it decreases the opportunity of processing the necessary inputs for self-correction (the modular effect). School board incumbents will consequently be defeated at election time.

Hypothesis 9. When an incumbent of a school board is defeated, open conflict on the board results. This conflict will be evidenced in:

(*a*) an increase in non-unanimous votes on the board, and

(*b*) a change in board leadership, initiation, and interaction patterns.

Hypothesis 10. Conflict will arise between the new member and the leadership group of the old board, particularly the superintendent himself.

Hypothesis 11. Marginal members of the old board will probably align themselves with the new member and under his leadership will influence the board's decision making.

Hypothesis 12. If the instability of the population that created the original shift in the district continues, the new board's leadership will be characterized by a degree of instability.

Analysis of the Situation in April, 1960

The model presented above was derived in part from the Robertsdale case. An analysis of that portion of the case plus certain measures

Chart III

**ROBERTSDALE SCHOOL DISTRICT
ASSESSED VALUATION**

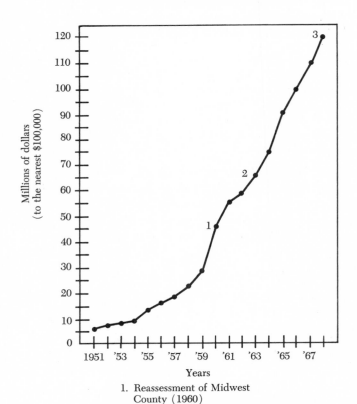

1. Reassessment of Midwest
   County (1960)
2. Annexation of Midmeadows (1963)
3. Projected as of July, 1967

of the stability or growth of the district should indicate how the statements in the model emerged from the data. These theoretical statements were extended by additional studies to be reported later in this chapter.

In Chart III the assessed valuation of the Robertsdale School District is shown over a period of seventeen years. This includes the ten years before Prentice's election to the Board, the year Prentice served on the board, and approximately six years after Prentice's election. All years from 1951 to 1956 except one show an approximate gain in assessed valuation of $1 million. From 1956 to 1962, even excluding the year of reassessment (1960), the average growth is about $5.7 million. Since 1962 the rate has continued to accelerate with the average gain being $12.2 million. Thus, a picture of relative stability and slow growth unfolds until 1956, followed by a period of accelerated growth between 1957 and 1962, and even more rapid growth after 1962.

Another measure of growth is the school numeration. These figures are presented in Chart IV. Taking the same time periods when analyzing the district's assessed valuation, one finds an increase of 280 school-age children per year in Robertsdale from 1951 to 1956. From 1956 to 1962 there was an average increase of 500 school-age children per year, almost twice as many as in the prior period. Since 1962 there has been an average increase of 1700 school-age children per year. Even though one of the years coincides with the annexation of Midmeadows, this period still shows a significant acceleration over the previous period. Excluding Midmeadows annexation year, this is an increase of 1400 children per year, approximately three times the 1956-62 period and five times the growth of the 1951-56 period.

If the statements in the model are correct, periods of rapid growth of a school district should be followed, under certain conditions, by increasing conflict in school district policymaking. The voting pattern of the Robertsdale Board should provide an insight into the conflict exhibited on the board—whether or not it should be considered closed.

The voting pattern of the board was not followed during the first year after Prentice's election. On the basis of some assumed lag between change in district population and the emergence of conflict, we will average the years 1951 to 1958 and 1959 to 1961. During this first period there was an average of only 2.1 per cent of the total school board votes without complete unanimity. During one year, none were recorded. Between 1957 and 1961, however, this non-unanimous vote increased to 5.9 per cent, more than twice as many as the previous period. During Prentice's first year, 8.1 per cent of the votes were not unanimous.

Chart IV
ROBERTSDALE SCHOOL CENSUS

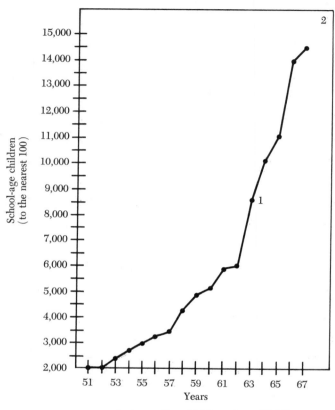

1. Annexation of Midmeadows (1963)
2. Projected enrollment (not census) for 1980's 20,000 pupils

Turning now to the case data, there is further evidence of relative stability in the district until the mid-1950's and continued stability and closure on the board during the year of Prentice's election in 1960. Little growth had taken place in the district prior to the mid-1950's. Much of the area was still under cultivation. In the one area that had been developed (St. Joseph), homes ranged in price from $9,000 to $12,000. The people purchasing these homes were largely blue-collar workers and of the upper-lower and lower-middle class. In the mid-1950's things began to change. Large tracts of land were developed. Homes in the tract developments ranged from $16,000 to $35,000. The people purchasing these homes were largely lower-middle and middle class individuals. The residential expansion was accompanied by increased commercial development and actual and projected increases in municipal government and services.

Coupled with the increase in population and the shift in the socio-economic class of the district (based on percent) was a change in the aspiration level of parents for their children's education. One would expect that there would be a considerable lag between a change in the parents' aspiration and a change in the percent of high school pupils entering college. Chart V depicts this shift but only considers the five-year period beginning with the 1963 graduation.

Chart V

**ROBERTSDALE HIGH SCHOOL GRADUATES
ENTERING COLLEGES**

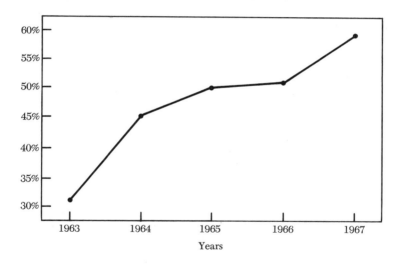

While the social composition of the district changed, and new areas with new people holding different educational aspirations emerged, the board, the superintendent, and the educational program tended to reflect the stable pattern of some years past. The school board was composed entirely of blue-collar workers (although some were supervisors) or small business owners. As will be seen later, many of these members had linkages into the old social structure of Roberts-dale dating as far back as twenty-five years. No linkages with the new communities (with the exception of Clubb, who was from St. Joseph) had been established. Nor had the board elected by the old community responded to the different aspirations of the changed and new community. Chart VI depicts the courses offered in the high school curriculum and provides data regarding the board's response to the changed aspirations of the new community.

Chart VI

NUMBER OF COURSES OFFERED IN ROBERTSDALE HIGH SCHOOL (1954-1967)

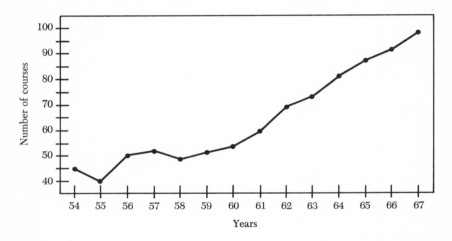

Years

Prior to 1959 no new trend had been established. Through a series of ups and downs, a total of four courses had been added to the curriculum in five years. Although less than half the graduates entered college, the curriculum was traditionally oriented toward college preparatory pupils. While not geared to the newer approaches in science or math, the school did offer advanced Latin and German. Including the 1960 curriculum established under the board prior to Prentice's election, a total of nine courses had been added since 1954, about one per year. Between 1961 and 1966 a total of forty-four courses were added, averaging about six courses per year. This represents a considerable change in board responses since Prentice's election and demonstrates the lack of response of the old board.

In summary, there are similarities in the data presented in the charts. There had been almost constant growth during the period. In 1956-57, all indicators of growth were accelerating and continued in that direction. Increase in size, coupled with changes in socioeconomic class as well as a move from rural to suburban status, allowed (perhaps required) the development of new points of tangency in the social structure of the school district.

As conditions promoting new points of tangency became more prominent, one might predict that the school board would have developed a different or modified pattern of interaction. But as indicated, strong linkages with powerful points of tangency had been developed in the past and these continued largely without modification. The linkages of the decision-making subsystem of the Robertsdale district had remained relatively constant while the larger system had changed. Thus, the decision-making system (the school board, including the superintendent) was a relatively closed system that effectively excluded inputs from the newly developed points of tangency. If a new pattern did not develop and include these new points of tangency, one would expect to find new board members elected who would represent the new points of tangency in the social structure. While it takes some time for this to occur, the election of April, 1960 was an example of the election of such a new member.

Hypotheses 1–8 emerge from the data presented up to this point. The school board and the school district developed stability between 1938 and 1950 (Hypothesis 1).[18] The board and the superintendent had established a stability demonstrated by the board's continued support of the superintendent through the extension of the superintendent's contracts and confidence in his recommendations (Hypothesis 2). There was a consensus pattern within the board demonstrated by the unanimous voting pattern of the board prior to 1958 (Hypothesis 3). The consensus between the board and the superintendent was reflected in the superintendent's continuing position and other data emerging later in the case (Hypothesis 4). Only the length of time served by individual board members tends to support the stable conditions of board membership. Some evidence is presented later that tends to confirm the prediction that the superintendent enters into the selection of board members (Hypothesis 5). The community changed in terms of population increase and socioeconomic class, and citizens attempted to change the board by suggesting and backing new candidates. This was political action on the part of the new community (Hypotheses 6 and 7). The result of this action was Prentice's election (Hypothesis 8). The resulting increase in board conflict was demonstrated by the increase in non-unanimous votes cast during the 1960-61 year (Hypothesis 9). This conflict is further demonstrated by

---

[18] Admittedly, the exact points in time are difficult to pinpoint. Perhaps the end of stability between the two is 1954 or 1955.

data in the continued case. Hypotheses 9, 10, 11, and 12 emerge more clearly from later developments in Robertsdale. But turning to these, the lessons Robertsdale offers about the road to incumbent defeat and evidence concerning the extent to which Robertsdale resembles other suburban schools may warrant our attention.

CHANGING SCHOOL DISTRICTS AND STATIC POLICY MAKING

The Robertsdale story suggests that the road to the defeat of an incumbent school board member begins with a near-equilibrium in the school board, in the board–superintendent relationship, and in the relationship between the board and its school district. From the late 1930's to the early 1950's, Robertsdale had behaved like a typical small town school district, reflecting rural values with low-pressure consensus politics under the established leadership of the superintendent. The board appears to have reflected the school district's political ideology as well as its values and aspirations for education. The low-conflict ideology and stability of the sacred community continues to characterize school board activities and the board-superintendent relationship in the 1960's and gives the appearance of a stable relationship between the larger social and political system, the school district, and its decision-making central subsystem, the school board. The growing population of Robertsdale through the 1950's and the related changes in housing indicated by changes in assessed valuation suggest that while the old stability is reflected in the pattern of unanimity of voting on the board, the larger community was undergoing rapid social change. Such changes suggest that the values and aspirations for education held by the community would also be undergoing rapid modification. The changes in high school course offerings and in the percent of Robertsdale graduates going to college further illustrates this point. So the appearance of a continued stability in the relationship between board and community is misleading.

The appearance of stability reflects the internal relationships of the board and the board–superintendent relationship established during the two preceding decades but does not reflect the changing community. Stated another way, the board was a relatively closed system reflecting the past and responding very little, if at all, to the present. The community was an open system with new and different population inputs. Hence, it can be seen that a gap was developing between the board and the community. The decision-making center of the school district and the district's changing population were drifting further apart.

Placed in this context, the election of Prentice did not just happen. His election reflected certain changing community values and aspirations and interest in education. It was the product of conflict, however muted at this stage, between the old values exemplified by the defeated incumbent and the new aspirations personified in Prentice. Moreover, if Prentice's election illustrates a common process of school district change, one in which the changing society becomes more effectively represented in educational policy making, then communities must incur population changes prior to defeating an incumbent school board member. This would be expected to occur often enough to reveal the statistical significance reflecting these generalizations. It is conceivable that similar changes may come about in values concerning education without such population shifts. However, it is unlikely that major population changes will take place in communities without being reflected in the values held by the community. These population and value shifts are often not reflected in governmental bodies to the extent that these bodies continue to represent the established social system of the community. In Springdale the prevailing power holders in the invisible government and governmental boards, including those of the school, represented the prevailing core values of the community. Similarly, the Jefferson School Board reflected the prevailing values of their community. So long as the actions of members in school government are consistent with the value system of the community, the central decision-making subsystem of the school district will remain in control. But school districts and communities change, especially in suburban areas surrounding metropolitan centers like Robertsdale. The urban centers change more slowly. Newcomers bring with them backgrounds, experiences, dreams, and fears, as well as hopes for their children. These feelings may be different from those held by the old residents of the community. The newcomers may represent different religions, races, occupations, ethnic origins, and associational ties. Such differences, especially when they produce differences in the perceived need for education, are likely to demand changes in educational policies and decision making resulting in demands by the new group to participate in educational policy making. These population changes will result in pressure on established policy-making organizations. Since established boards reflect the social systems of the past and remain closed to the newcomer, these boards will fail to modify their behavior to meet the new demands of incoming populations whether in white suburbia or in Negro urban centers.

When the governing structure fails to respond to a new set of values of an incoming population, groups representing the new set of values are likely to develop a new, competing structure. Conflict between the old and the new structures will result, eventually focusing on the governing boards. But a lag generally exists between change in community and school district populations and the development of competing social systems. Thus, the translation of the societal base in school districts into an effective and competing political system will take time. In essence, changes in social and economic elements in a community will require changes in educational policies and practices of that community. However, if the school district has developed a relatively stable decision-making central subsystem in its school board, it is likely that the board will reflect the past rather than the present pressures, fending off these present pressures enough to be characterized as a closed subsystem. This forces the new population to develop social and political mechanisms that can successfully challenge the old power groups in the district and defeat an incumbent school board member, as Prentice did in Robertsdale. It is precisely these developments that characterized the road to incumbent defeat in Robertsdale.

The lag between significant changes in a school district's population and the development of competing power systems is likely to be followed by political conflict in the district. The lag may continue after the development of such conflict until the conflict is resolved, most often by a victory of the new over the old. In school districts where there is little or slow population change, such conflicts will seldom occur, and such districts will display long periods of stability. In districts which are undergoing rapid social change, the conflict and competition may display several changes during a similar period of years. Finally, some districts may spend a long time in conflict and competition before resolution takes place. In any event, the central lesson of this chapter, as seen in Robertsdale with Prentice's victory at the polls, is that the defeat of an incumbent school board member after an extended period without incumbent defeat results from a gap between the educational values and aspirations of the community and those reflected in school board policies. Areas undergoing rapid suburbanization are likely to provide good opportunities to test these ideas.

From Socioeconomic Changes to Political Action[19]

Richard S. Kirkendall, using the Robertsdale story and its theoretical background, developed indicators of social and economic

---

[19] This section owes much to Richard S. Kirkendall, "Discriminating Social, Economic and Political Characteristics of Changing versus Stable Policy-Making Systems in School Districts" (Unpublished Ph.D. dissertation, Claremont Graduate School, Claremont, California, 1966).

changes as well as political indicators along the road to incumbent defeat. Kirkendall hoped that discovering such predictors of incumbent defeat would help avoid unnecessary political conflict and help community leaders, superintendents, and school boards to take action to change school policies and programs before disruptive conflict could take place. He felt that a community value system is characterized by the dominant core of values held by the citizenry within the school district community. It has been demonstrated that the prevailing power structure is linked with the prevailing value system of the community.[20]

In his description of the monolithic pyramidal power structure of Regional City,[21] Hunter describes school board members as second-line power figures. In communities smaller than Regional City, school board members, like mayors and city councilmen, probably enjoy a higher rank in the local power structure than they do in larger cities. But whether of first or second order, the school board members are elements of the formal power structure of the community. As such, they are susceptible to the pressures brought about by changes in the value system of the community resulting from changes in the community itself.

The groundwork of the theory stimulated a search for evidence of antecedents to change in the pattern of school board elections of a community. Kirkendall's statement of the theory follows. (References are to Chart VII.)

1) Social, economic, and political conditions within a given community (Point *B* in Chart VII) affect the values, aspirations, and interests of the society encompassed by said community (Point *C* in the Chart). These conditions give evidence of their nature through visible characteristics or indicators (Point *A*).

2) A community's values, aspirations, and interests exert a dominant influence over the decision-making processes of the community (Point *D*).

3) The former power structure of the community (Point *E*) responds to the influences exerted by the value orientation of the community. The school board is an important element in the formal power structure. Therefore, its composition responds to the influence exerted by the value orientation of the community (Point *F*).

4) The chief school officer, as a policy maker, plays a political role. Therefore, his tenure is affected by changes in the membership of the board of education (Point *G*).

---

[20] Arthur J. Vidich and Joseph Bensman, *Small Town in Mass Society* (Garden City, N.Y.: Doubleday & Co., Inc., Anchor Books, 1958), Chapters 2, 3, and 4.

[21] Hunter, *Community Power Structure* (Chapel Hill, N.C.: University of North Carolina Press, 1953), p. 21.

Chart VII

A DIAGRAMMATIC REPRESENTATION
OF THE THEORY

The School District Community

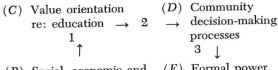

Points *A*, *F*, and *G* in the diagram represent the visible variables in the theory, while *B*, *C*, *D*, and *E* are intervening variables. Point *A* is the visible representation of Point *B*, *F* is the visible element of *E*, and *G* depends on *F*. The focus of Kirkendall's study was the potential relatedness of indicators of social, economic, and political conditions in school district communities, *A*, and the composition of school boards in those communities, *F*.

Although the theory suggests that a linkage exists between Points *A* and *F* (via *B*, *C*, *D*, and *E*), no attempt was made to investigate these linkages directly. Particularly, there was no attempt to measure the value orientations of communities, *C*, nor their decision-making processes, *D*. Neither was there an attempt to investigate the relationships between points *C* and *D*.

The primary question in Kirkendall's study is stated as follows:

> Can indicators of social, economic, and political conditions in school district communities be used to discriminate between those school districts in which changes in the composition of the school board occurs and those in which it does not occur?

As indicators are found which discriminate between the two kinds of school district communities defined in the primary question, two secondary questions with time dimensions become important. One relates to the chronological order in which these indicators discriminate between the two kinds of districts, and the other relates to their relative position in time with respect to the defeat of school board incumbents. These two secondary questions are stated as follows:

In cases in which indicators of social, economic, and political conditions in school district communities discriminate between those districts in which a change in the composition of the school board occurs and those in which it does not occur, do the social and economic indicators precede in time the political indicators?

Can some indicators of social, economic, and political conditions in school district communities be used to predict later change or non-change in the composition of the school board?

Kirkendall selected thirty-seven school districts from four growing counties in southern California. Nineteen of the districts were ones in which no school board incumbent had been defeated in a board election between 1952 and 1965. These nineteen were randomly selected from the California counties involved. They were compared with eighteen school districts, all the districts in the four counties in which one or more school board members had been defeated in the 1961 board elections and in which the incumbent of the superintendency changed within four years of that election. Eight of the eighteen districts in which a school board incumbent had met defeat in 1961 had never experienced incumbent defeat between 1952 and 1961. The other ten of these districts had experienced one or more incumbent defeats during that period of time. In addition, the districts chosen had five-member boards throughout the period, and unlike Roberts-dale, they had not undergone area reorganization or unification during the period from 1952 to 1965.

The four counties from which the sample was drawn had experienced a large population growth between 1951 and 1961. Most school districts in those counties experienced similar growth in population and in school enrollments during that period. Theoretical considerations led Kirkendall to believe that there would be numerous changes in the counties during that period. As most practicing school administrators know and often regret, there are practical limits to the kinds of socioeconomic indicators that practitioners can obtain without special resources or grants. Census data which might otherwise be good indicators of changing socioeconomic composition of the district are generally not collected often enough and suffer from the more serious limitation that census numeration districts rarely coincide with school districts. Kirkendall used three common descriptive characteristics of school districts: (1) assessed valuation, (2) average daily attendance, and (3) number of votes cast for each candidate at school board elections.

Average daily attendance is usually defined as the number of days each registered pupil in the district attended school divided by the number of days school was in session during the year. It is an indicator of the size of the educational enterprise. Increases or decreases in average daily attendance represent changes in the need for school housing, for teachers, for supplies, for equipment, . . . These changed needs represent potential pressures on the school board. With less certainty it may be said that changes in average daily attendance reflect changes in land use, most often suburbanization but sometimes shifts from residential to industrial use of land or perhaps increased urbanization. In short, changes in average daily attendance are likely to correlate with changes in either the population size or the social class of the district, or both.

Changes in average daily attendance within the same school district are roughly indications of changes in (1) the density of population, (2) the average number of school-age children per capita, and (3) the ratio of the number of children attending public schools to the number of children attending private and parochial schools. Significant changes in any of these are meaningful in regard to the educational values of the community. School districts which experience changes in the population density, the number of school-age children per capita, the ratio of the number of children attending public schools to the number attending private and parochial schools, or the use of land will feel different pressures than those districts not experiencing such change.

The assessed valuation of a school district is the sum of the assessed value of all the real and personal property in the district against which a tax is levied. A change in the assessed valuation of a school district becomes a measure of the changing gross wealth of the district. It is an indicator of the district's economic capacity to meet the stress of changing programs. It reflects change in land use and changes in assessment practices. Any or all of these reflect the socioeconomic conditions of a community. Generally assessed valuation per child in average daily attendance is the single most important indicator of the ability of a community to support its schools. A high assessed valuation per child in average daily attendance could result from a significant industrial or commercial use of an area within the district or from very expensive homes with a low number of school-age children per family. Either case suggests a specific socioeconomic type of community with its values and aspirations for education. Conversely, a low assessed valuation per average daily attendance would result from a predominantly residential community of low cost housing with little industry or from a high population density with little wealth. This indicator takes on a special meaning in the light of studies that indicate that dwelling type and value of housing are closely related to social status.

Changes in assessed valuation per child in average daily attendance bring about changes in the community's economic capacity to provide the education needed by its residents. They are probably stronger indicators of new building and change in land use than change in assessed valuation by itself. Changes in this ratio are apt to be sensitive indicators of changes in the social class composition of a school district's population. These have further implications for possible changes in public attitudes toward school board policies and educational practices.

Kirkendall suggests that changes in a community's values which do not result in changes in school board policies and educational practices will lead to pressures for changes in the school district's power structure as it focuses on the board. As stated in Hypothesis 7, when the school district perceives the progressive segregation of its school board, it will attempt to prevent further segregation. The district will attempt to reverse the process by initiating to the board in the hope that messages will be received. But the progressive segregation of the board from the district actually decreases its chances of engaging in self-correcting behavior. This situation decreases the probability that the board will be able to process the necessary messages for self-correction. Political action to change board membership is then likely to occur. This political action can be seen in changes in the number of voters in school board elections.

Generally, school boards are elected by a minority of the potential or eligible voters of a district. It is likely that the small number of regular voters in the school district's elections will be comprised of the supporters of the board and the district's established leadership groups. Students of voter behavior and political practices have known for some time that two-party elections depend to a significant degree on the turnout of those voters traditionally for or against a given party. Even in the absence of a two-party system, as in local school districts, it appears that the same behavioral aspects of voter choice operate, the differences here resulting from the lack of an institutionalized loyal opposition by the party out of office.[22] Small voter turnout is in part a reflection of the lack of organized opposition to the policies of

---

[22] In contradiction to the view of some analysts of educational voter behavior, Arnold Spinner has found that there is stability in voter behavior in school district referenda. These authors believe that other investigators will also find parallels between partisan political behavior and the politics of education. *See* Arnold Spinner, "The Effects of the Extent of Voter Participation Upon Election Outcomes in School Budget Elections in New York State 1957-1966" (Unpublished Ph.D. dissertation, New York University, 1967).

the established district leaders. The failure of the old board to represent a new population's educational values and aspirations is probably
the result of long stability at the board level and changes in the socioeconomic composition of the school district's population. Generally
speaking, an increase in voter turnout, specifically in ballots cast
against incumbents results prior to the removal of an incumbent from
office. Hence, Kirkendall's third basic element for developing measures
to identify and predict districts that will experience incumbent defeat
is as follows:

> It is logical to expect that a significant increase in the number of
> voters in a school board election would result in a higher ratio
> of votes against incumbents to total votes cast than would no in-
> crease in the number of votes.

Kirkendall used the ratio of votes cast against incumbents to total votes
cast in the elections during the decade prior to 1961 as one of his
measures. The ratios of incumbents and nonincumbents to positions
open indicates the degree to which nonincumbents are challenging the
old board establishment. These factors as well as the socioeconomic
indicators were used as a measure of change in each of the thirty-seven
districts and finally in the discriminate analyses of the data.

The eighteen school districts whose incumbents had suffered defeat
in 1961 can be statistically separated from the nineteen which had not
had incumbent defeat by 1965. This discrimination, significant at the
.005 level, rests on a combination of socioeconomic measures dating
from the early 1950's to 1958. Thus, these indicators could have predicted which districts were to experience incumbent defeat at least
three years before the event. When Kirkendall examined the eight
districts which had not experienced incumbent defeat from 1952 to
1961 from those ten which had had one or more defeats before 1961
and since 1961, he found that the eight districts more closely approxi-
mated the nineteen districts that had not experienced incumbent
defeat than did the other ten.

Thus, the examination of thirty-seven districts and their changes in
measures involving assessed valuation, average daily attendance, and
voting behavior strongly supports the Robertsdale findings. Further,
the strongest predictors of the 1961 defeats of incumbents were (1)
the percentage change in assessed valuation over the three-year period,
1951-52 to 1954-55, (2) the percentage change in average daily attendance over the three year period 1956-57 to 1959-60, and (3) the
ratio of votes against incumbents to total votes cast in the 1959 elec-

tions. Finally, the shift in assessed valuation preceded by some eight years the significant political shift in voting behavior.

In the midwestern Robertsdale case and in the southern California districts, changes in assessed valuation, then in pupil attendance, and later in voting behavior marked the road to incumbent defeat. If these are the sign posts which board members, superintendents, and other school people can read as warnings of impending school board defeat, the unified stable board—a closed decision-making subsystem—is the vehicle which takes schoolmen and experienced board members to that fateful election where old and new values meet. For most school districts the governmental process is best seen as a dynamic relationship between two types of dimensions—societal and governmental.

If this theory of political change is correct, then for a period of time school board membership and policies should remain rather stable. Political change requires change in the district's social and economic composition so that the societal and governmental dimensions drift apart. The reliable "yes" voters, reflecting the past as well as the local school establishment's values, reinforce the board's relatively static condition until the changing society upsets the old system through political action. Then the societal and governmental dimensions in education display a sudden convergence through political activities at the local school district level.

The specific political event, convergence or abrupt change in the governmental dimension, is the defeat of an incumbent school board member. When changes in a school district's populace take place without similar changes in the governmental policies, an election upset will occur which disrupts the internal alignment of the board and superintendent and changes the direction of educational policy. If the policies of a school district are largely the product of the district's superintendent of schools, then their destiny becomes his destiny. Incumbent defeat and closing the gap between the societal and governmental dimensions, places the chief school officer's tenure in danger.

Summary

The defeat of an incumbent is apparently achieved by a consolidation of opposition forces. This defeat leads to conflict on the board, especially between the new member and the superintendent. Usually within three years, the superintendent is out of office. His replacement is usually an outsider with a mandate to change the schools. Local districts exhibiting an intermittent pattern of change in the governmental dimension and a relatively constant pattern of change in the societal dimension will move along a collision course toward incumbent defeat, involuntary turnover of the superintendent and the selection of an outside superintendent.

This pattern, first found in case studies and then tested with verificational studies, confirms the capacity of local school districts to change themselves and their schools. The operation of even relatively blind forces follows social laws. In the case of the local school district, these forces do produce change, bringing a school into alignment with its society. It would be wise to eliminate the legal barriers which hinder this pattern of change. Efforts to institutionalize a loyal opposition in school districts may speed up the process. Better training of boards and superintendents can produce an awareness of early indicators for adjusting educational programs to the needs and aspirations of the citizens. In no way do the findings of these studies justify the conclusion that the local district "must go" because it cannot or does not change to meet its citizens' demands.

The process through which school districts cause their boards to respond to society is not completed with the defeat of an incumbent or two. The forces behind that election must continue and extend themselves, reaching further into the behavior of school administrators and teachers so that the old patterns and near-equilibrium of the closed board will not reassert themselves. Often it is only through these continued conflicts that the "Prentices" in changing districts learn where the center of opposition to their educational platform really is. The political effect of one incumbent's defeat is much greater than the one new school board member's voting power would suggest. The new man usually becomes the center of a new series of struggles with the established leader of the old power structure. In Robertsdale Prentice found that to validate his election and carry out the mandate of his election, he had to confront the established leadership and eventually struggle to take that leadership for himself.

5

After Incumbent Defeat:
The Fight for Power
on the Board

This chapter contains data about the Robertsdale School Board. In Chapter 4 the factors which lead to the election of Mr. Prentice to the Robertsdale School Board were set forth and examined. Here certain political aspects of school board action will be presented in a case covering a five-year time period. This is perhaps the largest span of time anyone has ever attempted to describe in a school district case. The case is also unique because of its method of development. The first section, "Notes from Prentice's Personal Diary," contains selected parts of a diary which Prentice kept while the events were occurring. The diary is written in the first person. The authors' interpretations and the latter portion of the case are written in the third person.

Regular board business such as roll call, minutes, and noncritical matters are not presented in this diary. One should remember that such items of business did take place. Usually eighty-five to ninety percent of the board's business caused no controversy. Unanimity was usual.

No observation can encompass the total interaction. Therefore, this diary records Prentice's observations of board interaction but does not include his total interaction. The diary includes only items that Prentice observed and felt were significant to relationships on the school board. These were generally items about which there was a difference of opinion on the board. One should not assume that this record is a complete description of all board business nor a representative sample of interactions of all board members.

Included here are several charts which should help the reader understand the diary: Chart VIII indicates the formal structure of the school board in April, 1960; Chart IX shows the division of board members into subgroups; Chart X is a map of Robertsdale indicating rural and suburban areas of the district showing the approximate place of residence of each school board member.

Chart VIII

FORMAL STRUCTURE OF THE ROBERTSDALE SCHOOL BOARD
APRIL, 1960

Mr. Mahan—	President	Mr. Wilke—	Treasurer
Mr. Chubb	Vice President	Mr. Scott—	Member
Mr. Dyke	Secretary	Mr. Prentice—	Member

Chart IX

GENERAL GROUP DIVISION OF ROBERTSDALE SCHOOL BOARD
NOTED IN PRENTICE'S DIARY

Old Guard Group	*Insurgent Group*
Mr. Dyke	Mr. Clubb
Mr. Scott	Mr. Wilke
Mr. Mahan	Mr. Prentice

NOTES FROM PRENTICE'S PERSONAL DIARY,
APRIL, 1960—NOVEMBER, 1960

Special Board Meeting, April 5, 1960. At the special board meeting on election day (April 5, 1960) I was welcomed by the defeated incumbent Jones and by board members Wilke, Clubb, and Mahan. Neither Dyke, Scott, nor Superintendent Joyce said a word to me. The following Thursday (April 7) was the regular meeting at which I was to be installed.

The day before the Thursday meeting, I received a call from Clubb informing me that the annexation of Midmeadows would be taken up

Chart X

RURAL AND SUBURBAN AREAS OF THE ROBERTSDALE DISTRICT

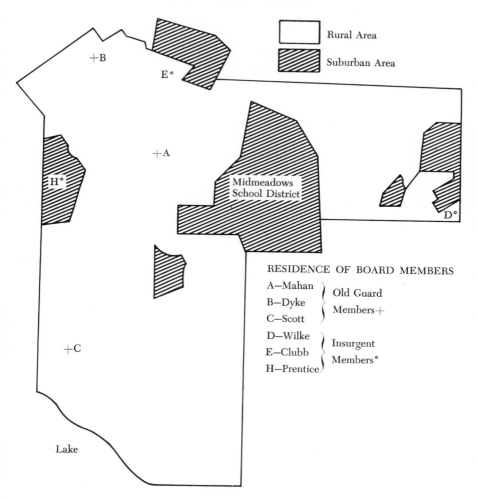

Rural Area

Suburban Area

RESIDENCE OF BOARD MEMBERS

A—Mahan }
B—Dyke   } Old Guard Members+
C—Scott }

D—Wilke   }
E—Clubb   } Insurgent Members°
H—Prentice }

Midmeadows School District

Lake

at the meeting the next day. Clubb's remarks made it perfectly clear to me that he favored the annexation requested by Midmeadows. He told me that by a vote of the Midmeadows electorate, it had become possible according to state law for the Robertsdale board to annex Midmeadows without a vote in the Robertsdale district. The Midmeadows vote was obtained in the April 5th election after the hard work of the citizens who favored the merger. *[A look at Chart X reveals that Robertsdale almost surrounds the small Midmeadows district. It is clear that Midmeadows could not survive as a separate district and still provide an adequate education at a reasonable cost.]*

Clubb continued to say that there were some jealousies and animosities between old residents of the two districts due to tradition and rivalries. In spite of the fact that the Robertsdale board could have annexed Midmeadows without a referendum, they had put the issue on their ballot. In a very small election it had lost by a narrow margin. Prior to the election, however, the Robertsdale Board had taken no position regarding annexation. In fact, they had disseminated no information as to what the election was about. Clubb informed me that legally we were not bound by the vote of either Midmeadows or Robertsdale.

Regular Meeting, April 7, 1960. This was the first school board meeting I attended as a member. The Midmeadows annexation was brought up and Superintendent Joyce handed out a set of figures indicating they had been supplied by the Midmeadows Superintendent. These figures showed a projected enrollment for Midmeadows anticipating an increase for September, 1960 of approximately sixty-seven percent over the present year's enrollment.

The entire Robertsdale board hoped to annex Midmeadows, but in view of the figures presented they could not see any possible way to do so at that time. The figures indicated a continued growth of approximately 65 percent for both the second and third years following the first year's projection. *[In the best sense of the word these figures were not school population projections. They had not been calculated on the basis of a formula or census data. They were guesses based on statements of builders indicating what they hoped to build in the following three years. When presented to the Robertsdale board, these figures were almost six months old.]*

Dyke made a motion that the Robertsdale board reject the annexation of Midmeadows due to the evidence before the board. I indicated that I would not vote at that time because the Board had already printed, in the local papers, a notice of a meeting to be held at the high school to discuss the annexation problem. The meeting was to be held April 21. The board agreed that they should not act before the meeting, and Dyke withdrew his motion.

As the meeting adjourned, all members seemed to agree that the figures presented to the board could not be correct, but if they were correct, it would be impossible to annex Midmeadows.

The following Saturday I was called by two residents of Mid-meadows and requested to tour the district with them to see the building presently underway. I agreed and then called Mr. Thoms, the Midmeadows Superintendent, and asked him about the figures that had been presented to the Robertsdale board. Thoms said that the figures were gathered six months before and might not be correct as of the time of annexation. *[There is no data to indicate that Joyce did not make an effort to discover the validity of the annexation information provided him by the Midmeadows superintendent.]*

The following Sunday I toured the Midmeadows district with residents of Midmeadows and spoke to builders at the subdivision sites. We obtained a count of what was built, what was under construction, and what would probably be constructed by September, 1960. These figures showed the original set of figures presented to the Robertsdale board to be three hundred percent too high during the first year. The Midmeadows residents obtained the signatures of two Midmeadows board members indicating that these new figures were correct. I then called Joyce, gave him the figures, and asked him to indicate on Thursday what these new figures would mean when considering annexation.

Special Meeting, April 21, 1960. The board met in executive session before the public meeting convened. *[Here is where controversy usually occurs among boards, as Vidich and Bensman discovered in their research[1] and as Prentice discovered in his review of the minutes of the April 21 and 28, 1938 meetings of the Robertsdale School Board.]* Superintendent Joyce had not revised his recommendation in view of the new figures. He recommended that the board reject the annexation. I then presented the new data. The entire board had agreed a week before that they would have annexed had not the projected enrollment been so high. Still Dyke, Mahan, and Scott refused to annex.

Mahan then interjected that the negative vote of the Robertsdale people should prevent annexation. This was the first time this had been mentioned and was a reversal of Mahan's position of the previous week. He now maintained that the board had agreed that they would abide by the vote of the Robertsdale electorate at the April 5th election, even though they were not legally obligated to do so. Dyke and Scott agreed. Thus, all three reversed their positions of the previous week. Clubb and Wilke strongly disagreed with the opinion that the

---

[1] Arthur J. Vidich and Joseph Bensman, *Small Town In Mass Society* (Garden City, N.Y.: Doubleday & Co., Inc., Anchor Books, 1960), pp. 175-8.

board had agreed to abide by the Robertsdale vote. *[Here we see disagreement as to decisions supposedly made by the board prior to April, 1960. The official minutes offer no indication of any such decision or even of a discussion of the notion pro or con.]*

After much discussion and no agreement, Dyke accused me of having some ulterior motive in obtaining the new figures on the Midmeadows projected enrollment. I replied to this accusation, and the matter was dropped.

Dyke made a motion to reject the annexation, and Scott seconded it. The roll call vote was Dyke, Scott, and Mahan "for" (rejecting annexation), and Clubb, Wilke, and myself "against" (rejecting annexation). Clubb suggested that Joyce could cast the deciding vote, but I objected that this was illegal. Joyce confirmed my objection. Clubb then excused himself from the meeting without asking for a recess. The meeting went on with the discussion of annexation. When Clubb returned, he asked what had happened. Finding the situation unchanged, he mentioned to Mahan that he could have called for another vote while he, Clubb, was out of the room and could have won 3 to 2. The board went before the public split 3–3 knowing that the county superintendent could legally be petitioned to decide the issue and that he favored annexation.

At the public meeting Clubb made some remarks as to why he favored annexation. His words showed definite personal antagonism toward Dyke. Dyke returned in kind, opposing annexation. The 3–3 split was then announced, and Clubb informed the public and the board that he would not sign the petition necessary to allow the county superintendent to cast the deciding ballot. Clubb had not mentioned this decision at the executive session. Since three signatures were necessary on the petition, the issue was ended and the meeting adjourned.[2]

During the following weeks, two articles appeared in a local newspaper urging the board to annex Midmeadows.

Regular Meeting, May 5, 1960. Dyke asked what was going to be done about Midmeadows. There was no hope of resolving the issue at that time, and I therefore offered the following resolution:

Whereas the Robertsdale School Board split 3–3 on the question of the Midmeadows School District annexation, and whereas there seems to be no likelihood that this tie will be broken in the next few months, be it resolved that the Robertsdale Board of Education notify the Midmeadows Board of Education of its release from

---

2 "Public School Laws of Midwest State, 1960," No. 10, pp. 115-16.

any possible annexation at this time and be notified that the entire Robertsdale School Board is ready to actively work for and support such annexation after a six-month study by both districts to discover and work toward the solution of the classroom shortage and other problems that may exist.[3]

I had hoped to commit the board to favorable action regarding annexation at the next possible occasion. Dyke seconded the motion and it was unanimously adopted.

Next I initiated a discussion of the district's mailing list. I felt that more could be done in getting information to the public. At this time only the parents of children in public schools received information. During the ensuing discussion there again seemed to be a 3–3 division of opinion. Finally, it was decided to use the registered voter list plus whatever other lists were available to develop a mailing list. Dyke made such a motion and all six members voted in favor. (It should be noted here that in spite of my continuous inquiries regarding the progress on this project, nothing had yet been done about it one year later at the meeting on April 7, 1961.)

Another order of business was the employment of new teachers. Names, positions of appointment, and salaries were presented, but no qualifications were indicated. I asked that in the future qualifications be presented in a short paragraph for each candidate. Superintendent Joyce agreed that it could be done, and the board agreed that this would be helpful.

Upon presentation of bills, I asked if, in the future, the area in which the expenditure was made could be indicated. This had not been a practice of the board. The board agreed, and the meeting date was re-scheduled for the second Thursday in each month in order to provide time to complete this information.

It was also decided to meet with the Midmeadows board on May 25th. A letter was to be sent to their board to this effect. (This was later changed to June 1st, due to a calendar conflict.)

[In rapid succession Prentice had made four moves calculated to obtain modification of the system. Although some proposals were minor and there seemed to be unanimous agreement to make the changes, it would be some time before any change took place. Social systems change slowly. "Agree quickly but do nothing" often seems to be the response of a system to the attempts of an agent of change.]

A discussion of the dedication of the junior high school under construction indicated further disagreement on the board. There had evidently been a discussion sometime before the April, 1960 meeting

---

[3] "Official Minutes of the Board of Education of Robertsdale," May 5, 1960.

(when I was elected) about dedicating the building and placing a plaque to Superintendent Joyce and his wife in the building. Mrs. Joyce had taught in the old junior high school until her recent death. Dyke, Scott, and Mahan insisted that the entire building was to be named "Joyce Junior High School." Clubb and Wilke insisted that no such discussion or agreement had taken place. After some discussion the entire board agreed that nothing could be done at this point since the name was already on the building.

[There is evidence here of decisions being made at informal meetings without all members attending. Official minutes provide no indication of agreement at any regular or special board meeting regarding the naming of the junior high. The February 18, 1960 minutes indicate approval of additional cost for lettering on the junior high building, but there is no stipulation as to naming of the building.]

Joint County Board Dinner Meeting, May 25, 1960. Joyce drove Dyke, Mahan, Scott, and myself to the meeting. The latter three sat in the back, leaving Joyce and me in the front seat. Neither Clubb nor Wilke attended the meeting. At the dinner, Dyke, Mahan, and Scott sat on one side of the table, and Joyce and I sat on the other side. Little of relevance happened at the meeting. I felt the exclusion, indicated by the seating pattern, which confirmed the voting pattern established to this point.

Special Meeting, June 1, 1960. Superintendent Joyce introduced Mr. Chris, the new assistant superintendent for business and finance. The minutes were then read. I asked why there was no record in the minutes of the agreement to furnish board members with the qualifications of new teachers upon their recommendation for employment and also why no indication appeared regarding the agreement to identify areas of expenditures when presenting bills for approval. Dyke indicated he did not feel that there was reason to place the coding of bills in the minutes since no motion was made, and he did not remember anything being said about providing information related to teacher qualifications. The minutes were approved, and the meeting continued.

Joyce presented a proposed school calendar for the following school year. According to this calendar, school started very early in comparison with most Midwest County districts. School was to close on May 26th, much earlier than the vast majority of the Midwest County districts. The calendar, Joyce said, encompassed 186 teaching days. I believed that it was impossible that this many days fell within the specified period. Dyke took exception, saying that the board should not dispute the superintendent's word. To this I retorted that even a superintendent could make a mistake and asked that a calendar be produced so the days could be counted. (The calendar presented had merely listed certain dates; i.e., the opening and closing of school, etc.) Joyce's secretary was working that evening and was called into the meeting. She produced a calendar, and we proceeded to count the days. It was immediately obvious that one day was miscounted, bringing the calendar to 185 days. I suggested that Monday, January 2nd, should be a holiday since January 1st fell on Sunday in 1961. Dyke agreed, and the rest of the board concurred, making the calendar 184 days.

Counting Christmas as a school day, inasmuch as it fell on a Saturday that year, also seemed to me to be irregular. The law stated that it must fall on a school day to be counted. Joyce insisted that it could be counted and was counting it in the 184 days. Joyce stated that even if Christmas could not be counted he could arrange to count workshop meetings as teaching days, and in any case the state only required 180 days.

After the disposal of several items on the agenda, Dyke made a motion to accept the calendar as the superintendent had recommended with the modifications to make it a 184-day calendar. Scott seconded the motion. The calendar was passed at this time with five votes "for." I voted "no." I was stunned that it should even have been brought to a vote before the legal question was resolved. (Actually, neither Clubb nor Wilke voted, but according to law they were recorded with the majority.[4])

Several other items were taken care of before Clubb left the meeting in order to get some sleep before leaving on a truck run at 3 a.m. the next morning.

The meeting continued, and I asked that both teacher qualification and the coding of bills appear in the minutes of the present meeting. Dyke refused, saying that they were not motions. "It is easy to make that a motion," I said, "and I will be happy to do so." Dyke conceded that the coding of bills could be included in the minutes without a motion. The board president, Mahan, asked that it be made a motion anyway, and I presented it. It was seconded and passed. I then made a motion regarding teacher qualifications. Joyce said that no motion was necessary and that he would see that the board members received

---

[4] "Public School Laws. . . ," *op. cit.*, p. 116.

the information. Dyke agreed, saying all of this was on file. "I don't have the time to run up to the superintendent's office to look at the file," I said. "I want the qualifications along with the recommendation for employment." Joyce again tried to stop the motion by saying he would see that the board members received the information as requested. Mahan asked what he should do with the motion on the floor, and Wilke said he would second it. On the vote Wilke and I voted "aye." When the question "those opposed?" was asked, no one indicated opposition. The vote was recorded five "for" and none "against." The entire discussion left the superintendent very unhappy. His beet-red face indicated a considerable rise in blood pressure at the idea of being required to present teacher qualifications to the board of education.

[*An analysis of official board minutes reveals no conflict regarding the presentation of teacher qualifications or the coding of bills. The first time the two issues appear in the minutes, both are unanimously passed. Again there is evidence that simple analysis of the minutes can give no clear picture of the social systems in a school district or of the social system of the board of education. It is interesting that Mahan later told Prentice that he did not always support Joyce. Prentice should have perceived Mahan's support for this motion as an early indication of this—but he did not!*]

As the meeting adjourned, all the board members still in attendance and Joyce walked out of the board room (which was at one end of the superintendent's office) and turned left down the corridor toward the main exit of the high school. The 1960 graduating class picture which had recently been placed on the wall caught Wilke's eye, and he stood looking at it. I walked up, and a few complimentary remarks were exchanged regarding the picture. Joyce had also stopped and joined in the conversation. Meanwhile, Mahan, and Scott passed the three of us and went into the high school principal's office. (The principal was not in the building.) As they passed, Mahan said good night to Wilke and me. Joyce turned away leaving Wilke and me looking at the picture. Dyke had stopped momentarily at the picture as Joyce, Mahan, and Scott entered the principal's office. Mahan returned to the corridor, looked at Dyke and again said good night. Dyke then entered the office saying good night and leaving Wilke and me alone in the hall.

As we left the building, Wilke commented, "I guess you see they're having a private meeting to decide what to do. That's probably where they decided to name the junior high." Wilke continued saying that he would not again go along with extending the superintendent's contract. He indicated that he was "fed up." I remarked that we quite obviously were meant to be excluded from the meeting in the principal's office. Wilke concluded with, "If you and I pull together, we can change that in the next election."

During the next few weeks I tried to persuade Joyce to investigate the matter of counting Christmas as a school day. In fact, I did some checking myself. I called the county superintendent, who believed that Christmas could not be considered a school day. He said he would call the state office and check. He called back shortly to inform me that the state ruling was that Christmas could not be counted in 1960.

Upon receiving this information, I called Joyce and informed him of the situation. Joyce still believed that Robertsdale could count Christmas since they had previously counted a holiday in a similar situation. Seeing no other resolution, I said that I wanted the calendar placed on the agenda for the next meeting so that the difficulty could be straightened out. I insisted that the calendar approved at the last meeting which included Christmas as a teaching day, was an illegal calendar. After another attempt to sway my opinion, Joyce agreed to place the calendar problem on the agenda for the forthcoming meeting.

During the two weeks while I was checking on the calendar, I called Wilke to discuss the matter. Wilke agreed that, if Christmas could not be counted, something would have to be done. He went on to say that he had brought up a question concerning uncertified salaries at the last meeting because Clubb had asked him to do so. Wilke was upset because Clubb had given him no support when this issue was brought up, and so Wilke was left holding the bag. At least, Wilke saw it this way. He indicated that this was the usual procedure and he was sick of it. (Wilke had initiated such a discussion at the June 1st meeting. There was not much discussion, and no motion was presented or decision made.)

Later in the week I again called Wilke and brought him up-to-date on the situation. Wilke said, "I'm sure glad you're not a yes-man. I've never been one. What we need is more people who will do that."

Both Clubb and Wilke had now indicated that each felt he was the only one who could be counted on to act when the superintendent tried to push something through. Wilke, however, correctly pointed out that on two occasions, e.g., the annexation and uncertified personnel Clubb had failed to support his words with action. I discovered that both men were capable of such actions.

[*The group structure seems to be established at this point. Un-doubtedly the seeds of this structure were present before Prentice's election. He had some hint of this while he was campaigning. By now he was fairly sure of his ground. It is interesting to speculate what would have happened if he had not acted so quickly. As has been noted, the president of the board, Mahan, had acted at least once in his interest. If he had not been predisposed to certain behaviors, Mahan might have been won over. On the other hand, such a move may have driven Clubb and Wilke away from him, thus splitting the board into three groups instead of two. Social behavior is an inter-esting phenomenon. The after-the-fact guessing about the possible results of alternative actions provides an almost endless and pleasur-able game. Unfortunately, for participants in the actual social be-havior, they do not have the advantage of hindsight.*]

June 5, 1960.   Mr. James and his wife were guests in my home on June 5th. During the course of the evening, it was revealed that James, although living at the time in Midwest City had lived in Robertsdale as a boy and had attended the old two-room school. James clarified many of the things I had heard about the district. He confirmed that the former superintendent was fired due to an auto accident caused by drinking, that Joyce and the Little family were closely tied by mutual exchange of favors, and that Joyce (during the period James knew about) was active in the Baptist Church.

At Clubb's suggestion, Mr. Darst called me regarding the deposi-tory used for school district funds. Darst was an officer of the St. Joseph Bank, a new bank at that time and the only bank in the Robertsdale district. He asked me if I would come to the bank to discuss the depository. On June 17th, I complied, and the following situation unfolded. The large majority of the Robertsdale district's funds were deposited in the Community Bank, which was the only bank near the Robertsdale district before the St. Joseph Bank opened. During the summer of 1959, all activity funds were moved to the St. Joseph Bank, but the large teachers' fund and incidental funds re-mained in the Community Bank.

The Little family had been prominent in the Robertsdale district for many years and had on occasion served as school board members. Through long association, Joyce considered the Little family personal friends. The two older Littles seemed to be much closer to Joyce than were their boys. Jack Little, Sr., was a member of the Community Bank Board, and his son, Jack, Jr., was an officer at that bank. Her-bert Little had been a member of the Robertsdale School Board and the owner of a hardware store. One of his two boys was still operating that store. The School district still did business with both families.

There was at this time in Midwest State a law levying a bank tax on the business a bank did. The tax returned to the school district in which the bank was located. After a long talk with officials of the St. Joseph Bank, I asked that further information regarding the bank tax be obtained so that I could have complete information regarding it.

Special Meeting, June 22, 1960. This meeting was called because a reassessment in the district had made it necessary, by law, to reduce the school tax levy. The new levy would by reason of the increase in valuation due to reassessment bring in the same revenue as the old levy at the old assessment. During the discussion I was surprised to hear Dyke say he would not reduce the levy because the district was so much in need of money. Scott, however, was in favor of reducing the levy as much as possible. The law was clear, a reduction of thirty-five cents was made. I urged that a great deal of publicity be given the fact that the Robertsdale district had one of the lowest expenditures per pupil in the county and, while the reduction would help tax-payers that year, the board would probably have to seek a higher levy for 1960-61. [*In spite of Prentice's urging, however, only minimum publicity was given to this side of the tax reduction. As will be seen during the 1960-61 tax levy election, the electorate failed to understand why a high tax raise was necessary.*]

After this matter I again raised questions regarding the school calendar. Dyke countered that the board had already passed the calendar. I pointed out the changes which the superintendent had made due to new information received; I insisted that this was a new calendar and that due to a manipulation of days an extra day was picked up, although pupils were not actually in class. Superintendent Joyce continued to insist that Christmas could be counted as a teaching day. Only upon my objection did he say that he would not count it. Dyke interrupted the discussion: "I don't want to be rude, but we did vote that this calendar or this approximate calendar would be adequate. Therefore, I make a motion we approve this calendar now." Scott seconded the motion, and it passed three to one with my voting against the motion, Clubb and Wilke being absent from the meeting.

The final item on the agenda was approved: salary raises for maintenance men, mechanics, and cafeteria personnel. I asked if maintenance men and mechanics were on salary schedule or if each negotiated independently. Upon finding that there was no schedule, I suggested that good personnel practice indicated the necessity for a salary schedule.

Upon leaving the meeting, I spoke at length with Mr. Chris, the new assistant superintendent. Chris was working on his dissertation at Midwest University, having completed his course work. Chris said that he had come to Robertsdale because his advisor at the university thought very highly of Joyce. Chris himself thought that Joyce was a fine superintendent. The majority of Chris's remarks supported Joyce's behavior at the previous meeting. It was clear, however, that Chris and I had a great deal in common. Chris indicated that he hoped we could get together in the coming year.

Midwest County Joint School Boards Meeting, June 26, 1960. Joyce and I were the only ones from the Robertsdale district attending this meeting. Joyce picked me up at my home, and conversation on the way to the meeting was friendly. At the meeting a report on the status of certain school districts was presented which named the Robertsdale district without coding its name. Joyce was very unhappy about this since Robertsdale did not compare favorably with the two other districts in Midwest County used in the study. I said that the report was factual and that the thing to do was to try to improve Robertsdale's position. I felt that the district was in a position to do so at present. Joyce agreed, stating that the new communities would make this possible. He indicated that he felt it was very difficult to convince the older residents that more money was needed for education, but that the people moving into the new communities of Bluffview and Elm Grove believed in education and were willing to spend money for it.

June 27, 1960. I had an appointment to see Chod, who was to be part-time principal of the new Bluffview Elementary School as well as principal of Robertsdale Elementary School. I had called him at his home on June 21st to ask if we could get together for a discussion. I told him that I would like to know him better and that I wanted to find out if there was any way I could be of assistance to him. Chod suggested that I meet him at the high school on the afternoon of the 27th as he expected to be working there at that time. However, he cautioned me that he might be at his own school, Robertsdale Elementary. I said I would locate him, and on that afternoon set out to do just that.

I first went to the high school and, not finding Chod, inquired and was told that Chod was at St. Joseph Elementary School. I drove to St. Joseph and finding no one, went on to Robertsdale Elementary. I was told that Chod was at the high school. I returned to the high school but could not locate Chod. Chod never gave me an explanation for his failure to keep our appointment.

Mr. Darst, an officer of the St. Joseph Bank, stopped by my home on June 28, 1960 with the information I had requested during our earlier meeting. I told him that I had heard that there were other factors involved in the selection of a depository than just where the district could earn the most money. Darst immediately came to the heart of the matter by indicating that Scott had told him that he wouldn't consider changing his personal account as he was a close friend of Little. "Of course, Mr. Joyce and Mr. Scott are very close friends," Darst said. "I could tell you how it would go if you were to vote on moving your money to our bank. Mahan, Dyke, and Scott 'against;' Clubb, Wilke, and you 'for.'" I stated that such a vote would not solve anything.

June 29, 1960. I returned the personnel handbook which Joyce had lent me. Joyce was not in at the time, so I left the book along with a note indicating that I felt a revision was in order, and if Joyce was interested, I would be happy to talk it over with him. I never heard from Joyce, but many changes were made in the handbook which came out the following year.

On this same day I had a conversation with Mr. Troy, a neighbor of mine. Troy was a member of the Lakeside City Council and a long-time resident of the community who had moved to the Bluffview subdivision about the same time as I had. Troy knew a good deal about the community and helped me to understand the school district in the light of its past history. Troy owned and operated a gasoline station in the Bluffview Shopping Center which provided him with many contacts and made him somewhat of an information center.

Troy said that Lakeside had been run for many years by the Republican organization in the community. The Republican Club was composed of older men, the younger men of the community were in the Democratic Club. (It is interesting to note that during 1960 a group of young Republicans from Bluffview formed a new club, and both Republican clubs were functioning at the close of this diary.) Troy reported that the young men in the Democratic organization were rapidly causing this organization to grow in power.

Troy went on to relate that Herbert Little, Sr. had been on the board of education when Joyce was first hired. Troy confirmed many of the stories about the relation of the Little family to the district, and described another situation between the school district and the

Littles. James Little, now deceased, had owned a grocery store, and the district had always purchased their "Christmas treats" from this store. According to Troy, the only year that bids were taken on commodities to be purchased Troy's father got the business. After that year, bids were never again requested, and the business returned to Little. I was unable to check this story. However, bills indicated that for more than twenty years the district had been doing business with the Littles. [*During the period when data was collected, the district did not provide Christmas treats, so no current information was available. Whether or not the story is entirely accurate, it confirms what emerges in this diary as Robertsdale's community image.*]

Troy continued by tying the Little family in with certain aspects of the community and the school board. He said that Robert Little had once been president of the Republican Club and the school board. Further, Dyke, present member of the school board and strong supporter of Joyce, had also been president of the Republican Club. The incumbent president of the Republican Club was Tally, president of the high school P.T.A. at the time of my campaign. (Mr. Tally's wife was secretary to the high school principal and was hired by Joyce, not by the high school principal.[5]) Troy also said that Chod, principal of the Bluffview Elementary School, was hired at approximately the same time as was Joyce.[6]

Troy felt that Chod and Joyce were very close friends. He also felt that Joyce did quite a bit to control decision making in the district. As evidence, he said that Mahan's wife had told him that Mahan had not wanted to run for school board, but Joyce had urged him to run, saying that he needed Mahan on the school board. Mahan ran, won, and became president of the board.

July 3, 1960. I had a conversation with Mrs. Franz, one of the people who had held the meeting in December which had given me the idea of running for the school board. I told her that I understood that Joyce went to the Baptist Church in the community. Mrs. Franz replied, "Goes to the church! He is the church!" Mrs. Franz said that Joyce was a deacon and had a good deal to say about the running of the church [*There were two Baptist Churches in the community. Joyce had first been a member of one; during the period of this diary he was a member of the other. He knew both ministers well. It was*

---

[5] Conference with the high school principal.

[6] Confirmed by a review of the minutes of the Robertsdale School Board.

also apparent that Joyce was no longer as strongly tied to the Baptist Church at the time the data for this study was collected as he once had been.] Mrs. Franz recalled that Joyce had been elected to the superintendency after the former superintendent had had an auto accident and evidence indicated he had been drinking. Mrs. Franz verified Troy's statement that Robert Little was on the school board when Joyce was first hired and that the two were close friends.

[*Conversations such as these appear to substantiate the historical data in the former chapter. As has been mentioned, a member of the Little family was present at the April 21, 1938 board meeting when Joyce was first elected as superintendent of the Robertsdale School District. While this gives no evidence of the amount of influence exerted by the family, it certainly presents evidence that there was a long standing influence.*]

On this same day I also called Wilke and asked if he remembered any official board action on the employment of the new assistant superintendent, Chris. Wilke said he had no recollection of any action and suggested that we should get together to do something about this situation.

July 7, 1960. The Midwest County Bugle carried an article giving an account of a bridal shower for Scott's daughter. The only wife of a school official in attendance was Mrs. Chod. (Mrs. Joyce was deceased.) Joyce, Dyke, Mahan, and Clubb attended the wedding. Neither Wilke nor I were invited.

July 8, 1960. I spoke to Clubb for forty-five minutes regarding the forthcoming board meeting. We discussed the district depository and the probability that nothing would be done to change it. "It's not a matter of anything except friendship," said Clubb. "You must know by now that Dyke will do anything that Joyce requests of him. And Joyce is a close friend of Little."

Clubb agreed that he had heard nothing about the hiring of Chris and added that, although the Board received only the name of the teacher recommended, he felt that top personnel should interview with the board before being hired. I reminded Clubb that the board was supposed to receive a paragraph on each teacher to be hided. Clubb said: "I'll make you a little bet. I'll bet Joyce does it for a while and then drops it. That's what he always does with anything the board passes that he doesn't like or want. For instance, we voted to improve the football field, and he was against it. The thing strung out for months. Finally, one Saturday we called a special board meeting and went out and got the seed and hired the work done ourselves."

At the conclusion of the conversation, Clubb agreed to raise the questions of the attorney and Chris's employment, and I agreed to ask about the district's depository.

Special Meeting, July 14, 1960. A letter was read regarding the organization of a citizen's group interested in the public schools. The majority of these people were from the Elm Grove area. The letter assured the board that the people were anxious to help. (A year and a half before, citizens in this area had petitioned to leave the Robertsdale district and join the district to the south because they felt the Robertsdale district was not progressing fast enough).

Several routine items were taken care of before the dedication of the new junior high school was discussed. Joyce left the room and Edmonds, assistant superintendent in charge of curriculum, took over. Edmonds who was in charge of the dedication arrangements, presented the proposed program, which included ministers from both of the Baptist churches Joyce had attended. One minister was to open the program, the other to close it. Edmonds went on to say that there would be a section reserved for "special guests of honor." Clubb asked who these people would be, and Edmonds replied, "People like Mr. Brook [*the high school principal*] and Mr. Chod [*the Robertsdale Elementary Principal*]—people he has known for a long time. He wants Mr. Dyke to make the address." Dyke responded in a surprised tone: "He wants me to?" Edmonds replied, "He feels very close to you and would prefer someone like that." Dyke indicated that he thought Scott would be the logical person for the task. Scott objected, "He said something to me about it but I can't do it. It's too much like being one of the family. We're too close. His wife and mine were very close." At this point Dyke agreed to make the address. The discussion ended, and Joyce returned to the meeting.

Clubb, as he had agreed in his telephone conversation with me, raised the issue of Chris's employment. Joyce claimed that not only had the board voted to hire Chris but that they had seen his credentials. "I didn't see any credentials or vote to employ anybody," I said. "I think Mr. Chris is a good man, and we should take the correct formal action." Immediately Dyke, Mahan, and Scott agreed with Joyce that they remembered the entire proceeding, while Clubb, Wilke, and I claimed we knew nothing before Chris was presented as employed. I said to Dyke, "If we acted on his employment, find it in the minutes; I can't." Dyke started to look. Joyce told him just to make another motion. Dyke insisted that he could find it. Finally he admitted, "I can't find it but I know it's there!" Clubb replied, "Why isn't it in the minutes, then?" With no further comment Scott moved that the board hire Chris, and Clubb seconded the motion. The motion passed unanimously. [*A careful examination of the official board minutes proved Clubb, Wilke and Prentice right; no official action is recorded before the meeting of July 14, 1960.*]

The formal minutes of July 14th make this item look like an instance of full agreement among the board members. The official minutes state:

> Motion made by Mr. Scott and seconded by Mr. Clubb that Mr. Chris's employment be made a matter of record, his salary being $6,400. Ayes: Mahan, Clubb, Dyke, Wilke, Scott, and Prentice.[7]

As I read these minutes, I felt that they were purposively written so that it appeared that Chris had somehow been legally employed before July 14th and that the board was making this a matter of record.

[*Again there is evidence of the one group of board members being rather sure of obtaining data and taking official action, while the other group appears completely in the dark about the entire matter. There are two possible explanations for this behavior. Either the one group is very forgetful, or the other group is used to getting information, taking informal action, and forgetting to act formally in official meetings. (We reject the idea that either group is intentionally lying.) It appears that the lack of distinction among old friends concerning formal and informal action is the more likely explanation. This is, in part, the reason for the California law prohibiting informal meetings among elected representatives.*]

In the next item of business Dyke and Wilke, holding at the time the offices of secretary and treasurer respectively, were reelected without discussion, and Mahan was ready to adjourn the meeting. I asked to be recognized and initiated a discussion regarding legal advice and the board attorney. I said that in cases where legal advice was needed, such as with the Midmeadows annexation, either the attorney was not asked or else he had given incorrect advice. I suggested that the board investigate possible solutions to this problem. I also asked that our attorney contact the Midmeadows attorney to determine the state of annexation and what could be done at the present or in the near future. The board agreed with this action.

---

[7] "Official Minutes. . . ," *op. cit.*, July 14, 1960.

The district depository was then discussed and a great deal of interaction occurred. Joyce said that he felt it was good public relations to continue to use the Community Bank for all funds except the activity fund. He went on to say that the Littles had supported the district and had done favors for it. [*At this time there was no difference between the earnings paid at the Community Bank and the St. Joseph Bank except the bank tax mentioned before.*] Clubb finally replied to Joyce: "This business of good public relations amounts to this. These people are friends of yours and the other people here."

During the discussion, Scott moved that the meeting be adjourned, and Dyke seconded it. The motion passed, although Clubb and I voted no. (Wilke did not vote and was thus recorded affirmative.) Clubb became very angry and had sharp words with Mahan. Mahan said nothing could be voted on unless it was on the agenda. (It should be noted that this policy was never followed in any Robertsdale board meetings at that time.) Mahan said he would reopen the meeting, however, and did so. I asked Mahan how board members could know what was to be voted on under this "agenda policy" as they never saw an agenda until the night of the meeting.

Clubb then made a motion that the board have regular monthly meetings during the summer, but the motion failed with only Clubb and myself voting yes. I made a motion that tentative agendas be sent to all board members on the Monday before the board meeting. When the motion passed, Joyce's facial expression indicated that he was displeased with the idea.

After adjournment, Clubb, Wilke, and I agreed that there would have been no use in voting on the depository as it would only have resulted in another 3–3 tie.

The official minutes take little note of the confusion regarding adjournment and completely fail to mention that the discussion in progress during the first adjournment concerned the district's depository. The minutes state:

> After discussion of some items, motion made by Mr. Scott and seconded by Mr. Dyke that the meeting be adjourned. Ayes: Mahan, Dyke, Wilke, Scott, Nays: Mr. Clubb and Prentice.
>
> After some statements made by Mr. Clubb, the President with the approval of the motion, the second, and the affirmative votes declared the meeting open for business.[8]

---

[8] *Ibid.*

Mr. Chris called me on July 24, 1960 stating he had been offered a position in a small college. The new position paid half again as much as his present position. He asked if I felt the board would release him from his contract. I said that I would support his petition.

The issue of the school calendar was again raised when several of the residents of Bluffview complained to me about it. They said they had been told, however, that it would be all right for their children to miss the first few days of school as school was starting so early. Needless to say, I was very unhappy with this report after my stand on the calendar. They also asked where in Bluffview the boundary of the Robertsdale district ran. I assured them I would try to straighten out the situation. I called Joyce's secretary the following day and asked that these items be placed on the agenda.

July 29, 1960. Usher called me and asked to be placed on the committee to study the Midmeadows annexation. Usher had been an unsuccessful candidate for the school board for several years and felt this appointment would help him. He said that Dyke had told some residents of St. Joseph, who were unhappy with the calendar, that I had insisted on the early starting date.

Chris, the assistant superintendent, visited with me on August 7, 1960. We left the high school building to have a coke. At this time Chris indicated that he was having some difficulty in performing his job, particularly in paying bills, due to a conflict with Joyce's secretary. Chris told a story of misplaced checks and late mailing of checks signed and approved. Chris mentioned that many of the professional staff were talking about the situation between Joyce and his secretary and complaining that the secretary "hovered over him" so that principals could no longer confer with him about their work. Although Chris wrote out the checks, they were all handled by Joyce's secretary. She was in fact the bookkeeper in addition to being his secretary. I discussed with Chris the possibility of setting up an assistant superintendent title with a bookkeeper in Chris's office so that Chris could better perform his job. (Up to this point, assistant superintendents were called administrative assistants.)

Through a telephone conversation on August 9, 1960 Clubb and I struck up an agreement regarding Chris's problem. Clubb said he knew of an unpaid bill dating from May, and agreed to support the move to place all bookkeeping and matters of finance in an assistant superintendent's office with a bookkeeper and secretary to help him. Clubb also stated that a friend had come to him complaining about me because he thought I had insisted on the early starting date for the next school year. Clubb said he had assured his friend that this was far from true and that I had strongly opposed the calendar as it was approved. During the conversation Clubb said his friend had told him that he had received his information from Dyke. In trying to give meaning to the dissemination of the misinformation, Clubb asked, "Do you think they're running scared, Prentice?"

Special Meeting, August 11, 1960. Regular business was conducted as usual. Scott was absent. When communication regarding the school calendar was in order, I made known the information that I had received regarding the confusion about the boundary line in Bluffview as well as the fact that some individuals had indicated they thought the starting date rather early. I said that I wanted no credit for the present school calendar and wondered how anyone could get that impression when I had so often voted against it. Dyke said, "I don't understand how anyone could have gotten that information from anyone on the board." I did not press the matter.

There was considerable discussion about the motion to change the administrative assistant's title to that of assistant superintendent. When the question was called for, however, all were in favor. I noticed with some surprise that during the discussion Joyce offered no particular opposition to the changing of the titles, questioning only if organizing a separate office where all finances were to be handled was meant to bypass his authority. The board assured Joyce that they intended that all bills be processed in the new assistant superintendent's office but that he was to be responsible to the superintendent. [*At a later teachers' association meeting Joyce was to express some feelings about the changing of these offices.*]

At this meeting $2500 was appropriated for libraries, $1000 for the junior high and $1500 for the senior high. Account numbers to be used when approving bills were provided the board in accordance with the motion of a previous meeting.

August 22, 1960. I learned that the high school principal, Brook, had received no notification that he was to expend $1500 for improvement of library facilities. Neither had the junior high school principal been notified that he was to spend $1000, nor had any effective steps been taken to establish an independent office for handling the payment of bills.

During a discussion with Brook I suggested that the local teachers' association appoint a salary study committee and a welfare committee. Brook asked, "Who would protect them?" I questioned the meaning of his question and Brook indicated that up until that time anyone who initiated these steps would probably lose his job. If such action were to be taken, the individual teachers involved would have to be guaranteed job security. I gave this assurance to Brook.

Special Meeting, August 30, 1960. The board was informed that a bookkeeper had been employed. Since Joyce's secretary had worked many extra hours at this job as well as doing her own work over the past two years, the Board agreed, on Joyce's recommendation, to pay her $1000 for the extra hours. Clubb expressed the view that this procedure was irregular and that the practice of overtime should be discontinued. (Four months later I received a Christmas card from Joyce with the first "official" information that he had married his secretary.)

Clubb then asked about the school district requesting the St. Joseph Bank for some supplies. Clubb said he had found that the honoring of such a request was an infraction of regulatory banking laws. Joyce said that the Community Bank had always given the district these supplies. A discussion arose, regarding the two banks, which resulted in the approval of a motion forbidding the district to make such requests from banks. Only the fact that an editorial comment appears in the official minutes and that these are corrected minutes indicates the conflict which was so apparent at the meeting. The original minutes read, in part:

> . . . not to request supplies of the St. Joseph Bank. (Note: The rubber bands are of the right size and strength to use on currency without causing it to roll in the package.)[9]

Regular Meeting, September 8, 1960. Mahan and Wilke were absent, and Clubb presided. The first order of business which I initiated was correcting the minutes of August 30th, which appear in the quote above, to read "any bank" rather than "the St. Joseph Bank."

During the discussion of legal advice, the board unanimously agreed that there was no need to have an attorney present at every meeting. Rather, the district needed to make better use of the advice

---

[9] "Official Minutes. . . ," August 30, 1960. Note the editorial comment explaining the superintendent's action in making the request. Such editorial comments appear only when Dyke's group felt it necessary to defend their actions.

available to them. I made a motion that Cork be retained and that the superintendent contact him at least once a month to be sure that all matters needing legal advice be given professional consideration. Dyke said that there was no need for the motion inasmuch as the board already had such a policy. I replied that, although I had requested to see the policy book many times, I had never seen it. I knew from the advice which the board had received on legal matters that there was either no legal information available or else that when it was available, it was incorrect. I attributed this fault to the superintendent and the board and concluded, "I want Mr. Joyce to call Mr. Cork at least once a month, even if it's just to ask the temperature." The motion was seconded and carried unanimously.

Prior to this meeting I had talked to Clubb about the teachers' association forming salary and welfare committees and sending the board minutes to all principals to post in order to prevent any delay in dissemination of board policy, such as had occurred regarding library expenditures. Clubb had felt that these were good ideas, and now as presiding officer at this meeting, he recognized me to discuss these topics. I made the following motion:

> . . . that the board request the teachers' association to form a salary study committee composed of three elementary teachers, three secondary teachers, and one principal to develop a schedule and that they submit same to the board for their consideration no later than the regular November meeting. Further, that our educational plan be submitted to this board by the superintendent after consultation with his principals no later than our regular December meeting.[10] and that this plan include any additional curriculum or teaching aids which the group feels are sound. Further, that the principals attend the meeting to present their reasons for additions being implemented.[11]

There was considerable discussion regarding the motion and no one seconded it. Clubb finally asked if there was a second, saying he could not second it as he was chairman, (an incorrect assumption based on the board's operating by-laws). Scott said he could not second it as he did not understand it, and Dyke said he would not second it as he did not believe there was any necessity for a salary study committee because the teachers had in fact approved the salary schedule when they signed their contracts in the spring. He stated

---

[10] I said, "educational plan," for as we will see later, no plan had ever been developed in this manner before.

[11] "Official Minutes. . . ," September 8, 1960.

that anyone who did not like the schedule could have gone elsewhere.

At this point I was angry. I replied to Dyke, "You wouldn't have the nerve to stand before the teachers' association or the P.T.A. and say what you just said—that if teachers don't like our salary schedule, they can get out!" Dyke said, "I didn't say that, and if you say I did say it, I'll sue you for libel." I replied, "I know exactly what you said . . . and I'll repeat it any place I please. *I'm* not the one who's known for misquoting other members of this board." [*This was the angriest exchange which ever took place between Dyke and Prentice. It probably marks the high point of division on the board and the time which most closely typifies the board's group structure diagrammed in Chart IX. It is also the high point of editorializing in the minutes, a function entirely of the secretary, Dyke, perhaps with the help of the superintendent.*] The discussion was abruptly dropped here and the minutes record and editorialize that:

> The motion lost for want of a second. The reasons given were that any action by the teachers' association should be voluntary and that the second phase has been a practice of the superintendent except for having the principals present at the meeting.[12]

Clubb then initiated a discussion on sending board minutes to each principal to be posted on bulletin boards in the various schools. I made the motion, and this measure also lost for want of a second. Dyke indicated, however, that he would check with the attorney to see if this would be legal, and if so, he would not oppose it.

At that time I said I would continue to make these motions (those which had failed for want of a second) until they passed. I noted privately that the board could not afford to continue to oppose them in the light of public sentiment, particularly if visitors were to increase in number at board meetings.

As I left the meeting, I told Joyce that I had heard from several sources that the reason the teachers' association did not have a salary study committee was that there was some fear that those on the committee might not be rehired. Joyce denied that there was such a feeling. I commented that after what had happened at the meeting, I was inclined to believe that there might be something to the report.

The time was about 11:30 P.M., and I noticed that Joyce's secretary was just leaving the building. Clubb had made it very clear at a prior meeting that he thought the superintendent's secretary

---

[12] *Ibid.*

should not be asked to work late and that there was no provision in board policy to pay for these extra hours.

In the parking lot I spoke to Mr. Frank, the district's new assistant superintendent of business and finance, who replaced Chris. Frank said that some progress had been made toward initiating the handling of the bills in his office, but that Joyce's secretary was still handling some operations through the superintendent's office.

During my conversation with Frank following the board meeting, I discovered that Joyce had not seemed to accept the change when speaking to the certificated staff just after school had opened. Frank had been introduced as the new assistant superintendent in the area of business and finance. Joyce said that Edmonds had had his title changed to that of assistant superintendent. According to Frank, Joyce laughed and said, "I don't know why they're assistant superintendents, but that's what we'll call them because one member of the board decided that's the way he wanted it." Frank said Joyce then assured the staff that the jobs were just the same as they had always been and that there was no new authority connected with the jobs.

September 19, 1960. I received a call from Mr. Lindzey, president of Elm Grove P.T.A. He had heard of the lack of support for my motions regarding the educational plan and the teachers' association salary committee. He asked what he could do to help. I told him I believed that increased attendance at board meetings by members of the P.T.A. would be a great help. Lindzey agreed to do what he could.

October 5, 1960. Lindzey called to say that he had sent a letter to all P.T.A. presidents asking that each P.T.A. be represented at board meetings and that P.T.A.'s take a more active interest in the district's affairs.

October 11, 1960. I received a tentative agenda for the coming board meeting. The agenda called for a discussion of the salary schedule. After the last meeting, I was surprised at this and called Joyce to inquire about the item. Joyce said, "I'm throwing together several preliminary ideas in order to save work."

The following day in a conversation with Frank, I asked if the bills were being handled in his office as the board had designated. Frank said he was still having difficulty obtaining the previous balance and information regarding bills, some of which were long overdue.

This same day I called Hartman (the individual who had asked me to run and had managed my campaign) and told him that I felt no candidate from Bluffview should run in the April school board election. I suggested the president of the Elm Grove Elementary School P.T.A., Mr. Linzey, as a good candidate to support. I told Hartman that it would look better if Bluffview supported an incumbent. I also told him that Clubb generally supported my position. Hartman did not agree with this point of view but agreed to discuss it during the weekend.

[*Although not a part of the model used here to explain the political nature of school board action and educational change, a process of the "political mind" begins to operate at this point and should be noted. It is October 12; the next board election is six months away. Prentice is not only suggesting the names of possible candidates for this election but is stating three propositions which he believes should be followed. These are:*

1) *The power base that elected Prentice cannot oppose all incumbents if Prentice is to mobilize any support from incumbents.*
2) *Too many candidates from Bluffview would give the impression of a "power grab" and would be self-defeating.*
3) *Areas which supported Prentice and are a part of the power base should be cultivated for candidates.*

Clubb meets the first criterion. He is an incumbent who had offered some support. If his cooperation is rewarded, support from Clubb might increase and perhaps even entice other incumbents to trade some of their support for the support Prentice could lend them when they had to run for reelection. If incumbent board members who supported Prentice, at least in part, receive no help in the election, they could ask themselves, "Why bother?" Prentice would find himself alone unless he and his power group can elect a majority of the board members. At best, such a plan would take two years to bring about changes. Thus, Prentice suggested support for Clubb.

Clubb also meets criteria 2 and 3. He is from St. Joseph and might possibly bring that area into the power base supporting Prentice. Lindzey also meets criteria 2 and 3. He and Clubb have both been strong P.T.A. workers. Each could cement that linkage. Linzey is from Elm Grove, the area that strongly supported Prentice when he was elected but failed to get its own candidate elected. This is a chance for Bluffview to return that favor.]

On the day of the Board meeting I called Edmonds, the assistant superintendent for personnel, and suggested that he be present at the board meeting since he was in charge of certificated personnel and the board was to discuss the salary schedule. Edmonds seemed pleased by this suggestion; apparently Edmonds felt he was not consulted often enough in areas where he thought he should function. Edmonds closed the conversation by saying, "I'm glad to get this vote of confidence. Thank you very much."

Regular Board Meeting, October 13, 1960.   All members were present, and the meeting was moved to the library and out of the superintendent's office because of the large number of visitors. This was the first meeting held in the library since I had been elected. (Evidently Lindzey's letter had been effective, for the vast majority of the visitors were P.T.A. people.)

Two questions were raised during the meeting regarding finances, and in both areas, Wilke defended Joyce. I felt that the reason for this was that Wilke was treasurer of the board and thought he was being attacked by these questions.

Just before adjournment, I presented two motions. One called for the submission of an educational plan by the superintendent, and the other for distribution of a summary of the minutes of all board meetings to each principal. Both of these motions had been made at the September meeting and both had failed for lack of a second. This time both measures passed unanimously, apparently because of the visitors attending this open meeting. The minutes do not indicate this, however. The motion regarding the educational plan appears in the minutes of the executive session which followed, but there was no record of the motion regarding the summary of board minutes. Such a summary was sent to the principals, however. [*The minutes were still being sent to principals and posted in their offices as of July, 1967.*] I then asked permission to make a motion regarding the salary schedule, but the chairman ruled that it should be discussed in the subsequent executive session.

The board adjourned to executive session to discuss personnel problems. After several individual items were discussed, Joyce presented the material related to the salary schedule which he had told me he was preparing. The board minutes state ". . . a request for a general understanding of the desire of the board regarding the levy that might be approved was made." Joyce had said this proposal had nothing to do with my proposal for a teachers' association salary study committee, but should the board approve one of these plans or state an amount at which the levy might be fixed, there would be little use for such a teachers' association committee. This I believed to be an effort to avoid my proposal. I stated that I had made a mistake by not making my motion regarding the committee before the open session as I had planned. A good deal of discussion followed, and I made a motion that the teachers' association be asked to form a salary study committee and report to the board at their December meeting.

During the discussion of the motion, it became apparent that there were at least three votes in favor of the motion. Dyke indicated that he would vote for it. He said that regardless of what the teachers asked for, he would go along with their request. He added that he felt the request would result in a ridiculously high salary schedule that would require a tax levy higher than the voters would support. He stated that regardless of this, he would support the teachers' schedule and the district would have to operate without a tax levy as the people would never vote the levy necessary to implement the teachers' request. At this point Dyke seemed very bitter and resentful.

The motion was carried by the votes of Clubb, Wilke, and myself. Scott voted against it, and Mahan, who said he saw nothing wrong with the motion but nothing good about it, abstained. In spite of Dyke's proclamation that he would vote for the motion, he also chose to abstain. [*Prentice's prediction after the previous meeting is correct. Every motion that failed for lack of a second at the September meeting passed at the October meeting. Motions presented while a large number of P.T.A. members were present passed unanimously and without discussion. The only motion held until executive session (no visitors were allowed), passed without a unanimous vote and with bitter words.*]

Bluffview P.T.A. Meeting, October 24, 1960. I had been asked to speak at this meeting about the future plans of the Bluffview Elementary School. The meeting was an open house replacing a formal dedication of the building. Clubb had called and asked me to tell Mrs. Code, the P.T.A. president, that he was very sorry he could not attend. Clubb emphasized this request. It is likely that Clubb was concerned about obtaining votes from the Bluffview area in the April election.

Clubb also mentioned he had heard a rumor that teachers who served on the salary study committee would be advised to proceed carefully if they wanted to be rehired. I informed him that I would call the teachers' association president about the rumor.

October 27, 1960. I visited the high school and talked with Joyce. Later I had coffee with Principal Brook and Assistant Superintendent Frank. Both Brook and Frank indicated that they thought things were moving better than they had been. Next, I went upstairs to see Assistant Superintendent Edmonds. He also indicated that everything was moving ahead—both the educational plan and the teachers' association committee. Edmonds said that he felt these things had been a long time in coming.

Before leaving the high school, I spoke to the teachers' association president, Mrs. Hahn. I discovered that prior to the board motion and just after her election as president she had been warned that salaries were a board matter and that the teachers' association was not to interfere. No comments had been made since the board motion, according to Mrs. Hahn, and she was receiving Joyce's cooperation. I assured Mrs. Hahn that I supported the teachers' association in this matter and that she could call on me at any time.

That evening I received a message to call Mrs. Hahn. When I returned the call, Mrs. Hahn said that Brook was concerned because Joyce had told her that ". . . those of us on the salary committee had better be careful." Mrs. Hahn went on the say, "You know our teachers' association has never had any strength, or any recognition or rights. We feel this will be an opportunity to build up our organization." I again assured Mrs. Hahn that everything would be done to protect those serving on the committee and that I expected the committee to present their findings to the board.

November 5, 1960. A problem arose on this date that in itself was of no particular significance to the district but led to a significant development.[13] Wilke called to tell me that some noncertificated staff had supposedly been persuaded to quit their jobs. Wilke said that he had already called Clubb and that he felt there was a conspiracy to eliminate all people who knew or were friends of either Clubb or himself. Wilke suggested that Joyce and Assistant Superintendent Frank were working together in this. I stated that Wilke's accusation was somewhat strong, but it should probably be investigated. The following day I learned that Frank's bookkeeper had quit because of some unhappiness and that she and her husband were very close friends of the Wilke family. [*It appears that the matter of friendship, mentioned earlier by Clubb, was a matter of whose ox was getting gored.*]

---

[13] See the taping of board meetings incident in Chapter 6, pp. 145-146.

ANALYSIS OF THE FIGHT FOR POWER

Up until this point our analysis has tended to focus on the total school district. The school board has been considered a subsystem of that macrosystem. It is clear, however, that the school board is the focal subsystem and the legal subsystem of the school district.[14] It is now time to change the focus of our analysis to the board itself in order to examine the power shifts on the board which followed incumbent defeat.

It is no accident that the American political system is a two-party system. Even those political systems that purport to have multiple parties usually result in systems which exhibit two competing coalitions. In one-party systems like those in totalitarian states, factional splits tend to exist within that party which result in differences and occasional changes in national stands on major issues as well as purges in government. Erving Goffman has indicated that this "two-team" political action is the norm in all human systems. He says that not only does this political interplay take the form of action between two teams, but when the group presents itself before the public, it generally attempts to present a common front, becoming a single team while the public becomes the second team.[15] Such a description fits most school boards except during moments of transition. This concensus before the public—the public refusal to allow conflict to emerge openly—is the classic definition of the sacred as opposed to the secular social system. Such a notion may, in the long run, provide a viable explanation for the failure of the "educational establishment" to respond to what is increasingly becoming a more pluralistic and secular public.

Prentice as the New Member

The basic pattern of the Robertsdale board began to emerge even before Prentice was elected to the board. Clubb had indicated his position of "odd man out" when he talked with Prentice at the St. Joseph P.T.A. meeting. At the meeting when the April, 1960, election results were tallied, neither Dyke, Scott, nor Joyce said a word to Prentice. Prior to attending his first meeting, Prentice received a call

---

[14] Frank W. Lutz and Joseph J. Azzarelli, *The Struggle for Power In Education* (New York: The Center for Applied Research, Inc., 1966), pp. 67-68.

[15] Erving Goffman, *The Presentation of Self in Everyday Life* (New York: Doubleday & Company, Inc., 1959), pp. 86-90, 191-2.

from Clubb briefing him on the annexation issue. On an issue of this magnitude one might expect the superintendent or board president to have contacted a new member, but neither Joyce nor Mahan did so. When Superintendent Joyce presented his annexation information, Clubb and Wilke immediately disagreed with Joyce, and Dyke, Scott, and Mahan unconditionally accepted the superintendent's statements. Having avoided a vote at this meeting, Wilke put Prentice in contact with Midmeadows residents so that Prentice would become convinced that Joyce was wrong. In the first significant vote by the Robertsdale board after Prentice's election, the board split 3–3. (Prentice, Clubb, and Wilke opposed Dyke, Scott, and Mahan.) At this point, Prentice noted in his diary the composition of the two separate groups that composed the Robertsdale board.[16]

What Prentice did not note, and a fact that did not become apparent until much later, was that neither Clubb nor Wilke could be counted on to support any position. Clubb actually failed to support the annexation of Midmeadows by not signing a petition to allow the county superintendent to cast the tie-breaking vote. Perhaps this was one of the reasons that both were marginal members of the board prior to Prentice's election, the additional reason being that neither supported Superintendent Joyce.

Additional data emerge throughout the case indicating that both Wilke and Clubb were marginal members of the board's decision-making process. Neither had been aware of the decision (apparently made before Prentice's election) to name the new junior high school in honor of Superintendent Joyce. Wilke, Clubb, and Prentice were excluded from the informal decision and actual hiring of the new assistant in business. They and Dr. Chris were excluded from the private meeting after the board meeting on the night of June 1st. These and other data presented in the case tend to verify Hypothesis 10, that the marginal members of the old boards are likely to comprise the manpower of the new insurgent faction of the board led by the individual defeating an incumbent.

The marginal membership of Wilke and Clubb is established. The seeds of the new coalition rest in the old board. These men had felt rejected, regardless of the validity for that rejection. They were ready to coalesce. In other words, they wanted in on the decisions. It took but one meeting for the new structure to emerge. Now their votes made a difference. At least they could prevent the board from taking

---

[16] *See* **Chart II.**

action they opposed. The question of the leadership of the insurgent group is not yet clear, however.

If Prentice had been asked to run or if either Clubb or Wilke had supported them, it is likely that one of these men could have assumed the leadership. Such was not the case. Prentice had run as a representative of an emerging group in the district. He defeated an incumbent. This achievement in itself gave him power. In Prentice's case, he represented a public of middle and upper-middle class professionals. In another case, the victory over the incumbent might have represented another "minority" group such as Negroes, the taxpayers' association, etc. If such a minority is a growing minority, the newly elected member is likely to have considerable power. In any case, he is likely to be perceived as having power.

Prentice had an expertness about educational matters that was not available to the board except from the superintendent. Prentice was trained to be an educator. This expertness is usually inaccessible to challenging groups in public education. Traditionally, boards of education do not have their own staff of professionals. If they are to challenge the superintendent's recommendations, decisions, or administration, the board must do so as lay persons challenging the professional. If part of the board supports the superintendent, it is even harder for the other part of the board to make an effective challenge. Alluding to the knowledge of the professional expert in defense of policy and practice in governmental units is well-known in health and education. Thus, Prentice brought a rare quality to the challenging segment of the Robertsdale board and he used that quality during his first few months as a board member.

During the first few months Prentice prefaced every challenge with a question. His role is best described by "I'm a new board member and can't know what's going on—but!" This is the role he played when he favored annexation. The data were probably right but based on his past experience, they seemed high. "Could they be checked?" (It turned out they were three hundred percent in error.) Likewise, Prentice took the position, "The calendar could be right but might the days be recounted?" (They were incorrectly counted.) Also, "It might be that Christmas can be counted, but will you [Joyce] check with the county superintendent?" (Joyce didn't check but Prentice did; Joyce was wrong.) Could the board receive code numbers on bills and teacher qualifications? Was there any record in the official minutes of board action for naming the junior high school or hiring Chris? Was there adequate communication with the residents of the district? Shouldn't there be a salary schedule for nonprofessional personnel? Was the teachers' handbook an example of up-to-date personnel practices? Was the district receiving sufficient and proper legal advice? Not only did Prentice raise these questions, but a simple answer was not adequate if Prentice disagreed, because he had professional expertness. Not only could Prentice challenge the answer, but he could supply contesting information. Thus, he provided the insurgent group with a rare and vulnerable commodity, the quality of leadership, according to Homans.[17]

This service, coupled with the initiation of ideas; i.e., the coding of bills, teacher qualifications, teacher salary committee, the posting of board minutes, projected educational plans, pointed to Prentice as the emerging leader of the insurgent group. Dyke was clearly the leader of the old guard. Apparently, both board groups were aware of this leadership. The hostility between Prentice and Dyke at the September 8th meeting was the clash of the old board leader and the emerging board leader.

Having established some leadership within the board, Prentice moved into the community to reaffirm his power base and make that base clear to the entire board. Having told Dyke that "You wouldn't have the nerve to stand before the teachers' association or the P.T.A. and say what you just said," Prentice assured Dyke that if he ever made such a statement again, the teachers and the P.T.A. would be aware of the statement. Prentice established the practice of posting the minutes of each board meeting in every school for teachers and parents to view. Since parents and teachers were Prentice's major source of power, he felt he could increase their interest by improving communication between them and the schools. Lindzey's letter to all P.T.A. presidents had an even greater effect. At the board meeting following Dyke's remark about teachers' salaries the office generally used for board meetings was overflowing with interested public. The meeting was moved to the library. Never again was there room in the office for the board meeting. Even the physical territory of the old guard was affected.

The public exposure of the issues defeated at earlier meetings affected the behavior of board members. Without doubt the ability to decide in secret not only changes the process of decision making but also the decision itself. Perhaps public decision making does not result in the best decisions. There is little question, however, that

---

[17] George C. Homans, *Social Behavior: Its Elementary Forms* (New York: Harcourt, Brace & World, Inc., 1961).

legislators or school board members who are allowed to make agreements and trade-offs in "smoke-filled" rooms away from the scrutiny of the public eye cast their vote for reasons unknown to the public, and often that vote is quite different from the vote they would have cast in public. The fact is that the majority of Americans eligible to vote have no idea how their representatives vote either on specific issues or on general trends. A school board member's voting behavior is certainly no better known to the public. For a period at least, this was not to be the case in Robertsdale, and Prentice had planned it that way.

The result of public scrutiny of the board's voting behavior was amazing. At the first meeting two motions that had failed for lack of a second at the previous meeting passed unanimously. Perhaps the entire board had changed its mind, and in a period of one month all five members had decided the motions were a good idea. A very unlikely chance, however. But if one accepts even that one small chance, how can the third vote be explained? Three motions had been made by Prentice and all had failed to receive a second. Now before the public, two passed without a word of dissent. But the third motion was held for executive session. There was heated discussion involving this third motion. It finally passed, three members voting in favor, one in favor by silence, one abstaining from voting but bitterly opposed, and one voting against. It appears that in private there was still considerable opposition. Dyke avoided the public issue by abstaining, but in the privacy of the executive session he was adamant in his opposition. Scott, who later decided not to run for reelection, voted against the measure, and Mahan took no position whatsoever. It is not likely that chance alone was operating here. The spotlight of public scrutiny modifies the behavior of the actors on the stage of politics.

During the month of October, 1960, Prentice spent a good deal of time cementing relationships with the groups he perceived as supplying his base of support. Although it was not his usual practice to attend P.T.A. meetings, he delivered a speech to the Bluffview P.T.A. He spent a day talking to members of the professional staff of the Robertsdale School District emphasizing his support for a continued increase in the quality of the program and for greater participation in decision making by the assistant superintendents, principals, and teachers.

It is interesting to note the discrepancy between Superintendent Joyce's statements about the participation of staff members and the statements of others. Joyce claimed that he utilized his staff to the fullest extent in preparing recommendations and that teachers had never been warned against participating in salary considerations. He had told Prentice that the district did not use a marking system based on the normal curve. Yet Prentice discovered that some of the elementary school principals required their teachers to mark on a curve.[18] Several principals complained that they were never asked to report to the board. The president of the teachers' association said she had been told, upon her election as president, to stay out of salary discussions, and she was warned again when a salary study committee was established. The question arises—was Joyce deliberately lying? These authors do not think so. Rather, Joyce told certain half-truths that he "believed" to be the truth based on his beliefs about his own role and what education should be. When a present-day "Yankee" discusses the Civil War with a present-day "Reb," they soon discover discrepancies between what each believes to be the truth.

Perceptual differences often create difficulties between school boards and school superintendents. Neither intends to act in bad faith, but each may believe that the other is less than honest and fair. It is for this reason that both pre-service and in-service programs for superintendents have always stressed the necessity for the superintendent to "educate" his board. In practice this suggests that superintendents should provide their boards with information which causes boards to perceive educational matters in the same way as the superintendent. Certain modern-day politicians have referred to this process as "brainwashing." In education we have a kinder name. Thus, one can account for the superintendent who desires a "stable board," one that never, or almost never, changes. It also accounts for the establishment of an equilibrium between the superintendent and the board while the "less educated" public moves farther away from each, setting up the likelihood of incumbent defeat and superintendent turnover. Perhaps the "educate your board" process is not as good a procedure as it seems at first glance.

Hypotheses

Several of the hypotheses generated by this work help account for the data presented in this chapter. Both Clubb and Wilke were marginal members of the Robertsdale School Board. From the first meeting Prentice attended, it was clear that he would have their

---

[18] Conversation with two elementary school principals, supported by evidence from their files.

support in his attempts to challenge the *status quo* (Hypothesis 11). An item not discussed in the model is the behavior of such marginal board members. There must be a reason for someone being a marginal or low-status member of a group. Non-conformity is, of course, one reason but not reason enough. Persons who can provide rare or valuable services are never low-status members of a group. Nonconformity may lower the status of such members but will be tolerated if their activities are valuable to the group. When the person has no services to provide that are valued by the group and, in addition, will not or cannot conform to the basic group norms, that person is a very low-status member of the group and is sometimes eliminated from group membership.[19]

Not only were Clubb and Wilke low-status members of the formal board, but they were not members of the informal meetings after the board meetings. Why? Because in the eyes of the rest of the board they did not offer any valuable service to the board, nor did they conform. They were not reliable. While it may be that low-status members of a group have valuable services that are not desired because the leader supplies the services, this situation is not likely to be the case. Such a member is more often an isolate, not a low-status member. Isolates, often protected by the leader, need little from the group because of their capabilities. They are protected by the leader as payment for not challenging his leadership. If such an individual attacks the leadership, he may end up at the very bottom of the status heap in the formal group or out of the informal group completely.

This analysis is meaningful to the insurgent who, it is predicted, will receive the support of marginal board members. The man who defeats an incumbent, by that very fact, has some unusual characteristics. If he finds a marginal member who is an isolate on the board, there may be a contest between them for the leadership of the insurgents. Such a person will be a valuable ally since he will possess talents valuable to the insurgent cause. Much energy may be expended, however, fighting for leadership before a leader emerges. During this period the insurgents will probably not take effective action against the old guard.

On the other hand, the marginal members of the old board may simply be low-status members without many talents to contribute to the insurgent group. Then the fight for leadership will be shorter.

---

[19] This brief analysis of group membership is based on the work of George C. Homans, *Social Behavior: Its Elementary Forms* (New York: Harcourt, Brace & World, Inc., 1961).

However, they will not be much help to the new leader, particularly if one attribute of the marginal members is a lack of reliability in conforming to some voting pattern. Prentice faced a situation similar to the low-status member situation. The fight for leadership of the insurgents was short, almost imperceptible. It is likely that Clubb had some of the status attributes of an isolate. He was vice-president. He fought a short fight and probably resented the fact that Prentice won. Perhaps Prentice did not even recognize the struggle or the possibility that Clubb was hurt in the process. This must have made it all the more painful to Clubb. Prentice may have been a good social politician, but his psychological perceptions of individuals were not keen. He might have received more support from Clubb if they had been. He also missed some cues from Mahan. In any case, while one can predict that the insurgent who defeats an incumbent will receive support from marginal members of the old board, this support is almost as marginal as are the old members.

Hypothesis 10 refers to the fact that the clash between the insurgents and the old guard will focus on the new member and the leadership of the old guard, particularly the superintendent. This was true of Robertsdale. As Joyce was not the active leader of the old guard, much of the fight was between Prentice, the leader of the insurgents, and Dyke, the leader of the old guard. Without question, the fight will finally focus on the superintendent. Often the conflict will center between the superintendent and the individual who defeated the incumbent sooner than it did in Robertsdale. This is because of the qualities of leadership inherent in two persons, one who can unseat an incumbent in sacred politics and another who can rise to the position of chief executive of a large formal organization.

Regarding Hypothesis 5, there are few data available in the Robertsdale case. Prentice was not asked nor would he be asked to run by either the superintendent or the old guard. It was not likely that data confirming this hypothesis would be available to Prentice if Joyce could prevent it. There was a considerable amount of hearsay evidence that Joyce and other old guard members did invite certain candidates and supported their candidacy. Once Prentice reports a resident stating that the wife of the board president said that her husband had decided to run for reelection only after Joyce had urged him to do so.

One final comment about the case thus far provides insight into the process of politics on the Robertsdale board while Prentice was a board member. For the first eight months, Prentice was busy demonstrating the qualities he possessed that could be useful to a school board, particularly to an insurgent group on a relatively closed board. This role of Prentice's steadily increased hostility between him and the old guard group, particularly Dyke and Joyce. In addition, it steadily strengthened Prentice's position as leader of the insurgents. This assumption of minority group leadership on the board may be considered the first phase in effecting school board policy change. As this period draws to a close (there is nothing magic about the actual eight months), Prentice has consolidated that leadership position and extended his base of power in the P.T.A.'s, in the teachers' association, with certain administrators in the district, and in two neighborhood communities. The next logical step is for the minority party to take over the leadership of government. In Anglo-American politics, this can still be done through the elective process.

6

After Incumbent Defeat:
A New Board Leadership

In Chapter 5 we saw how Prentice moved to the position of leader of the insurgent faction of the Robertsdale board. He accomplished this by a procedure of questioning and challenging the advice of the superintendent. He probed the vulnerable spots and was sure of his ground before he acted. He not only questioned, but he was right when he did. Finally, he chose to use this procedure before important segments of the school district. The old guard began to look bad. They began to lose issues, an experience not familiar to them or to their liking. The minority party was gaining power and the old guard was beginning to recognize that fact.

NOTES FROM PRENTICE'S PERSONAL DIARY, NOVEMBER, 1960—APRIL, 1961

Regular Board Meeting, November 10, 1960. A large number of visitors were present at the Board meeting again. [*After the October meeting, it would be rare if visitors did not attend.*] No unusual interaction took place during the regular meeting except that Mahan criticized Joyce for the way he handled a problem concerning pumping water at one of the elementary schools. This was the first time Mahan had criticized or opposed anything Joyce had done since I had been on the board. After the board adjourned into executive session, the following things occurred. Again, the official minutes make no mention that this action went on behind closed doors.

As stated in the official minutes, Wilke "expressed his displeasure" at the situation involving the resignation of Frank's old bookkeeper and, most particularly, the hiring of someone new at $50 per month more than Wilke's friend had been receiving. There was much discussion; Dyke said the board had indicated that they would go as high as $350 per month, if necessary, to hire a bookkeeper. (This is what the new bookkeeper was paid.) I said that I had some recollection of this and perhaps I was the one who had made the statement. I added that this problem of misunderstanding would always occur as long as the board failed to keep more complete records of meetings. Wilke made a motion that the new bookkeeper should receive no more per month than the former bookkeeper; Clubb seconded it. The motion carried with Dyke voting against, Mahan and Scott abstaining. I later told Clubb privately that I felt Dyke had been correct, but the only way to keep peace among the three of us (Clubb, Wilke, and myself) was to vote for the motion. Through the discussion I tried to play the role of arbitrator between the opposing factions of the board.

[*Although Prentice had not always received the support he felt he should have from Wilke or Clubb, here he was acting in an attempt to establish a solid front. As with his recommendation to support Clubb in the next election, Prentice is attempting to create a solid voting block.*]

After the board meeting Mahan privately mentioned to Clubb and me that he knew that "some of the board members" thought he did everything Joyce wanted him to do. He mentioned the water pumping exchange at the meeting as an example of the fact this was not true. "I give him plenty of trouble, actually, at times other than the meetings," Mahan said.

November 19, 1960. A White House Conference on Education was held in Midwest City. At this meeting Dyke approached me. He said that something had to be done about the situation that had occurred over the hiring of the new bookkeeper and that some people had simply lied about what the board had said previously. I agreed that misunderstandings were unfortunate and said that I felt this had not been the first time such a thing had occurred, mentioning the naming of the junior high as one other example. I suggested that meetings could be taped, thus eliminating differences of opinion as to what had been said. Dyke immediately agreed; I said that if Dyke wished to present such a notion, I would support him. [*Dyke did propose this idea and with Prentice's backing it became the method of operation for the Robertsdale board that is still followed today. This was the first instance of agreement between Dyke and Prentice.*]

December 1, 1960. Clubb phoned me and said that the situation involving Joyce and his secretary was as bad or perhaps worse than it had been. Clubb said he had heard they were to be married at Christmas. I replied that would be fine as it would resolve the situation. According to board policy, husband and wife could not work in the same building.

During the first few days in December, I received the proposed salary schedule and discussed it with Mrs. Hahn, president of the teachers' association. I also received a call from Clubb who wished to discuss the teachers' proposal. On December 4th I visited Clubb in his home; he agreed to go along with the professional growth requirement in the proposed schedule. [*As will be seen, Clubb did not live up to this promise at the Board meeting.*]

On this day I also received the following note which was sent to all board members regarding Joyce's secretary:

> Jane will not continue her employment with the school district as we plan to be married sometime in the near future. We had planned that she discontinue her employment at an earlier date, but the problem relating to the bookkeeping in the school district, the completion of the State Supervisor's Report, and the employment of a secretary for the office had made it seem advisable in the interest of the school district for her to continue to work to this time. It will be necessary for Jane to return to complete the Federal M & O report and to assist, on occasion, the new secretary and the new bookkeeper. Jane wishes to express her appreciation for her employment with the district for the past ten years as it has been a very pleasing experience.

[*If any board member attended the wedding Prentice did not know it. His only notification of the event was after the wedding. He received a Christmas card signed in such a manner as to indicate the two were married.*]

Regular Meeting, December 8, 1960. Regular business was handled as usual. There was again some discussion of steps toward the annexation of Midmeadows, which I initiated. There was total agreement among the board members on this issue.

The salary schedule developed by the teachers' association was presented by the chairman of that committee. A discussion ensued regarding the schedule, but no action was taken at this meeting.

Wilke indicated that he was concerned with a noncertificated personnel problem. He made a motion giving these people more holidays than they now had. Clubb seconded it, and the motion passed unanimously. This measure is mentioned as another example of Wilke and Clubb's interest in problems in which I had no primary interest.

After the meeting adjourned, Wilke and I walked out of the building. Wilke said, "Dyke is really trying to butter you up. Mahan too!" I said that both had seemed more agreeable lately. Wilke added, "You can't trust Dyke. I've seen him too long. He'll say one thing and do another."

December 13, 1960. Clubb called to discuss several problems. One of these concerned questions from teachers in the district regarding the board's feeling about the salary schedule their committee had presented at the last meeting. He said the teachers had told him they hoped the board would not act "in the old pattern and throw it all out the window and expect us to be happy!" I said that the board intended to do the right thing regarding the proposed schedule.

Special Meeting, December 15, 1960. This meeting was called to discuss changes in curriculum. A move toward a more academic type of curriculum was indicated. Included were additions to the foreign language program, science program in laboratory sciences, and a basic remedial program in the junior high school.

The elementary school principals submitted a preliminary report regarding equipment needs for the coming year. The board approved the submission of an $850,000 bond issue. There was some disagreement when Clubb wanted to earmark money for building permanent stands on the football field. I said that I would like to see the stands, but only after the classroom needs were satisfied. There was also a discussion, initiated by Wilke, questioning whether or not the addition on the Elm Grove School proposed in the bond issue was adequate.

As the meeting adjourned, Chod, who was present at the board meeting in his official capacity as principal of Robertsdale and Bluff-view Elementary Schools, came up to me with some papers in his hand. He said that these were recommendations for equipment in his schools, and he would like me to have a copy. Chod said that he had only made two copies, one for the superintendent and this one;

so while he couldn't give all board members a copy, he wanted me to have this one. This was quite a change in Chod's attitude from the time during the summer when he had failed to respond to my invitation to talk with him.

December 20, 1960. Mahan called to indicate that additional classrooms would be needed at Elm Grove and that the board should temporarily hold off on additions to the high school. He said that the board had a problem in addition to this. He indicated that the superintendent and his secretary (now his wife) were still working together in violation of board policy. I said that I did not know, except by way of a Christmas card I had received a few days before, that they had been married. I also did not know that a new secretary had not been hired. I reminded Mahan that Joyce had indicated in his original memo to the board that he would probably need to retain his secretary for a period of time in order to break in a new secretary. Mahan then replied, "They knew this was coming. It did not happen suddenly. They knew the policy. If he doesn't mention it at the next meeting, we'll have to. We can't let it ride without any idea of when it will end."

I agreed and then reminded Mahan about the renewal of Joyce's contract. I said that because of the opposition last year and indications of considerable opposition again this year, it might be better if the extension of the contract was not mentioned. I said that I didn't know how I would vote if there was a motion to extend the contract that year. Mahan said he wasn't sure how he would vote either. (Without an extension Joyce would still have a two-year contract.) I again suggested that perhaps the best thing to do was to fail to bring the matter up and therefore not embarass Joyce.

Mahan then told me that he did not plan to run for reelection to the board in April. He felt he had done his part and wished to retire for personal reasons. I expressed my regrets but indicated that I felt Mahan had certainly earned the right to retire from office.

January 5, 1961. I spent a day at the high school and visited with the principal, both assistant superintendents, and the superintendent. In my conversation with principal Brook, several interesting points were raised. Brook said that several recommendations he had made as part of the educational plan had never gotten to the board, nor had he been told that they would be withheld. He also indicated that Joyce's recommendation on administrative salaries would increase Brook's salary quite a bit above his own recommendation. (Frank and Edmonds had said the same thing regarding salaries.) Brook went on to say that this was the first year there had been any group curriculum planning. Until this year there was "never any planning." He indicated that in the last few years "absolutely nothing had been accomplished in educational planning" by the superintendent. Joyce had run the board meetings during the last several years his own way. "He [Joyce] structures everything," Brook said. "He calls Dyke, he used to call Mahan, and now he calls Scott. He primes them and sits there and pulls the strings."

Then I said that Dyke agreed with everything Joyce suggested, but Brook disagreed, "Not so much as you think, anymore!" I said I felt that the board should call on other members of the professional staff for their help and guidance; Brook said that, including the past meeting which he attended, he had only been invited to attend three meetings in his twelve years as high school principal. He continued: "We've made more progress in the last year than we had in the previous five years." Regarding the library and its improvement, he said, "We haven't done anything until this year."

After talking to Brook, I visited with Edmonds in his office. He corroborated many of Brook's statements—the district had made more progress in the past year than it had in all the previous years when he had been in the district. He went on to say that a salary study committee and principal participation in the educational plan would previously have been "just impossible. It would have cost someone's job."

The conversations during this day shed no new light on the school district situation. They merely validated the opinions I already had. It should also be noted that the information given was, in all cases, in answer to direct questions from a school board member and in none of these cases could the respondent have avoided answering the questions.

Regular Meeting, January 12, 1961. Cork, board attorney, was present to discuss several items in which he was engaged for the school district.

The attendance report indicated that one elementary school classroom contained thirty-six pupils. The board was assured that by the next regular meeting an additional teacher would be hired, and this classroom would be divided into two rooms. Another room had grown, in attendance, to thirty-two pupils. Joyce was instructed that should the enrollment increase, the parents should be given the opportunity to have their children transported to a school where class size would be smaller. During the previous year, class size at this same school had increased to forty pupils with no adjustment.

Several other matters were discussed before I asked about two items not on the agenda—a letter that was supposed to go to Midmeadows and an insurance report which the Board had requested. Joyce indicated that the letter had been sent to Midmeadows, but he had received no reply. The insurance people had asked if they could make their report at the end of January.

Because of the number of items on the agenda, salary schedule, budget, and tax levy were proposed for consideration at a special meeting to be held on January 19th.

At this point Mahan asked if Joyce and both assistant superintendents would allow the board to meet without them for a few minutes. After they complied with the request, he brought up the situation regarding Joyce's wife, who was still serving as his secretary. The board agreed that they would be willing to pay up to $300 per month (a higher rate than secretaries received) in order to get a capable person and alleviate the present situation. Mahan then brought up the item of the superintendent's contract, as he had agreed to do, stating that it had been suggested that the board fail to take any action on the present contract which still had two years to run. Dyke made no commitment. He thought there was no reason, at this time, to decide not to extend Joyce's contract. Scott, however, after hearing the discussion, agreed that perhaps it would be better not to take any action during the year. The board, with the exception of Dyke, agreed that this was the best way to handle the situation. During the discussion, Scott had indicated he was still very close to Joyce.

The superintendents were called back, and Joyce was told that he might go as high as $300 to employ a secretary and that he should proceed with this hiring as quickly as possible. No indication was given at the meeting as to the discussion regarding Joyce's contract, nor was anything recorded in the minutes.

After the meeting was adjourned, I drove Wilke home. We had a conversation regarding the composition of the board after the coming April election. Wilke said he felt I should be president of the board. I immediately asked about Clubb, and Wilke said he had already talked to Scott about electing me as president and Scott had been agreeable.

January 15, 1961. I called Edmonds and Clubb regarding the salary schedule. I also spoke to Mrs. Hahn about the schedule and a proposed insurance program in which the teachers might participate. On the 16th I called Joyce and, being unable to get him, gave a salary schedule to Assistant Superintendent Frank with the message that he give the schedule to Joyce and ask him to duplicate it for all board members. Frank said that he was pleased about the teachers' participation in the salary schedule. He said, "I've heard a lot of favorable comments about letting teachers sit in on the salary schedule. A lot of bouquets have been passed." The teachers, Frank indicated, were pleased that they were permitted to attend the meeting at which the board would act on their schedule. This had never been done before. He also indicated that the principals had been urged to attend the meeting of the 19th in order to protect their interests regarding their salary schedule.

School Bond Election, January 17, 1961. The people of the Robertsdale district voted in favor of an $850,000 bond issue to construct new buildings. The bond issue was to cause no increase in the tax levy due to the increased valuation of the district. The vote was 473 for and 164 against, a two-thirds majority being necessary to carry. When I asked why it had failed in certain areas, Dyke said, "A lot of old residents came out to vote."

Chart XI

BOND ELECTION RESULTS ON JANUARY 17, 1961— $850,000

	Robertsdale	Lakeside (Bluffview voted here)	St. Joseph	Mt. Olive	Elm Grove	Totals*
FOR	94	90	65	37	186	472**
AGAINST	83	8	37	17	19	164

* Two-thirds majority required by law for passage
** One absentee vote "for" was cast

[Small voter turnout is the usual pattern in all school elections— those elections concerning school taxes, bonds, and board members. The election referred to in Chart XI is an excellent example of this phenomenon.]

Special Meeting, January 19, 1961. The board met in executive session to handle a pupil–personnel problem. Upon completion of this business, the board returned to regular session.

Since the major reason for this meeting was a discussion of salary schedule, many teachers and principals attended. Joyce presented a salary schedule which he said he had been working on and which he felt was a good one. The schedule was exactly like the schedule I had wanted to present to the board just two days before, except for the recommendation about administrators' salaries. On the pages which contained the administrators' schedule, each principal and assistant superintendent had been listed and after each name were five columns of figures. The columns had these headings: Present Policy, Normal Increase, Principal's Recommendation (This column contained a salary schedule which Joyce said the principal had recommended.), Requested Schedule, and Recommended Schedule. The last three columns were interesting. Four of the eight administrators listed had requested a figure less than the principal's recommended column indicated. The requested schedule contained the adjustment factors.[1] In the column which I had asked to have applied to principals' salaries, all factors were applied as though the administrators had no experience. In other words, all administrators were placed at the beginning of the schedule. I had not suggested this nor had it even occurred to me that this would be done. In the superintendent's recommended column the same adjustment factors were applied but with the correct placement of administrators with regard to experience. Thus, Joyce was recommending exactly what I had suggested, but it did not appear so in the recommendation. I raised a question about the difference between the two schedules. I clearly indicated that I felt Joyce should place administrators at the appropriate step. I asked why there were two recommended columns. If Joyce had followed through on my request, there would have been no reason for the last column because it would have been exactly like the one preceding it. Joyce quietly admitted that they were, in fact, alike.

[Prentice later said that Joyce's actions here supported a statement which had come to him from one administrator, that Joyce had told the principals that they had better be at the meeting to defend themselves because Prentice was against giving them the salaries to which they were entitled. Prentice felt this may have explained the procedure Joyce used here.]

---

[1] The term "adjustment factors" used here refers to the fact that principals were to be paid on the same schedule as were teachers, except that the salary was to be multiplied by an "adjustment factor" to compensate for added responsibility and actual time on the job.

The recommendations for the salary schedule made by the superintendent were approved. It encompassed practically all of the recommendations the teachers' association had made and was, with one exception, in accordance with my proposed schedule. This exception is interesting. The teachers' association had recommended that a certain number of college credits be required of each teacher every so many years in order that the teacher might advance on the schedule. I argued that sometimes activity other than college courses might be beneficial to teachers and asked that this requirement be one of professional growth rather than college credits. Clubb, who had agreed to this in private conversation, completely abandoned me and the idea, and my motion lost for want of a second. More interesting is the fact that the minutes called my motion a probation motion. The minutes state:

> A motion was made by Mr. Prentice dealing with the probation of teachers resulting in withholding their increments upon the recommendation of the principal. The motion failed to receive a second.[2]

January 24, 1961. Mrs. Troy, wife of the gas station owner, called me to request some rerouting of the buses in Bluffview, stating that such a change would be advantageous to many residents. The following day I called Frank and asked him to check and see if the request was in order. On the 26th Frank called back to say that he had personally checked the matter. The request had been in order, and the bus involved had already been rerouted.

January 28, 1961. I had a talk with Mr. Troy who said that he understood that someone was to file for the board from the St. Joseph area who would have the total support of the Democratic Club in the township. The reason for this action, Troy speculated, was to obtain political favoritism. He further indicated that he did not like this policy and would not work for this person. This was the first time to my knowledge that Troy had ever spoken out against anything the Democrats had done. Troy urged that Bluffview consolidate with a candidate from another area in order to beat this Democratic-sponsored candidate. He suggested they work with Hartman again.

I told Troy that Mrs. Hartman had recently said that they would be happy to do what they could but that her husband, who had wielded a good deal of influence in the new Presbyterian Church in Bluffview, was no longer on the board of the church due to a disagree-

---

[2] "Official Minutes of the Board of Education of Robertsdale," January 19, 1961.

ment with the minister. She pointed out that they would be unable to be of as much help as they had been during the last election when I had been elected. Troy, however, felt that Hartman could still be of tremendous help.

January 31, 1961. Wilke called to tell me that a vandal had broken into the high school the Friday before.

During this conversation another question was raised. Joyce had recommended earlier that the money allotted to individual schools for supplementary supplies be spent in a uniform manner in all schools. This category of supplies he called "Category I." I had taken exception to this procedure, arguing that individual schools differed in their needs, but I had received little support from the other board members. Since that discussion, Joyce had called back some science equipment from the Elm Grove School because it was not standard equipment for elementary schools. As this was Wilke's area, he indicated at this time his support of my stand on the "Category I" issue.

February 5, 1961. Troy said he had asked Mr. Becker if he would run for school board in the coming election. Becker had said that he would. Troy had nothing but praise for Becker, saying that he had served well on the Bluffview zoning board, was a college graduate, and had children in the Robertsdale public schools. Troy went on to say that there were three men running from the St. Joseph area: Clubb, the incumbent; Usher, unsuccessful candidate in three former elections; and Farley, the person whom the Democratic Club supported.

All three candidates were members of the Democratic Club, but two of them had taken the position that partisan politics should play no part in school elections.[3] These two were to receive no help from the Democratic Club.

I called Becker, who stated that he had attended Casper University, that he would work hard to be elected, and that his only interest in the election was the improvement of the schools in the district. I warned him that only on this platform could a resident of Bluffview hope to win and only on this platform would I support anyone.

The following day I called Mrs. Code, president of the Bluffview Elementary P.T.A., and told her of Becker's intention to run for the

---

[3] According to a political advertisement in the March 30, 1961 edition of the *Midwest County Bugle*, letters in the April 6, 20, and 27, 1961 editions indicated Farley's image as a partisan Democrat. Clubb and Usher dropped their membership in the Democratic Club as a result of its involvement in the 1961 school election. Farley, who took no such stand, was appointed vice-president of the Democratic Club shortly after his election to the school board.

school board. Mrs. Code was not enthusiatic since Becker had not been active in the P.T.A., but she agreed that possibly he was the best candidate under the circumstances. She added that no one in the community expected Joyce to be rehired after his contract ran out and that even Chod was not very close to him anymore. She indicated that Joyce was no longer able to "run things" as he used to do.

[Between October 12th and February 9th, Prentice records no effort on his part to follow up his suggestions for candidates. Perhaps there were some minor efforts but if he did not feel them important enough to record in his diary, one is led to believe that they were at best half-hearted and feeble. Perhaps he was too confident of his influence; perhaps he was not confident enough. Now he has fumbled the ball. Troy is initiating another candidate and Prentice does not even seriously object. In doing so, he violates two of the three generalizations derived from his original suggestions. Becker is from Bluffview and not a P.T.A. member. Prentice appears more concerned about Becker's personal qualifications at this point than about the political phenomona he previously operationalized. Perhaps neither would have to have been sacrificed. Prentice's actions are not political in this case but school boards are political.]

Regular Board Meeting, February 9, 1961. During the first order of business I insisted that the item be corrected which indicated that I had suggested that teachers be held without salary raise. With this correction the minutes were approved.

A letter from Midmeadows was read which invited the Robertsdale board to meet with them February 20, 1961 to discuss annexation. The board directed Joyce to indicate their acceptance.

Joyce then presented the budget for approval by the board. Frank, who had prepared the budget, assisted in the presentation. I suggested that the board delay approval in order to give members time to study the proposal. The board agreed. Here again the minutes fail to indicate what happened. They say:

> Mr. Frank presented a summary of the budget for the board's consideration and approval at the next board Meeting.[4]

Actually, it was clear that Joyce intended that the board act, but on my request that the board delay until the proposal could be studied, he offered no objection.

After approval of the reemployment of the present administrators, the question of employing new principals and where they would be

---

[4] "Official Minutes. . . ," February 9, 1961.

placed was considered. Joyce felt that two of the elementary schools, Bluffview included, should have a full-time principal, but that one school should have a teacher-principal. I took exception to this idea and was surprised to find that Dyke immediately agreed. Joyce backed down and said that he agreed and that all principals would work full-time.

The final filing date for candidates in the April election was set as March 10, 1961, and it was agreed that the polling place for Bluffview residents would be in Bluffview. It had formally been in the Lakeside Elementary School. This polling place was to be eliminated at the April, 1961 election.

February 19, 1961.   Clubb called about a problem concerning contracts for noncertificated personnel. The contracts had been changed from those previously issued, which were detrimental to the employees. Clubb said, "I keep running into the same thing. Employees are told not to take their problems to board members and particularly not to Clubb." Clubb said that he had several calls that evening regarding noncertificated contracts and that Wilke had told him that he had eight calls that evening about the contracts.

After a long discussion about this, the conversation turned to the budget and spending in "Category I." At this time Clubb agreed with me that schools differed in their needs and should not be required to be uniform in their purchases. He described the areas in this way: "The St. Joseph area is an urban area and many people there are factory workers, while most of the Bluffview and Elm Grove residents are professional people who are interested in sending their children to college. The rest of the district is mostly rural." Clubb then suggested that perhaps an effort was now being made to get more Catholics into school district jobs. I mentioned that this did not seem to coincide with Joyce's background and Clubb commented, "He married a good Catholic, didn't he?" *[The religion of Joyce's new wife was later confirmed by several sources.]*

Clubb again said that he thought that Joyce and Dyke made many decisions at private meetings rather than board meetings and that Joyce recommended for employment whomever Dyke wanted. I said that I thought it was Dyke who went along with Joyce rather than the other way around. Clubb agreed that it was undoubtedly a reciprocal relationship.

Following the call from Clubb, I called Wilke and then Frank. Frank explained that he had looked in the policy book and had found no written policy regarding what should be contained in the contracts. He then had his secretary check with Joyce and Joyce gave her the figures that she used to type the contracts. Joyce signed the contracts designating Frank as the immediate superior, according to board policy. The afternoon the contracts were delivered, Frank said he had received several calls questioning changes in the contracts of which he was unaware. Frank said he passed the information on to Joyce and later that afternoon his secretary overheard Joyce call his wife (the former secretary) to ask what the old contracts had called for. Joyce's wife evidently indicated that the contracts as written were not correct, and she gave him the correct information. The contracts were then rewritten according to this information and were ready to be sent the following day.

I called Mahan, who stated that he had heard nothing about the situation and was very upset with Joyce because he had not let him know. Mahan said he would call Joyce and, if necessary, would call a special meeting about it.

The following day when I was checking further, Brook, the high school principal, who had known Joyce for a long time and had been in a position to observe him closely during the past few years re-marked, "Well, that fits the pattern!"

February 17, 1961. Troy said that the person who was to file from the Republican Club had decided not to run and was to support Becker, the Bluffview candidate. There was also an indication that a member of the Democratic Club who lived in the old Robertsdale area intended to support Becker. Tally, president of the Republican Club, would also support Becker, according to Troy. I said that I did not believe that Tally or the other Republican Club member would support anyone whom Dyke did not support, and that Dyke would not support anyone from Bluffview. According to Troy, Tally also intended to support Clubb. This was, I thought, impossible. I predicted that Tally would support neither of these candidates. *[A later conversation with Troy showed Prentice's prediction to be correct.]*

Later in the evening, Mahan called to say that he had been to see Joyce and had "raised heck with him" because the information needed for noncertificated personnel contracts had not been in the policy book. He had told Joyce that people in the area were saying it was really Joyce's wife who was running the school district. Mahan said he wasn't going to put up with that anymore. He closed by saying the contract situation was now corrected.

February 21, 1961. In a telephone conversation Clubb told me he would like to support Becker in the coming election. I said that I was doing what I could for Clubb and Becker and knew that Troy was also. Clubb then told me that Farley was running because Mrs. Gram, wife of the Democratic committeeman, was in the insurance business. She wrote some of the district's insurance and wanted to write more. *[This comment received validation three months after Farley's election. He requested to be placed on a board committee to study the district's insurance program. At the October and November meetings Farley made recommendations which, had they been accepted by the board, would have allowed Mrs. Gram to write $500,000 additional insurance.]*

Clubb also said that he believed that Tally would work for him in the coming election, and again I said I didn't see how this could happen. Later that evening I called Wilke and discussed the coming meeting to be held in conjunction with the Midmeadows board. Wilke said that he would like Becker to call him as he would like to take him to the Elm Grove and Mt. Olive P.T.A. meetings and introduce him to people he knew. Wilke said he was working for Becker and Clubb.

Joint Meeting of Robertsdale and Midmeadows Boards, February 20, 1961. This meeting, which showed general agreement about annexation, produced one notable comment. For the first time there was general agreement among members of the board that annexation should occur. The president of the Midmeadows board said: "In the length of time I've been associated with this community [it was obvious that he was including both districts], the unprecedented change which this meeting signifies is hard to believe."

February 24, 1961. Clubb called to say that at the recent meeting of the P.T.A. presidents, who had met to organize a P.T.A. Executive Council, all candidates for the board had spoken with the exception of Becker. Farley had received rough treatment at the meeting and could probably not count on any support from this group.

[This meeting was interesting for three reasons. First, Prentice had urged ever since his election that such a group be formed. Second, it was another phase in the pattern that was to cause Prentice's predictions of who would be elected to go completely afoul. Becker did not attend this meeting. He had told Prentice in their first conversation that he would attend all P.T.A. meetings from that time on. His wife became ill, and he attended only one of the nine P.T.A. meetings he should have. He became a closed subsystem to those subsystems on which he had to rely if he was to be elected. Becker was taking the first step in demonstrating that he would not fulfill the criteria which Prentice had set. Becker would not use the energy necessary to campaign. Third, Farley received no encouragement from these people and

he would never receive any. He would look to those who nominated him in the first place for support.]

March 5, 1961. Mr. Lindzey, president of the Elm Grove Elementary P.T.A., called me to say that he had been asked to run for the school board. *[In October Prentice suggested Lindzey's name to Hartman as a running mate with Clubb. Prentice's failure to take action was undoubtedly a mistake.]* Lindzey asked how much time it would take to perform the duties of a school board member and inquired about his chances of winning. I told him that it was rather late to file, that four men had already filed, and that most of the people who were willing to work in school elections were already committed. I urged Lindzey to wait until the following year when he could receive more support. Lindzey said he would call me again.

I called Becker and asked him if he had been going to P.T.A. meetings. Becker said he hadn't but planned to during March. He also said he planned to talk before the Lakeside Businessmen's Association, an association which represents the older elements of the community. It occurred to me then that Becker was asked to run not just by Troy but by a faction concerned with politics in Lakeside. This faction is actually made up of both Democratic and Republican men since Lakeside elections are nonpartisan. Apparently, Becker was chosen not for his ability but because he pleased these men. I again reminded him of the importance of attending the P.T.A. meetings and of getting some statement of what he believes about education before the voters in the district.

Later the same day, the editor of the Bluffview community paper called me to ask who was running for the board. Becker had not bothered to call her, and so I gave her the information. *[The community paper carried the names of Becker as a resident of Bluffview and Clubb as an incumbent.]* I called Troy and Wilke and indicated that perhaps it would be better for Becker to withdraw if he were not going to work.

[Prentice is beginning to recognize his mistake. Not only has he lost the political assets he would have gained by nominating Lindzey but those factors are now likely to work against him inasmuch as Lindzey himself is thinking of filing. Besides this, Becker is making it clear that he does not meet the criteria set by Prentice.]

Regular Board Meeting, March 9, 1961. I again offered a correction to the last month's minutes regarding my vote. The minutes were approved as corrected.

The insurance underwriters were present to make a report. I questioned the length of time it was taking to get the report and the fact that, while some buildings were not fully covered, other buildings were overcovered or had overlapping insurance. The insurance men publicly blamed this on the fact that Joyce had not allowed them to manage the insurance but had told them what he wanted them to do. Joyce later denied this. No extensive report was available. *[The report was finally made at the July meeting.]*

The annuity plan which I had been pushing for several months was next on the agenda. Some teachers had indicated that they wished to participate and the board unanimously adopted the plan. *[It is interesting to note that up until now each time this plan is mentioned in the minutes, the minutes carefully state that this is the same plan which the superintendent had offered the teachers in September but which no one had wanted. Actually, the federal government ruled that plan illegal and it did not take effect at this time.]*

With regard to the budget I made two motions, both concerning "Category I." Clubb seconded both of these motions. Joyce strongly opposed allowing any choice outside of "Category I" to the individual schools. Dyke and Scott backed Joyce strongly, but Mahan took the position that it really made no difference either way. I proposed that schools be allowed to spend money outside of this restrictive category if they felt it was educationally desirable. When the vote was called for on these two issues, only Scott voted against them. Dyke, failing to indicate his vote either way, was recorded with the majority as being in favor of the motions. With the passage of these motions individual schools would determine their own expenditures in this area.

Nothing appeared on the agenda regarding the tax levy and I asked if it wasn't necessary at this meeting to adopt a levy for presentation to the voters in the April 4th election. The superintendent and most of the board felt this matter had been taken care of, but the minutes showed no record of such action. A levy of $3.52 was unanimously adopted.

Dyke read a list of names of candidates for the coming election, and Lindzey's name appeared on the list.

The president then indicated it was necessary to go into executive session. (Again the minutes do not indicate this. It appears as if what follows were handled in open session.) In the executive session Scott said that inasmuch as the board was talking about annexing Midmeadows and they had extended their superintendent's contract, he moved that the board extend Joyce's contract. Dyke seconded the motion, and Wilke immediately agreed that under the circumstances the board should extend Joyce's contract. (Wilke later apologized for "speaking out of turn" about the extension.) During the discussion, Clubb and I both spoke against the motion. When the vote was taken, Clubb and I voted against. Dyke then suggested that since Joyce's contract would be extended anyway (by a 4-2 vote), the board might want to make it unanimous. I reluctantly agreed, but Clubb would not go along with the idea.

March 11, 1961. Becker called me and said he had talked to Wilke, and Wilke felt that Becker must do more if he were to be elected. When he promised to get to all of the rest of the P.T.A. meetings, Wilke was satisfied, Becker said.

On the following day Mrs. Master, resident of Bluffview, called. She and my wife had been sorority sisters in college, and we had visted in one another's homes. Mrs. Master was active in many social clubs.

Mrs. Master said she wanted to do everything she could to help Lindzey get elected to the school board and she asked for advice. I told her that it was rather late to start—less than a month before the election. I gave her what help I could.

March 13, 1961. Lindzey called to tell me he was going to run; he asked for whatever help I could give him. I repeated what I had told him before and what I had told Mrs. Master. I said I could not openly support anyone, but I felt Lindzey was a good candidate and would say so if asked.

Later, Wilke called to discuss the coming election. Wilke said that a friend of Lindzey's had called, and Wilke had told him that it was too late to do much of anything now. We agreed that there was no way those on the board who had opposed the things we had both supported could benefit from the election. There was no one running who could support or who would support their views if elected. Wilke said that Scott had agreed to work for Clubb and Becker. Both Wilke and I felt that Lindzey's filing would probably hurt both Clubb and Becker and that this was the thing we had hoped to prevent.

[Prentice has been neutralized. Realizing he cannot continue to support Becker in the face of the Lindzey candidacy, he takes himself out of the game. Instead of insisting that Becker withdraw and throw his support to Lindzey, he begins to rationalize. Either Prentice is not a true politician, or he is not sure of his power, or both.]

March 23, 1961. Troy confirmed my suspicions of a month before. Neither Tally nor the other old resident from the Republican Club was supporting Becker. Troy was very angry not only about this but also because Becker was not working to be elected. I again asked if Becker would withdraw in favor of Lindzey. Troy and I both agreed that at present both of the candidates whom Troy and I had backed would have a tough time winning and that Lindzey would probably have a better chance if Becker withdrew.

Just before the board meeting on March 23, 1961 Clubb called to inform me about a meeting of the Lakeside Businessmen's Association. This organization was strongly against the tax levy and supported candidates who apparently were not friendly to Joyce. I asked Clubb how this could be true since one of the younger Littles was an officer of that association. Clubb said, "Something in this marriage deal got between them! . . . He's banging at the Old Man's head."

Special Board Meeting, March 23, 1961. Bids were opened and approved for the construction at the Bluffview and Elm Grove schools. Approval was also given to waiting four days, as the law allows, to reorganize the board after the election. The reason given was that the signing of the bonds recently sold would be void if Mahan were not on the board at the time of signature. As Mahan was not running, he most certainly would not be on the board.

I privately mentioned to Dyke and Scott the idea of presenting retiring board members with certificates of appreciation from the school district. Wilke had previously agreed to this.

March 25, 1961. I attended a meeting of the Lakeside Businessmen's Association. All candidates and board members had been invited, but of the five candidates only Farley and Lindzey were present. I was the only incumbent board member present. Farley attacked everything from board members, teachers, and administrators, to noncertificated staff. Lindzey, while contending that progress could be made, supported the tax levy and the teachers of the district. I made a plea for support for the tax levy and the meeting adjourned.

March 27, 1961. A coffee was given for Lindzey at the home of Mr. and Mrs. Master in Bluffview. My wife attended, as did Mrs. Code, the Bluffview Elementary P.T.A. president. My wife thought that Lindzey made an excellent impression on those who attended.

Wilke called in the afternoon and asked if Becker was campaigning yet. He and I agreed that Lindzey's filing would hurt Clubb both in Elm Grove and Bluffview and would hurt Becker in Elm Grove. Both of us thought it would be better if Becker withdrew.

When I called Troy later that afternoon, I again suggested that Becker withdraw. Troy said that both members of the Lakeside Council from Bluffview agreed and that he had spoken to Becker but Becker had refused, contending that he would still win. Late in the afternoon a meeting was held which Troy, Becker, a member of the Lakeside council (not from Bluffview), and I attended. The council member dominated the meeting. I remarked to my wife after the meeting that I felt I had been "sold a bill of goods" on Becker. I insisted at the meeting that Becker distribute literature saying he supported excellent public schools and mention how he would obtain them. Wells, the councilman, insisted that Becker appeal to taxpayers without children who wanted to keep taxes down. Wells and I were miles apart, and I was even more unhappy with Becker than before.

Lindzey attended the latter part of the meeting and talked with Becker. Each gave passive agreement to helping the other in his own area. At this late date it is doubtful that either will do anything.

[In the early morning hours of the 28th, Prentice was stricken with appendicitis and taken to the hospital. He remained there through the election of April 4th and until the afternoon of the board reorganization on April 7th. With two exceptions he had no interaction with school district members during the rest of the period of the diary. Most of the information for these next few days comes from his wife.

Just before the election, Lindzey distributed circulars throughout most of the district. This circular is shown in Chart XII. The Masters painted and put up about a dozen signs supporting Lindzey, but just before the election a building ordinance was invoked forcing all signs to be removed until Lindzey's supporters had applied for and paid for the necessary permits. This ordinance had never been invoked before, and it is interesting to note that Wells, who backed Becker, served as building commissioner on the Lakeside Council. After the payment of a dollar for each sign, the signs were replaced.

Becker attended his only P.T.A. meeting of the campaign on April 3, 1961, the day before the election. He distributed circulars (see Chart XIII) the day before the election. It followed Wells's suggestions and completely disregarded any of Prentice's suggestions.

On this same day it was discovered that Becker was not a graduate of any college. His only comment was, "I went to Casper University," meaning that he had attended that university for a short period of time. Lindzey jumped at this opportunity and distributed circulars to that effect throughout Bluffview. Prentice said, upon learning this fact, "Becker now has no chance in Bluffview."

On April 4th, Joyce made a special trip to the hospital to bring Prentice an absentee ballot. Later that night Prentice received a phone

Chart XII

JAMES LINDZEY CANDIDATE FOR ROBERTSDALE SCHOOL BOARD*

Mr. Lindzey is a long term resident of the Midwest County area. He was graduated from Northwestern University with both Bachelor's and Master's degrees in Chemical Engineering.

Mr. Lindzey's interests and abilities in education are evidenced by:

Instructor at University of Illinois, University of Oklahoma, University of Mississippi, 1953–57.

Assistant Professor, Midwest University, Industrial Engineering, 1952–57.

President, Elm Grove Parent-Teachers Association 1960–61.

Regional Representative for Elm Grove Cub Scout Pack.

Educational Representative, Board of Deacons, Oak Chapel.

Chairman of Parent's Advisory Board, Green Nursery School.

Mr. Lindzey is now employed by ABC Chemical Company as an Engineering Supervisor. He was president of Midwest Chapter of the Association of Computing Machinery for two terms.

Mr. Lindzey has four children, the oldest of whom is now in first grade at Elm Grove School.

His platform includes:

1. Improving communications between the Robertsdale School Board, the educators, and residents.

2. Avoiding unnecessary tax increases by better long-range planning.

3. Improved vocational guidance and training as well as college preparatory work.

VOTE FOR BETTER SCHOOLS & VOTE FOR JIM LINDZEY
APRIL 4

---

* Circular distributed in behalf of candidate.

Chart XIII

VOTE FOR ROBERT C. BECKER YOUR LAKESIDE REPRESENTATIVE*

What

Robertsdale District School Board Election

Where

Bluffview School	St. Joseph School
Robertsdale Elementary	Mt. Olive School
Elm Grove School	Blue Ridge School

When

Tuesday, April 4   From 6:00 a.m. to 7:00 p.m.

Why

$3,000,000 of your tax money is spent annually by the School Board. You pay this tax whether or not you have children in the public school system.

Don't let a few decide who will represent many.

YOU owe it to your pocketbook.

IT'S YOUR MONEY AND YOUR VOTE! SPEND THEM BOTH WELL!

---

* Circular distributed in behalf of candidate.

call at the hospital from his wife saying that Usher and Farley had been elected and that the tax levy had failed. The results of this election are shown in Charts XIV and XV. Later that evening at the board meeting, Wilke made a motion, seconded by Scott and unanimously passed to resubmit the same levy to the district on April 19, 1961.

It has become evident that Becker did not meet the criteria for candidacy established by Prentice. The suggestion that he met these criteria was a lie. He did not attend P.T.A. meetings, he did not have

*a formal education past high school, and he supported "tax guarding"
rather than educational improvement. These violated the three criteria
Prentice had established. Yet there is no reason to blame Becker;
Prentice had failed to act and is now suffering the consequences.]*

Prior to my visit to the hospital, there had been some talk about
reorganizing the board after the election. Wilke had told me that
both he and Scott thought that I should be president. It had been
difficult for anyone to reach me while I was in the hospital, and nothing more had been said about the matter.

Special Meeting, April 7, 1961. I left the hospital at 4:30 p.m. and
after a brief stop at home attended the special meeting, which was
called to order at 7 p.m. After a few preliminaries, which included the
board's acceptance of the tabulation of both the board membership
and the tax election, Superintendent Joyce was appointed temporary
chairman so that board reorganization might proceed. The minutes
reveal that

> Nominations were asked for the office of President. Mr. Farley
> [newly elected member] nominated Mr. Wilke who declined the
> nomination. Mr. Usher [the other newly elected member] nomi-
> nated Mr. Prentice. The nomination was seconded by Mr. Wilke.
> Motion made by Mr. Scott and seconded by Mr. Wilke that the
> nominations cease and that Mr. Prentice be elected by acclama-
> tion. Ayes: Dyke, Wilke, Scott, Prentice, Farley, Usher.
>
> Mr. Scott was nominated by Mr. Wilke for the office of Vice
> President. The nomination was seconded by Mr. Dyke. Motion
> made by Dyke and seconded by Prentice that the nominations
> cease. Ayes: Dyke, Wilke, Scott, Prentice, Farley, Usher. The
> Chairman then asked for a vote on Mr. Scott as Vice President.
> Those in favor were: Dyke, Wilke, Scott, Prentice, Farley, Usher.[5]

The only other item of consequence was a motion to limit discussion at forthcoming public meetings about the tax levy to five minutes
per individual. This motion was unanimously passed. A letter from the
teachers' association was read which supported the tax levy. This
letter was to be circulated in the community by the association. The
board expressed its appreciation for this help. The meeting was adjourned at 8:27 p.m.

*[This ends the personal diary section kept by Prentice. Additional
sections of the case will be developed in two parts using slightly different methodologies. Up until this point the reader has been presented*

---

[5] "Official Minutes. . . ," April 7, 1961.

with something unique in the literature of educational administration. This part of the case has presented a board member's own perceptions, based on his personal diary, and the board minutes of a complete year of board membership. While it represents one person's thoughts, these thoughts are tempered with actual board minutes and official board records as well as newspaper accounts. In addition, the case was submitted to an administrator in the district and one community member for verification. These persons offered no recommendations for change.]

ANALYSIS OF "A NEW BOARD LEADERSHIP"

On November 10th Prentice played the role of arbitrator for the first time. In addition, he voted for a motion that he really did not favor. He let Clubb know that he did this because Prentice felt it necessary to support Clubb and Wilke. Prentice began to exercise a new kind of leadership function on the board at this point. He cast his vote with the party but let it be known that he was trying to be the peacemaker between the parties. While educational politics is factional rather than partisan, the action and result are the same. Almost immediately, members of the old guard group began to recognize this fact. Mahan went out of his way to explain his relation to Joyce, "I give him plenty of trouble, actually. . . ."

About a week later, for the first time in six months, Dyke approached Prentice to ask his advice about a problem. Not only did he ask advice but at the following meeting he demonstrated that he had taken the advice by proposing the motion to tape the board meetings. Prentice seconded the motion, and it passed unanimously.[6] Wilke recognized the more affable relationship and commented, "Dyke is really trying to butter you up. Mahan, too." Chod's behavior at the December 15th meeting was in striking contrast to his refusal to meet with Prentice during the summer of 1960. Chod had not spoken to Prentice since he had broken their appointment the previous summer. Now Chod had prepared one extra copy of a report he had orally presented to the board and said he wanted Prentice to have the copy. When one considers that Chod was Joyce's first appointment in the district, this is additional evidence that Prentice was increasingly felt to be the emerging leader of the board. Mahan's call on December 20th was the first time he had informally contacted Prentice. At the January 12th meeting, both groups appeared to have agreed to Pren-

---

[6] "Official Minutes. . . ," December 8, 1960.

tice's suggestion regarding the handling of Joyce's contract. Prentice is emerging in a new role as board leader rather than merely faction leader.

One of the most difficult things for the fighter to learn is when to stop fighting. It is not likely that Prentice perceived his gains at this point. On the other hand, while winning leadership on the board, Prentice had not accomplished the change he had desired. Perhaps board leadership was not a goal for Prentice but a means to a goal. The goal of change was not accomplished. Early in 1961 members of the professional staff perceived more change than Prentice did. Much remained to be done. There would still be a fight over the salary schedule, problems about Joyce's new wife and former secretary, difficulty in changing insurance practices, opposition to the annexation of Midmeadows, and of greatest concern, controversy and consternation about Joyce and his continued employment. Prentice, however, had assumed a new role on the board (although unofficial) as of January, 1961. This role was formalized when he was elected board president in April of that year.

The Election of April, 1961

Brief comments regarding the election are interspersed throughout the case. Since the election is very important, an additional analysis is made here. For a man of Prentice's ability, he was completely inept in this election. Only his stay at the hospital at the critical time excuses him at all. It is interesting that in our culture the hospital is a place into which individuals can escape, avoiding the consequences of their mistakes. Even this Prentice did not plan. Chance and the cultural norms joined forces to save him. With more practiced politicians, the retreat to the hospital is a well-used and a well-planned tactic in times of political crisis. In such cases it is said that the mayor, or the school superintendent, or the governor cannot be blamed—"The poor man was in the hospital due to illness, probably brought about by his dedication to duty and overwork." Not every trip to the hospital is so calculated; some are and some are not. Almost all are so used, however.

Months before the election, Prentice began to plan strategy. He contemplated the pros and cons of supporting incumbents as opposed to nonincumbents. He discussed this problem and the geographic composition of the district as it might affect the school board election with the individuals who had supported him in 1960. Prentice does not note in his diary that he gave consideration to these problems up until a month and a half before the 1961 election. By this time a party-oriented individual who had supported Prentice had already chosen Becker as the candidate he wanted. Most of the information on Becker Prentice records as being unreasonable and difficult to understand, yet he agreed to support the candidate. Clubb jumped in probably to get Prentice's support and the Bluffview vote. With hardly an argument, Prentice abandoned his position and supported Becker and Clubb.

Prentice's predictions regarding the necessary qualifications to win, as well as his speculations about supporting incumbents and geographic factors in the election were well-founded. His predictions about the support Becker would receive also turned out to be correct. The political adage, *Leopards don't change their spots,* is not completely true. *Leopards seldom change their spots, and then only for very good reasons* is true, however. The support which Tally indicated he had marshaled for Becker crossed party lines, geographic lines, and probably friendship and traditional community lines. Such support is not very likely, and if it did exist, it would probably be ineffectual. At best Becker could have hoped that such "support" would take the form of not opposing him and not supporting someone else. This is not a poor scheme but hardly one that in itself can elect a man. A politician "buys" such a package only after he has marshaled substantial positive and active support. Prentice bought "a pig in a poke" and one he apparently was suspicious of from the beginning. As of the end of February, Becker and Clubb were supposed to have had the support of some P.T.A. members, a Bluffview resident who was a Democrat and a Lakeside city councilman, the former president of the Republican Club who was an old-time resident of the community, the businessmen's association, and three incumbents of the school board. In addition, one candidate, Clubb, was an incumbent board member, so the total structure of the board was not under attack. The other candidate, Becker, was a new candidate and a resident of Bluffview and might be seen as representing the new movement in the district. Becker was reportedly a college graduate, representing the increased interest in quality education. These were not bad qualifications had they all been true. Even though Prentice was doubtful, he did not bother to check. He allowed others to do his work, a mistake that causes the downfall of many political figures.

As early as February 24th, data began to appear confirming Prentice's suspicions about Becker. Prentice felt sure that Becker's support must come largely from P.T.A. groups. He had struggled to open that system to nonincumbent candidates. He had insisted that any candidate he supported must campaign at all P.T.A. meetings and support the move toward a higher quality of education (and consequently, higher cost). Becker missed his first opportunity, a meeting of all P.T.A. presidents.

On March 5th additional data began to indicate that Prentice had made a mistake in agreeing to back Becker. Lindzey, the P.T.A. president who had strongly supported Prentice, called to say he had been asked to run for the board. He wanted Prentice's support. This was the man Prentice had suggested as a candidate. Now Prentice was committed to Becker. With the advantage of hindsight, it is clear that Prentice should have switched his support on May 5th. Instead, he asked Lindzey to wait a year and run in 1962. Prentice then attempted to start the machinery running for Becker. He called Becker only to find that Becker had not attended any P.T.A. meetings. Becker promised that he would attend all P.T.A. meetings during the month of March. He emphasized his support from the conservative businessmen's organization. Prentice noted in the diary his growing unhappiness, but he failed to take positive action.

May 5th held other surprises for Prentice. He found that Becker was the only candidate who had not bothered to call the editor of the weekly local. Since this editor strongly supported Prentice, she called him to obtain information on Becker. Becker's failure was too much even for Prentice. He called Troy and Wilke and suggested that they ask Becker to withdraw. No agreement was reached.

At the regular board meeting of March 9th Prentice discovered that Lindzey had decided not to wait until 1962 to run for the board. Lindzey had not called Prentice to tell him he was filing for election. His name was among those read at the meeting as candidates for the coming election. During the following week, Becker again indicated that, although he had not attended any previous P.T.A. meetings, he would attend subsequent meetings. At this point Wilke also became concerned. In addition, members of the community began to support Lindzey actively. Both Wilke and Prentice were called in an effort to obtain support for Lindzey. Both pointed to the lateness of Lindzey's filing as a reason for not giving complete support, but they indicated they would give some inactive support. At this point each should have either withdrawn their support from Becker and backed Lindzey or given no support to Lindzey and more active support to Becker. Their decision not to act in a positive way helped every candidate except Becker and Lindzey.

On March 23rd Troy reported that the support promised by Tally and the businessmen's association had not materialized. Becker was left with no organized support. P.T.A. support would go to Lindzey. Now only the fact that Becker was a Bluffview resident and that residents of areas perceiving themselves as communities tend to support their fellow residents gave Becker any hope of support. An analysis of the Robertsdale election results of 1960 indicates precisely that this phenomenon took place. Every candidate did better in his home area than any other candidate—even losing candidates.

On March 27th Troy asked Becker, at Prentice's suggestion, to withdraw from the race, but Becker refused. Becker, Troy, and Prentice got together with councilman from Lakeside to discuss the situation. It would appear that the councilman was the person who originally suggested Becker. The councilman made it clear that his expectations for Becker were quite different than those Prentice had. At this point Prentice should have withdrawn support and done everything possible to get Clubb and Lindzey elected. The voting results make it appear that this would have been possible. Lindzey received only 167 votes from Bluffview, while Becker received 247. Clubb received 76 votes from Bluffview. Forty more votes would have elected Lindzey, and twenty more would have elected Clubb. Lindzey undoubtedly hurt Clubb in Bluffview. If Prentice had openly and actively supported Clubb and Lindzey during the last week of the campaign, he might have been able to influence at least forty votes. Perhaps Prentice would have come to this decision. He had become increasingly disenchanted with Becker. We can only speculate because Prentice entered the hospital early on March 28th and did not leave until after the election. Thus, he was absent from the scene at the critical moment.

There was considerable political activity during the week before the election. Circulars were distributed in every area of the district. Lindzey's circular supported quality education. Becker's supported a "guard your tax dollar" notion of boardsmanship. Then the fact that Becker had misled certain people about his educational qualifications became known. He had only attended college for a brief period of time. Lindzey made political capital of this discovery. Lindzey's backers held several coffees in support of his candidacy and posted campaign signs supporting him. The city councilman who supported Becker ordered the signs removed under an ordinance never before invoked. The tax for posting signs was paid and the signs went up again.

The election was a complete disaster for Prentice. Both Clubb and Becker were defeated. Lindzey was also defeated. In addition, the tax levy was defeated. As for Clubb, without Lindzey's candidacy he would have polled at least one hundred more votes in Bluffview, more than enough to be elected. If Prentice would have actively supported Lindzey, Lindzey would have polled more votes in Bluffview. Lindzey's and Clubb's votes totaled 245—within two votes of what Becker received. This is strong evidence that Bluffview was split by Lindzey. When one considers that only Bluffview and Elm Grove passed the tax levy and that Becker and Farley opposed increased spending, one might expect that Becker and Farley would have done poorly in both areas. In Elm Grove Farley received 83 votes, and Becker received 52, while Lindzey (the leading candidate) received 268 votes. But in Bluffview Farley got only 73 votes, while Becker received 247 votes. Prentice could have changed the voting pattern in Bluffview, if nowhere else. Undoubtedly the tax still would have been defeated. Prentice had only himself to blame for the election of Farley over Clubb and Lindzey. Whether or not either could have defeated Usher is questionable, but both would have pulled more votes than Farley. This mistake cost Prentice during the next year and a half.

The reorganization meeting of the board confirmed the emergence of Prentice as leader. Instead of being leader of a board that was

Chart XIV

ELECTION RESULTS IN THE APRIL 4, 1961 ELECTION

	Clubb	Farley	Becker	Usher	Lindzey
Mt. Olive	57	49	49	99	66
Robertsdale	166	208	114	251	99
St. Joseph	236	227	22	340	37
Bluffview	76	73	247	139	167
Elm Grove	145	83	52	60	268
Blue Ridge	22	87	19	51	50
TOTAL	702	727	494	940	687

Chart XV

THE TAX ELECTION RESULTS APRIL 4, 1961

Mt. Olive		Roberts-dale		St. Joseph		Bluff-view*		Elm Grove*		Blue Ridge		TOTALS	
Yes	No	Yes	No	Yes	No	Yes	No	Yes	No	Yes	No	Yes	No
47	127	116	345	151	336	195	175	187	154	30	115	707	1207

*—Carried for the levy in the teachers' fund
yes—For the levy
no—Against the levy

solidly behind his objective, however, he was president of a board in which Farley was a member. Farley was to be a thorn in Prentice's side until he resigned from the board. The cost of Prentice's political naivete was substantial. Perhaps it cost the district more than it cost Prentice but that is the problem of failing to recognize the political nature of education.

Hypotheses

Hypotheses 9 and 10 are the concern of this section. There is no question that conflict was both apparent and overt during the first year following Prentice's victory over the old incumbent board member. Not only did the non-unanimous votes increase, but the discussions of motions often became openly hostile. The height of this hostility, according to Prentice's diary, was at the September meeting when Dyke and Prentice exchanged words over the establishment of a teachers' salary study committee. This hostility was indicated not only by an increase in verbal exchanges but also by an increase in the number and percent of non-unanimous votes of the Robertsdale board the year following Prentice's election.

Peaking in September, hostility diminished until mid-November when Dyke first asked Prentice his opinion about solving a board problem. During the months between September, 1960 and April, 1961, members of the insurgent group and members of the old guard group increasingly sought Prentice's advice. The emergence of Prentice as leader followed the pattern suggested in Hypotheses 9 and 10. Almost immediately, Clubb and Wilke teamed with Prentice. Both men were low-status members of the old guard board. Neither of them had taken part in such decisions as the naming of the junior high school. Early in the spring of 1960 Prentice was responding, at least in part, to the initiation of these men. Soon afterwards, however, Prentice assumed the initiation (e.g., the calendar, code numbers for bills, teacher qualifications, changing the financial organization, etc.). Prentice was soon perceived as the leader of the insurgents. This realization may have been a factor in the hostility between Dyke and Prentice as one challenged the other for the leadership of the whole board. The emergence of Prentice as the leader of the total board is confirmed by his election as board president in April, 1961 with both Dyke and Scott voting for Prentice. Hypotheses 9 and 10 can account for the shifts in the leadership pattern on the Robertsdale board. Perhaps one of the reasons Dyke and Scott were willing to elect Prentice was a desire to co-opt him. As president, Prentice had to represent the entire board more than was the case when he was the leader of the insurgent faction.

Prentice had assumed the leadership of the board, but he had failed to consolidate his gain by assuring a win for his "party" and thus a clear majority on the board. Prentice had brought the factions of the board somewhat closer together during the year but in the election both of the candidates whom he had supported lost. Clubb, Becker, and Lindzey all lost. Usher, one man whom Prentice could have supported did win but he owed Prentice nothing. Farley was the candidate from the Democratic party with whom Prentice had refused to run in 1960.[7] To some extent these events are explained by Hypothesis 11. The instability in the social system that elected Prentice created the situation that prevented the new board leadership from being more stable. While Prentice was to act during the next twenty months to bring more stability to the new leadership, the very factors which created the instability and incumbent defeat in the first place would continue to work against that steady state.

---

[7] *See* Chapter 3.

7

"Mene, Mene, Tekel, Upharsin"

When the incumbent defeat pattern results in a power shift on the board and an opening in the board's decision-making system that widens community influence, the new-comers elected will most often find the key to resistance to change in the person of the chief school officer. Individuals who defeat incumbents may or may not begin with the intention of struggling against the superintendent. However, since the superintendent is a key figure in establishing educational policies and goals that the new board member seeks to change, the member is likely to find that his chief opponent is the superintendent. If the new, emerging power system finds itself harrassed and thwarted by the superintendent as it seeks to carry out its election mandate, then a struggle for control of the board will take place. The struggle involving the new power system and the old will become sharper and more clearly focused on the superintendent and the new board member. If the new power system, as in Robertsdale, continues to gather greater public support while the old system rests on the power base in the old community—a condition that further narrows the power base —the result is predictable.

Belshazzar saw the handwriting on the wall but was unable to interpret it. He called Daniel who made the following translation:

Mene: God hath numbered thy kingdom and finished it.
Tekel: Thou art weighed in the balances and art found wanting.
Peres: Thy kingdom is divided and given to the Medes and Persians.[1]

Like Belshazzar, many school superintendents see the handwriting on the wall but have no Daniel to interpret it. As the school district grows and changes and the formal structure of the board and the administration continue to reflect the past, the days of the "establishment" of the superintendent are numbered. The voters weigh the situation and, finding it wanting, elect new representation on the board. This divides the establishment between the old guard and the insurgents. Many a superintendent's kingdom has fallen thus.

PRENTICE AS PRESIDENT OF THE BOARD

For the one and two-thirds years that Prentice served as board president, he failed to keep a day-by-day diary. The authors have based this chapter on the occasional notes which Prentice made, his recollections, a scrapbook of articles that appeared in the metropolitan daily and in two local weekly newspapers, and a complete set of board minutes covering the period of Prentice's presidency until his resignation from the board. This section will deal with several of the issues in the school district in chronological order. These will include the defeated tax levy in 1961, the insurance program in 1962, the hiring of a new high school principal, and interwoven through this discussion, the fate of Superintendent Joyce.

The Tax Election of 1961

Following the original canvas of ballots indicating the loss of the tax levy and the election of Farley and Usher, the board decided it should again present the same tax levy to the electorate. (Prentice was in the hospital at the time and did not attend the meeting.) Farley had campaigned on a platform of lower school taxes. Both he and Usher (who had not campaigned for lower taxes) received their heaviest

---

[1] King James Version of the Bible, Daniel 5: 26-28.

support in the areas that defeated the tax. The next referendum was set for April 19th, the earliest date under state law that a tax could be submitted to the electorate.

Prentice left the hospital on April 7th and was elected president of the board on that date, just twelve days before the tax election. He officiated at his first meeting on April 13th, just six days before the second referendum. The minutes of that meeting indicate no discussion of the referendum. Prentice recalled that he had told the board that the referendum date had been set too early since not much could be done to influence the voters in such a short time. He also stated that the school administration had done virtually nothing during this period to insure passage.

At Prentice's suggestion, notices were sent to parents indicating that four meetings would be held to explain and discuss the proposed tax levy. The meetings were held in different areas of the district in order to provide ease of access for the electorate. One was held at the Blue Ridge School on the 13th, another at the high school on the 14th (St. Joseph-Robertsdale area), the third at Bluffview School on the 17th, and a final total district meeting at the junior high the evening before the election. Both major daily papers carried notices of the meetings in the April 12th issues, and both weekly papers carried front page articles on the 13th. The meetings were well attended, the attendance ranging from 100 to 300 people at each meeting. Superintendent Joyce took no part in the meetings except to answer questions directed to him. Prentice chaired the meetings and answered most of the questions. The majority of the board attended all meetings.

On the evening of April 19th the board held a special meeting to canvas the ballots of the second tax referendum. The results of this ballot appear in Chart XVI.

Chart XVI

RESULTS OF THE APRIL 19TH REFERENDUM

Mt. Olive		Roberts- dale		St. Joseph		Bluff- view*		Glen Grove*		Blue Ridge		TOTALS	
Yes	No	Yes	No	Yes	No	Yes	No	Yes	No	Yes	No	Yes	No
102	144	208	338	233	269	242	181	248	132	83	101	1116	1165

*—Carried the levy
Yes—For the levy
No—Against the levy

The tax levy lost for the second time. There was a substantial increase in *yes* votes (more than one and a half times those of the April 4th vote). However, not a single election area changed its previous position on the levy. It is interesting to note that the *no* votes actually decreased by forty-two votes. A public meeting was to be held to discuss what should be done about the defeat. A special board meeting was scheduled on April 26th for this purpose.

Dyke's earlier prediction appears to have been correct. The increase in teacher salaries required a tax levy which the voters turned down twice. Yet Dyke had supported the levy, at least in public. Farley had openly opposed the levy in both referendums, and the organizational potential of the district had done nothing to promote the passage of the levy.

During the special board meeting the board was polled and was unanimously in favor of the defeated tax levy. Even Mr. Farley supported the levy, the increase being mainly due to the teachers' salary schedule. It was he who introduced a motion to implement the salary schedule in spite of the tax defeat. The minutes read, "The sentiment was expressed that at present we could not justify a reduction [in the tax] as it is our responsibility to offer leadership for good schools."[2]

At the April 19th meeting notice was given of a public hearing on April 26th when the board would again discuss the levy. This notice was carried the next day on the front page of one weekly newspaper with the comment, "In a roll call vote, all six board members went on record as saying, 'We see no way to reduce the levy without seriously curtailing our educational program."[3] The Daily Sun also carried an article describing the defeat and announcing the open hearing on the 26th.

The hearing of April 26th was attended by 300 people. Again Prentice assumed the leadership, and Superintendent Joyce remained in the background. Prentice made an initial statement concerning the levy and answered audience questions for approximately one hour. He outlined the areas of the educational program that the board had decided would be eliminated if the levy were reduced. These included, "kindergarten, audio-visual education, interscholastic athletics, field trips, and library projects. . ." He concluded, "We feel all these are an essential part of our educational program."[4]

---

2 "Official Minutes of the Board of Education of Robertsdale," April 19, 1961.
3 *Midwest County Bugle*, April 20, 1961.
4 *Ibid.*, April 27, 1961.

The board then voted to resubmit the same levy for a third time on May 17. Wilke made the motion, Usher seconded it, and Prentice, Scott, and Dyke voted in favor of it. Although Farley had made the motion to implement the higher teachers' salary schedule that required the increased levy, he voted against the levy stating that the "fat" should be trimmed out of the budget. This comment stimulated an angry exchange between Farley and Prentice that was reported, in part, in a series of letters to the county weekly in the following manner:

> I asked Mr. Farley for suggestions as to what could be cut. His first reply was "Kindergarten—it's only babysitting anyway." I explained that we could not consider such programs as reading and reading readiness as just baby sitting. Mr. Farley's next comment was "Well, then cut something else, anything. I don't care, just so we reduce the tax. Why don't we cut librarians? We don't need them!" At this point I saw no reason for going further for I could come to no agreement with anyone who believed that kindergartens and librarians constituted the "fat" of an educational program.[5]

Prentice probably did not realize the prophesy of his comment. He would *never* come to agreement with Mr. Farley. This would plague the district even after Prentice left.

The opponents of the school tax found an unexpected ally in the metropolitan morning daily. Always a champion of the conservative point of view, it took an editorial position opposing, not the levy itself, but the resubmission. They editorialized in part:

> This month, Robertsdale voters twice turned down a request to raise the school tax. . . But will this settle the matter? Not at all. . . The school board's strategy is to harrass the voters. . . This unjustified tactic of calling repeated elections. . .is an expensive form of pressuring. . . Midwest's State Legislature should outlaw it.[6]

Prentice immediately answered the editorial. The letters to the editor carried part of the answer. He pointed out that the school board had no choice but to resubmit a tax levy, because if it did not, the tax would revert to one dollar per hundred according to state law. Under these circumstances, ". . . the school district could not possibly operate. The only question is what levy should be resubmited." He pointed out that no reduction in the requested levy could be accomplished without

[5] *Ibid.*, May 11, 1961.
[6] *Midwest Daily Sun*, April 29, 1961.

eliminating what the board considered essential educational programs. He concluded, "If boards of education would be legally prohibited from resubmitting a levy once defeated, any district that might lose its levy once might just as well close its doors."[7]

The *Sun* responded editorially by reaffirming their position but sympathizing with the Robertsdale board. They said, "The Robertsdale Board of Education faces a very real crisis." The editorial emphasized the unfairness of proposing the levy for the third time. "Whatever else, the American people cannot afford to downgrade the importance of the ballot box, even if it means a temporary crisis in Robertsdale."[8] Prentice, believing that he had come out as well as he possibly could, did not respond to this editorial.

Both of the local weekly papers backed the third levy submission. Each carried a front-page headline in the issue just before the referendum date. One daily interviewed citizens in the community. Excerpts from twenty interviews were quoted. A long list was printed of "businessmen in the area" who supported the levy.[9]

The district P.T.A.'s and the teachers' association gave their support to the levy. Many of their members made a canvas by telephone of lists of P.T.A. members and other citizens who were believed to favor the levy, urging them to vote. "Poll watchers" used these lists at the polling places on May 17th. Car pools were organized to help people get to the polls. Individuals who were thought to favor the levy and who had not voted by 5 p.m. would be called and asked to vote. Prentice directed that a special newsletter about the levy be sent to all district residents.

With the help of P.T.A. officers and teachers' association officers, Prentice coordinated the effort to pass the levy on this third attempt. He made it clear that it would not be submitted a fourth time. Educational services would be reduced if the levy was defeated.

On May 16th, the day before the referendum, Prentice was the guest on "The Sounding Board," a local radio program. He answered questions about the levy and discussed it with the host of the program. This was followed by a fifteen-minute audience question-and-answer session. On the day of the election, Prentice and Lindzey, the Elm Grove P.T.A. president, toured the district in support of the levy. They used a sound truck supplied by Lindzey. Other P.T.A. personnel campaigned outside every polling place by distributing literature supporting the levy. The board met that evening to canvas the ballots. The results are reported in Chart XVII.

---

[7] *Ibid.*, May 2, 1961.
[8] *Ibid.*, May 5, 1961.
[9] *Midwest County Bugle*, May 16, 1961.

Chart XVII

RESULTS OF THE MAY 17TH REFERENDUM

Mt. Olive		Roberts- dale		St. Joseph		Bluff- view°		Elm Grove°		Blue Ridge		TOTALS	
Yes	No	Yes	No	Yes	No	Yes	No	Yes	No	Yes	No	Yes	No
178	192	263	427	427	366	357	240	350	142	146	126	1719	1493

°—Carried for the levy
Yes—For the levy
No—Against the levy

As an anticlimax to the tax levy issue, the weekly newspaper later carried the following headline: SCHOOL BOARDS CUT TAXES: ROBERTSDALE TAX IS 23¢![10] After two defeats the tax finally passed. Two months later reevaluation necessitated a reduction in the Robertsdale tax levy just as it had a year before. This time the voters were informed by newspaper headline and school bulletin!

Prentice's first campaign as board president was successfully completed. Several patterns were established that would continue throughout his presidency. (1) Farley opposed the tax levy. Although he had fought a losing battle, he never gave up the fight. On opposite sides of almost every issue, Farley and Prentice often engaged in open personal verbal battles. At one point during his presidency, Prentice was to tell Farley at an open meeting, "I'll not allow you to use this board to further your political ambitions! Everytime you do, I'll rule you out of order." Prentice could have made life more tranquil and perhaps gained Farley's support for some educational issues. (2) The P.T.A.'s and the teachers were solidly behind Prentice. (3) In general, Prentice held the leadership of the board.

Prentice's board leadership occurred partially by default. Neither the old guard nor the new force, represented by Farley, could have obtained the office of board president. While the remaining old guard found Prentice more acceptable than they had earlier, it would be difficult to believe their admiration was unbounded or their support well established at the time he was chosen president. But the tax victory increased Prentice's support inside the board as well as in the community. It validated his right to leadership as a public official. Much of his power rested on his vigorous activity and restless energy which had defeated an incumbent and placed him on the board in the first instance. His chief power resources were the initial mandate given him in his election and his capacity to enlist P.T.A. and teachers'

[10] *Ibid.*, July 13, 1961.

association support. The situation could still have reverted to its former condition if Prentice weakened or his support slackened. Neither happened; both became stronger.

The more Farley, Joyce, and the others let Prentice carry the tax campaign, the greater Prentice's political risk but the higher still would be his political stock if he carried the day. As Prentice's star shone brighter, Joyce's grew dimmer. Yet for at least a year Prentice did not see that Joyce and he were locked in a struggle for control of the Robertsdale policy-making system. Perhaps he never fully saw it until years later. He had begun as a candidate supporting the professional chief officer of the district. The obvious initial hostility of the old guard had been less obvious in Joyce's case because of the formal requirements of his office. As Prentice's first year drew to a close, the clashes over factual matters and specialized knowledge began to indicate the contest for board leadership. Prentice still interpreted this conflict as centering on Dyke's leadership, with Joyce as merely a member of the old guard rather than its leader.

Joyce's behavior during the tax campaign violated the traditional behavior of schoolmen in search of resources. Perhaps he understood that Prentice's leadership, and thus his own leadership, was at stake. Prentice's victory resulted in Joyce's becoming what his legal office was intended to be—chief employee of the board rather than its leader. This adjustment required greater personal flexibility than Joyce could muster at this point in his Robertsdale career. Superintendent Joyce would not again take an active and open leadership role in the district. He would use his influence (usually against Prentice) but never where it could be seen. Never again would he publicly be for or against anything.

The Insurance Program

The insurance program of the Robertsdale district was a continuing issue during the entire time Prentice was on the board. Joyce initiated the issue at the September 8, 1960 meeting. He suggested a method to reduce insurance costs and by a unanimous vote the board asked him to pursue the matter. After his 1960 defeat Usher asked Prentice for an appointment to the insurance committee in order to gain more visibility for his 1961 campaign, but no committee was formulated. The superintendent and the insurance agents made several reports prior to April, 1961, but nothing had happened. The insurance agents had accused Superintendent Joyce of not cooperating with them.

Immediately following the April, 1961 election, a board committee was appointed to investigate the district's insurance plan. This committee was composed of two board members and two cooperating agents who had written insurance for the district. At the July 6th meeting the former president of the board, who had declined to run in the April election, made an insurance presentation to the board. The board took no action after the presentation and the matter was never again touched upon.

On August 10th at the regular board meeting Assistant Superintendent Frank reported the status of insurance on school building contents. Lists of property were given to the insurance agents. At this meeting Usher presented the report of the board committee on insurance. Based on the report, the following motions were made.

> Motion made by Mr. Dyke and seconded by Mr. Scott that the Board of Education take bids on insurance to include specific rates, average rates, and any other plan which the agent thinks would be to the advantage of the district. [The motion passed unanimously.]

Up until this point the school district's insurance agents, as well as Dyke and Joyce, had insisted that all insurance rates were by law the same. Therefore, bidding was a waste of time, they said.

> Motion made by Mr. Farley and seconded by Mr. Usher to appoint John Barell as Agent of Record.

Only Prentice voted against the second motion. He indicated that he did not necessarily oppose Mr. Barell (who was presently writing insurance for the school district) but felt it inappropriate to appoint an agent of record for the district's insurance when the board had just voted to take bids on insurance.

It is important to understand the general status of the district's insurance program. This was reported to the board for the first time in a document dated July 10, 1961. The district owned approximately $3,000,000 worth of insurance. There were six insurance agents participating in this business. Four of the agents, Mr. Barell being one, wrote between thirty and thirty-five policies each, totaling approximately $700,000 worth of business for each agent. A fifth agent wrote one policy for $16,500 and a sixth agent wrote two policies totaling $80,000. No other agents in the district carried school insurance for the district.

The sixth agent was the wife of the Democratic state representative and district committeeman. It should be recalled that Farley was president of the Democratic Club and received help from that club in his successful campaign for a seat on the board. He informally let it be known that he wanted this agent to write more of the district's insurance. Formally, he said that he wanted the district's insurance divided more equitably among all insurance agents in the district.

At this point an unexpected alliance developed on the board. Farley wanted more insurance for his friends but was not interested in better rates for the district. He wanted the business restricted to agents in the district. Dyke, Scott and Joyce preferred the preferential treatment of their four old friends who had been writing almost all the insurance. If the district's policy toward insurance was not preferential, how can the fact that each of the four agents wrote almost exactly the same number of policies for almost exactly the same total amount be explained? Let us keep in mind that for all practical purposes other agents were excluded and no written policy regarding insurance existed prior to Prentice's arrival on the board. Prentice and now Usher felt that the restrictive and discriminatory insurance practices were deplorable and cost the district considerable money, but neither wanted Farley's friend to reap the benefits of Farley's election to the board. Thus, Farley, Prentice, and Usher all wanted a change in the way the insurance was handled. They did not agree as to what the change should be. Dyke and Scott, with the support of Joyce, wanted no investigation or change in the insurance program. Wilke appeared to have no interest in the matter except that he opposed Farley.

Following the report of the board's committee on insurance, which included a recommendation that a lay citizens' committee be appointed to carry out further investigation and propose a program, it was decided that this committee should complete its work by the next meeting and be dissolved. Farley objected. He wanted a standing insurance committee of the board on which he might serve and to which the lay citizens' committee would report. At the August 17th board meeting, Dyke made the following motion:

> No standing committees shall be appointed or maintained by the Robertsdale Board of Education.[11]

Scott seconded the motion and during the discussion Farley proposed the following amended motion:

---

[11] "Official Minutes . . . ," August 17, 1961.

> The President, with the authority of the board, shall have the authority to appoint any committees, which shall be dissolved when the committee has completed its work.[12]

The amended motion passed unanimously.

At the October 12th meeting the insurance committee of the board was ready to report. Prior to the meeting a five-page recommendation was sent to every board member. The heart of the recommendation was the appointment of a lay committee of six persons with overlapping terms. This committee was directed to (1) make a study of the school district's present insurance, (2) recommend an agent of record for the district, (3) obtain new information on rates, (4) devise a new program, (5) submit a written report to the board, and (6) purchase and supervise insurance as directed by the board. The report contained a statement regarding the duties of the agent of record and policy-writing agents, the types of insurance to be purchased, and the distribution of commissions.

The board, with minor revisions, accepted the recommendation of the committee and directed that "all qualified underwriters be sent a copy of the existing insurance program and asked to make application with the district if they were interested in participating."[13] Information was also released to the newspapers through the school newsletter and posted on P.T.A. bulletin boards.

Prentice objected to an item eliminating participation by anyone but "brokers who live or maintain an office in the school district and shall have been a resident property owner of the district for at least three or more years. . ."[14] His attempt to revise this item met with no success but the minutes note his objection.[15]

The board's insurance committee noted with some displeasure that they felt they had not received full cooperation from the present insurance agents. One of these agents was present at the meeting and stated his views about the newly adopted policies and said he felt all agents had cooperated except on one item because they had not understood the information desired. Having approved the recommendations as policy, Prentice, acting for the board, disbanded the board committee in compliance with the motion of the previous month.[16]

Applications for membership on the lay insurance committee were sought during the weeks between the October board meeting and the

---

12 *Ibid.*
13 "Insurance Program, Robertsdale School District," October 12, 1961.
14 *Ibid.*
15 "Official Minutes . . . ," October 12, 1961.
16 *Ibid.*

meeting of November 9th. At the November meeting Farley moved that Assistant Superintendent Frank begin to equalize the district's insurance business without waiting for recommendations from the committee. The motion received no second.

A representative of a mutual insurance company asked if he could make a statement to the board. The board granted him five minutes to speak. He stated that he objected to the exclusion of mutual companies from participation in the district's program. He indicated that mutual companies could write the same insurance at a lower rate. The board directed that he talk to the lay committee about this matter.

Scott moved with a second by Dyke that Superintendent Joyce be empowered to renew policies that came due before the next meeting. Neither Prentice nor Usher wanted to continue under the present plan but the board was not ready with a new plan. Most of all, they did not want Farley's political friends to gain any business. The motion passed with all except Farley voting in favor of the motion.[17]

At the November meeting Superintendent Joyce reported that fewer than six names had been submitted for appointment to the lay insurance committee. The board deferred action on appointing any members until more names could be obtained. At the December meeting Joyce reported a sufficient list of names but indicated that he thought some of the people were insurance agents. A discussion of whether or not insurance agents should be on the committee insued, and the board asked for additional information before making appointments for the committee.

The Lay Insurance Committee was finally appointed at the January 4th meeting. Each member appointed was required by board action to receive the votes of four board members. The vote was by secret ballot and it required four ballots to elect the six members from the list of eight. As it was a secret ballot, Prentice did not know who voted for whom. He recalls that a person nominated by Farley was not elected. Dyke's old friend, the president of the Republican Club, was also eliminated, with two members (presumably Dyke and Scott) still voting for him. It was directed that the board notify the elected individuals and thank the others for their interest. The committee was to meet with the board on January 11th.

The January 11th meeting with the committee was uneventful. The lay committee received a brief account of the work the board committee had completed prior to its dissolution. They received all written materials including the new insurance policies and a listing of all

---

[17] *Ibid.*, November 9, 1961.

policies in effect. Assistant Superintendent Frank was directed to provide the committee with every assistance, and the meeting adjourned. The meeting evidently left some confusion regarding the duties and powers of the committee. At the February 1st meeting, the board directed Prentice to write a letter "clarifying the position of the Insurance Committee relative to the Board of Education and matters in general. . ." Prentice dictated the letter at the meeting for board approval.[18]

The board had decided not to allow insurance agents to hold membership on the committee in order to guard against a conflict-of-interest situation. This decision was appealed by an agent at the February 14th meeting. The agent felt the exclusion of all those experienced in the insurance business would be detrimental. He was referred to the insurance committee, "as they will be making recommendations to the board. . ."[19]

On March 1st the board approved two recommendations of the committee. One recommended that "Mutual companies may write insurance for the district if other qualifications are met." The other recommended that an agent of record be approved in order to assist the committee in its deliberations. Both were unanimously approved.

Two new members were elected to the board and sworn in on April 5, 1962. These were Mr. Lindzey, former president of the Elm Grove P.T.A. and unsuccessful candidate in 1961, and Mr. Master, resident of Bluffview and close friend of Lindzey and Prentice. Their campaigning and election is described below. At this meeting Prentice was also reelected board president.

Following the reorganization of the board, action on the recommendation of the committee was tabled until the April 23rd meeting to allow the new members time to become familiar with the matter. During the interim, Superintendent Joyce was directed to have ". . . the current writers of insurance write one-year policies covering the builder's risk policies which could be transferred."[20] This covered the new building and additions which the board was having constructed.

The recommendations of the committee were discussed at length at the April 23rd meeting. Several questions were not clarified to the board's satisfaction and the board directed, ". . . that written questions [from board members] shall be submitted to the Insurance Committee for their discussion and within 30 days a special board meeting shall

---

[18] *Ibid.*, February 1, 1962.
[19] *Ibid.*, February 14, 1962.
[20] *Ibid.*, April 5, 1962.

be called for the purpose of meeting jointly with the Insurance Committee representatives to discuss these questions."[21]

Insurance was not discussed at the May 3rd meeting except for a letter from one agent about a specific policy. The letter was referred to the committee. At the June 13th meeting the board directed that the committee meet with them on June 19th in order to discuss the questions submitted to the committee.

A special meeting was convened at 7:45 p.m. on June 19th to discuss the report of the committee. As a result of the discussion, the board decided to obtain bids on the district's insurance, allow nonresident brokers to bid, and affirm their new policy of allowing mutual companies to bid. They directed Assistant Superintendent Frank to prepare bidding specifications with the help of the agent of record.[22] On July 14th, this work was evidently completed because a motion was made and passed to pay the agent of record "$100 for services rendered in preparing the bid specifications. . ."[23] However, at a meeting just three days later the minutes indicated, ". . . the motion which had been tabled July 14th concerning the insurance consultant's fee be put to a vote at this time" passed unanimously. This was followed by a motion to pay the agent of record "$100 for services rendered. . ." Both Dyke and Farley are recorded as opposed to the motion.[24]

There is no explanation for this discrepancy in the board's minutes. Prentice was unable to supply any insight into the matter. It most certainly is additional evidence of the failure of official board minutes to describe the business of school board decision making clearly.

Following the item to pay the agent of record, Farley moved that the adoption of the July 19th board concensus be interpreted as the board's insurance policy. Dyke seconded the motion and Master made a motion for a significant amendment which the insurance committee had proposed. Lindzey seconded this motion. It required that ". . . bidding brokers shall be licensed brokers for at least three years and shall provide records to substantiate this." This amendment barred Farley's friend from bidding. The amendment passed four to two, Farley and Dyke voting against it. The amended motion was then passed with Farley and Dyke voting against it.[25]

Between July 17th and August 14th, bid sheets were sent to qualified bidders. These were opened at the August 14th meeting and

21 *Ibid.*, April 26, 1962.
22 *Ibid.*, June 19, 1962.
23 *Ibid.*, July 14, 1962.
24 *Ibid.*, July 17, 1962.
25 *Ibid.*

immediately turned over to Frank in order that he might prepare summaries for action at the August 23rd meeting.[26]

Prentice was absent from the August 23rd meeting. Dyke left the meeting shortly after 11:00 p.m. in order to go to his job. At about 11:15 Usher, presiding in Prentice's absence, introduced the insurance bids. Two minor bids were accepted by unanimous vote of the four members in attendance totaling only $4,255.21. Lindzey then moved to table the bids until the next meeting. This was unanimously approved. Farley then moved to disband the Lay Insurance Committee but failed to receive a second for his motion.[27]

On September 27, 1962 the board passed a motion, effective October 1, 1962, accepting the low insurance bid on the school buildings in the district as recommended by the insurance committee. Only Dyke voted against the motion. At the October 9th meeting, the superintendent read a memo from the agents who had written the district's insurance prior to September 27th, asking the board to pass a motion that would formally cancel all prior policies, ". . . if that is what the board wants." The following motion was made and seconded:

> That we cancel the existing policies written on a short-term basis and write insurance with Mr. Jones of the Guardian Mutual Insurance Co., authorizing Dr. Frank to notify agents of this action as a representative of the Robertsdale School District.[28]

So a new insurance program and a new set of policies were enacted by the Robertsdale School Board one year, one month, and seven days after the board committee had made its first report and more than two and a half years after the issue was first introduced.

Midmeadows Annexation

Prentice was installed as a board member on April 7, 1960. He voted in favor of ten motions, all passed unanimously, during that meeting. Two weeks later, with no information from Joyce about the issue, Prentice voted against a resolution which would have rejected the annexation of the Midmeadows School District. He voted with Clubb and Wilke, thus deadlocking the board.

It will be recalled from Prentice's diary that Clubb had contacted Prentice prior to the April 21, 1960 meeting and had petitioned his vote in favor of annexation. Between that meeting and the May

---

[26] *Ibid.*, August 14, 1962.
[27] *Ibid.*, August 23, 1962.
[28] *Ibid.*, September 27, 1962.

meeting Prentice gathered data on his own which disproved Superintendent Joyce's contention that the Robertsdale district would have to have split sessions if they annexed. Joyce refused to use the data, and Dyke, Scott, and Mahan refused to consider those data in making a decision.

Following the split vote that deadlocked the board, the *Midwest Morning Star* carried an article urging the Robertsdale Board to reconsider annexation of Midmeadows. Joyce had reported that the 3–3 vote was decisive. The paper questioned, "How can a tie vote be decisive?"[29] What they did not know was that Clubb was backing out. During the insuing month Prentice worked to secure the necessary switch to pass annexation or get the three members to petition the county superintendent to cast the deciding vote. (It was known that the county superintendent favored the annexation.) However, he could obtain neither.

After a pre-meeting executive session on May 5, 1960, it was clear that Robertsdale would not annex Midmeadows at that time. Prentice proposed a motion to turn down annexation which contained a critical phrase he thought would assure annexation in the not too distant future. The motion read in part, ". . . the entire Robertsdale School Board is ready to actively work for and support such annexation after a six-month study. . . ."[30] This motion passed unanimously, and Prentice felt he had lost the battle but won the war. The entire board was publicly committed to work for annexation.

This was Prentice's second meeting. He had a lot to learn about the "politics of education." Neither voting for the motion nor future statements of support committed some board members, nor did the board's vote commit the superintendent.

On October 13th at the regular board meeting, Superintendent Joyce read a letter from the Midmeadows board regarding the need for a traffic light on a major highway that ran through both districts. The secretary of the board was directed to express Robertsdale's willingness to cooperate.[31] Until this time, four months after a motion favoring a six-month study, nothing had been done to advance the annexation.

Regional University undertook a study of the entire county, and Robertsdale agreed to participate. The board committed itselves to its share of the cost.[32] At the December meeting Prentice made a motion asking the Midmeadows district to join in establishing a joint

29 *Midwest Morning Star,* May 4, 1960.
30 "Official Minutes . . . ," May 4, 1960.
31 *Ibid.,* October 13, 1960.
32 *Ibid.,* November 10, 1960.

lay committee ". . . to study the problem of annexation."[33] On February 6th Joyce read a letter from the Midmeadows superintendent requesting a meeting on February 20th. The board directed Joyce to indicate its willingness to attend.[34] The meeting was held and both boards again indicated their hopes for the future annexation of Midmeadows by Robertsdale. As of Prentice's election as board president one year after his initial vote to annex Midmeadows, Prentice felt he was at last on the way toward annexation. He directed Joyce to continue contacts with the Midmeadows board in an effort to get a joint district lay committee together to study the problem.

On June 8, 1961, Prentice could only report ". . . that Midmeadows had been contacted regarding annexation and that later communication would follow after parts of the Regional University Study were completed."[35] At the July meeting he reported ". . . a communication from the Midmeadows Board of Education indicating their desires to delay further discussion on the future annexation of their school district until word from the Regional University Study [was] received.[36] Reports reached Prentice that Dyke and Joyce had informally contacted Midmeadows board members and expressed their opposition to the annexation. No evidence could be found to confirm or deny these reports. The Midmeadows superintendent would only say that he favored action but his board had decided to wait. At any rate, this report would account for the contents of the communication Prentice had received from Midmeadows. As of the April, 1962 election of Robertsdale board members, nothing more had been done. Two years had passed and little, if any, progress had been made. Of those members who had voted on the issue in April, 1960, only Prentice and Dyke remained on the board.

During the spring of 1962 Regional University completed its study. The study supported Robertsdale's annexation of Midmeadows and several other school district annexations in Midwest County. Copies of this report were delivered to Robertsdale board members. The minutes of the September 11th meeting indicate some discussion of the report and a plan for further discussion ". . . when long range plans are discussed." Prentice read a letter from the president of the Midmeadows board ". . . indicating they would meet with the Robertsdale board at 9:00 a.m. on September 22nd to discuss annexation."[37] All members of both boards were present at this meeting. A two-hour

---

[33] *Ibid.*, December 8, 1960.
[34] *Ibid.*, February 9, 1961.
[35] *Ibid.*, June 8, 1961.
[36] *Ibid.*, July 6, 1961.
[37] *Ibid.*, September 11, 1962 and August 23, 1962.

discussion of a possible merger took place. The Midmeadows board seemed to prefer reorganization to annexation because they would then have a chance to be represented on the newly organized board. Most of the Robertsdale board preferred annexation. Prentice indicated that he would resign his seat to provide a place for a Midmeadows board member if that would help accomplish annexation. The Robertsdale board concluded the meeting by unanimously voting that it would "be receptive to a recommendation from the Midmeadows board first for annexation and second, if not for annexation, then for reorganization."[38]

The Robertsdale board was informed at the September 27th meeting that Midmeadows would resubmit the annexation question to its voters in October. The Robertsdale board responded, "The board feels that Robertsdale should give Midmeadows annexation all the support possible since each board member feels that is the right thing for the Robertsdale district to do—the right educational move. Mr. Joyce will prepare a 'Special Newsletter' to be approved Friday night and mailed immediately so that our patrons will be familiar with the board's feelings and have an accurate account of the facts."[39]

Prentice was still laboring under the delusion that public committment would effect voting support on the issue. Such will never be the case, although it may increase the likelihood of obtaining the vote of the public official. Prentice had learned, however, that he could not rely on a superintendent who was at best uncommitted and probably opposed to the issue favored by the school board.

In October, 1962 Midmeadows held a referendum on the annexation. The vote favored annexation by Robertsdale, 394 to 299, about the same margin in favor of annexation as was the case in the 1960 vote.[40]

A large delegation of Robertsdale patrons were present at the October 9th board meeting. They had heard of the approaching Midmeadows vote concerning annexation and wanted to know what their board was going to do. The group was largely composed of residents from Elm Grove but included some of the old-time residents of the district. Elm Grove residents were concerned because they were the nearest neighbors of Midmeadows.[41] The "old-timers" were concerned that their traditional rivals would become a part of their district. By board action, the public was allowed thirty minutes to ask questions

---

[38] *Ibid.*, September 22, 1962.
[39] *Ibid.*, September 27, 1962.
[40] *Midwest Morning Star*, November 16, 1962.
[41] See Chart X.

and make statements about the possible annexation. The entire group appeared to be against annexation.

It is generally the case that groups appearing at school board meetings are opposed to something the school district is doing or about to do. Occasionally they have a positive approach. They may want a change, a substitution in the program. More often, however, they will simply be opposed to something—the budget, the bond issue, the way busses run, or new math. Rarely will a group appear simply to approve board action. This demonstration in opposition is not novel to educational politics; it is often seen in national politics, e.g., anti-Vietnam or anti-poverty program.

As the discussion period ended, the board announced that it would "hold public meetings prior to any action relative to acceptance or rejection of the petition presented by the Midmeadows Board of Education should the people in that area vote in favor of annexation."[42]

At the November 25th board meeting the dates and places of the open meetings were set by the board. There was also a discussion of how the meetings were to be conducted. It was decided that Prentice should run the meetings and speak for the board. Superintendent Joyce asked not to participate. The school district architect was assigned the job of assembling information on building and facility needs, Assistant Superintendent Edmonds was to handle curricular needs, Assistant Superintendent Frank was assigned tax structure and transportation, and the new director of research and guidance was to handle the Regional University Study as it affected annexation.[43]

Meetings were held at the junior high on November 10th and at the senior high school on November 12th. As planned, Prentice chaired the meeting and had the help of the administrative staff in answering questions (with the exception of Joyce). Both meetings were attended by several hundred people. The Elm Grove residents were strongly opposed to annexation. They were concerned that their children would be forced to use the run-down facilities of the Midmeadows High School and that the quality of their education would be lowered.

Some residents of Midmeadows who had fought annexation in their own district attended both meetings. These individuals never identified themselves as Midmeadow residents. They intimated that Midmeadows had a "Negro problem" and had been forced to obtain police protection at several high school dances. (A check of the racial distribution of the districts indicated that Robertsdale had approxi-

---

[42] "Official Minutes . . . ," October 9, 1962.
[43] *Ibid.*, October 25, 1962.

mately 3 percent Negroes and Midmeadows had approximately 5 percent. Both the county police and the Midmeadows police indicated that they had no record of a disturbance at a high school dance. Nor did the Midmeadows administration's records show any such disturbance.) One individual claimed that a certain survey showed that "less soap was sold in Midmeadows than in Robertsdale." The implication was obvious.

The Elm Grove residents challenged the board to place the issue of annexation on the ballot as they had done in 1960. Prentice responded that he would oppose a referendum. He claimed that by law it was the board's responsibility to decide the issue and not an issue to be passed to the electorate. He further stated that if a referendum was held, he would not feel bound by its results.

On this issue there was again an unlikely alliance. *Politics makes strange bedfellows* is as true for educational politics as any other kind of politics. Elm Grove residents had always supported Prentice and the two new board members, Lindzey and Master. These two vehemently opposed both Dyke and Farley. Now Elm Grove residents favored only Lindzey and Master and fought Prentice on the issue of annexation.

Prentice and residents of Elm Grove had several informal discussions about Midmeadows. The difference in viewpoints clearly centered on the issue of the good of education in the long run as opposed to the immediate good for children in Elm Grove. There seemed to be no disagreement if they could agree to concentrate on one rather than the other, but they could not. Prentice insisted his duty as a board member was to support quality education for the total electorate and he could not show favoritism in one area even if that area supported him on other issues. He said, "You can buy Farley. He'll vote the way you tell him. Why not elect six Farleys? Then you can tell the board to do just as you like. That is not what you elected when you elected me." While the Elm Grove residents agreed that they did not want six Farleys, they could not be convinced that the annexation of Midmeadows was a good thing. Prentice could not be convinced otherwise.

On November 13, 1962 Prentice achieved his goal of two years and seven months. By a vote of four to two, with Dyke and Farley still opposed, Midmeadows was annexed by Robertsdale.[44] Immediately the Elm Grove group who had opposed annexation pledged continued support of the board in their effort to achieve quality education.

---

[44] *Midwest County Bugle*, November 15, 1962.

It is noted again that public commitment in the form of a statement or pledge to support a political action is no guarantee of the vote of a politician. Both Dyke and Farley on numerous occasions had pledged their support for annexation. Perhaps by their vote they were trying to gain the favor of Elm Grove, an area that had not supported them. Perhaps Dyke was merely showing his continued support of the "old community." Motivation is hard to pinpoint. Voting behavior is not. Both voted against annexation and in opposition to numerous statements indicating they would support it.

The School Board Election of April, 1962

Prentice's election in 1960 and the election of 1961 have been described. One will recall that Prentice's successful campaign in 1960 was followed by a failure to elect either of the candidates he supported in 1961. He determined not to make the mistake of losing by being passive again. If he was to lose again, Prentice would lose because he had campaigned, not because he stayed in the background. Such a defeat would be more visible but would be one that Prentice could accept.

Wilke had decided, in spite of Prentice's opposition, to run for his fourth three-year term. Scott had decided not to run for reelection. Clubb, having suffered defeat in 1961 with Prentice's passive support, decided to run again. Wilke and Clubb wanted Prentice's support. Both had minimally supported Prentice's goals. Prentice had learned, however, that he could not count on either. Wilke had voted for the extension of Joyce's contract after agreeing not to do so. Clubb, after petitioning Prentice's support for Midmeadows in 1960, had pulled out. On several occasions each had failed to be present to vote on important issues. Both were more interested in the noneducational aspects of the program than Prentice was (e.g., custodians, secretaries, bus drivers, and buildings). Neither was as interested in the educational program as Prentice. Clubb was from the St. Joseph area, the area from which Usher and Farley were elected in 1961. If he had been elected, three of the six board members would come from the same area. Although Wilke was from the Elm Grove area, he did not typify the norms of the area. In addition, he was known in Elm Grove and Bluffview as a heavy drinker. Prentice refused to support either of these men and told them so. Instead, he asked Lindzey and Master to run again. After some persuasion, each agreed.

While the P.T.A. groups and their executive council could not take a position favoring any candidate, they could and did invite candidates to speak. Both Lindzey and Master were very verbal and made a good presentation at these meetings. The leaders of the executive council of the P.T.A. formed an unaffiliated group called C.A.R.E. (Council to Accelerate Robertsdale Education). Prentice was the initiator of this group. His sole intent in doing so was to formulate political action to support and elect what he considered "good" school board candidates.

For some time Prentice had publicly expressed his disapproval of individuals serving on the board for an extended period of time. He also opposed the procedures established by the board that tended to perpetuate incumbents. At the January 4th meeting Dyke read the names of three individuals who had filed for election to the board. They were Wilke, Clubb, and Sail, a resident of St. Joseph who had run Usher's campaign in 1961. The board voted March 1, 1962 as the closing date for candidates to file for the April 4, 1962 election.[45]

The next motion proposed by Scott and seconded by Farley was the type that perpetuated incumbents and one that Prentice had opposed for two years. It read: ". . . that the election ballots for the Robertsdale Board of Education be printed with the incumbents' names appearing first and all other candidates following in alphabetical order."[46] It is well known that the candidate who heads the ballot is in a position of advantage. Individuals going to the polls to vote for one candidate but not knowing what to do with their other vote will most often vote for the candidates who head the list. This fact does not go unnoticed by incumbents in educational politics. Prentice made some comments opposing the motion but they were to no avail. Every board member except Prentice voted for the motion.

Another practice that had the 'flavor' of incumbent control of school board elections was one which allowed incumbent candidates or members of the administrative staff to pick up the ballot boxes at the polling places and deliver them to the board room for official canvassing. Prentice had been working informally with the board to get this practice changed. At the February 1st meeting Dyke introduced a motion directing the payment of an extra two dollars to one judge and one clerk at each polling place to deliver the ballot boxes. The motion passed four to two with Farley and Usher voting against the motion.[47]

---

[45] Official Minutes of the Robertsdale Board of Education, January 4, 1962.
[46] *Ibid.*
[47] *Ibid.*, February 1, 1962.

Upon Prentice's recommendation both Lindzey and Master waited until the last minute to file for election. In the meantime, another Bluffview resident phoned Prentice, indicated his desire to run for the board, and asked for Prentice's support. Prentice had known the man as the chairman of the Bluffview Recreation Committee and was not impressed with his work. Prentice said that he had already committed his support to two other candidates, one from Bluffview, and that another Bluffview candidate would split the Bluffview vote. Upon Prentice's suggestion, the man agreed not to file. The final list of candidates included the original three—Clubb, Wilke, and Sail—plus Lindzey, Master, Weiss (another candidate from the old Robertsdale area), and Shuster (a school teacher who lived in the St. Joseph area who had solicited Prentice's support).[48]

During the month of March the CARE organization interviewed candidates wishing their support. They chose to support Lindzey and Master. Both men had better educational and business backgrounds than the other candidates. There is some doubt as to whether CARE could have supported another candidate. Prentice had established CARE to support outstanding candidates. Prentice had the obligation of presenting acceptable candidates and CARE owed their allegiance to support them.

Neighborhood coffees were given to introduce Lindzey and Master to the voters in four areas of the district.

The final "Meet the Candidates" meeting was held at the junior high school on the night before the election. During this meeting Clubb, who was supposedly working with Wilke for reelection, told Prentice, "Tomorrow we'll show you how to run a campaign. I'll bet you ten dollars we beat the pants off your boys." Prentice responded, "You're the politician. I'll just wait and see." Prentice knew that Clubb and Wilke had also promised to support at least one candidate other than Becker. This candidate was Usher's friend.

On April 3rd the people of Robertsdale cast their ballots. The results of this election appear in Chart XVIII.

There are two ways to analyze an election. One method attempts to explain what was done to achieve victory for the winners. The other asks why the losers failed. Of course, both questions have relevance. CARE was an obvious success, but several other factors must be considered. True to their board voting behavior, neither Clubb nor Wilke lived up to their agreement to totally support the other. In addition, there were three candidates from the St. Joseph area running

---

[48] *Ibid.*, February 28, 1962.

Chart XVIII

THE SCHOOL BOARD ELECTION OF APRIL 3, 1962

Candidates*	Absentee	Bluffview	Mt. Olive	Robertsdale	Blue Ridge	St. Joseph	Elm Grove	TOTAL
Wilke	0	36	135	119	31	101	166	588
Sail (Usher's friend)	0	34	34	166	24	75	16	349
Shuster (teacher)	0	63	51	94	20	75	30	305
Lindzey** (Prentice's candidate)	3	342	55	119	60	95	270	944
Clubb	1	27	46	147	53	283	14	521
Masters** (Prentice's candidate)	8	388	62	192	90	135	219	1090

* These are not in alphabetical order because of the code names used in this case. They were alphabetical on the ballot with the exception of Wilke, the incumbent.
** Won election.

for the two available seats. This situation had to split the St. Joseph vote. In addition, there were already two residents from St. Joseph on the board. Voters from other areas must have considered this. Because other groups were fragmented, the CARE group could win.

On April 5, 1962 Lindzey and Master were sworn in as members of the Robertsdale Board of Education.[49] These two men would provide welcome support for Prentice until the time of his resignation.

Selection of a New Principal

One additional episode took place shortly after the 1962 board election. As is the case in most school districts, the board seldom questions the superintendent's recommendations for employment. Thus, a high school assistant principal is hired without much concern on the part of the board. Late in the spring of 1962, Principal Brook died. The board indicated to Joyce that they wanted several names presented to them for consideration as candidates for principal. On June 19th

---

[49] *Ibid.,* April 5, 1962.

the minutes indicate the beginning of an unpleasant series of events that finally made Prentice decide that there was no hope of improvement as long as Joyce was superintendent.

Never before had Joyce volunteered any information about the educational program of the district. In fact, he had consistently resisted the efforts of board members who wanted such information. On June 19th "Mr. Joyce presented each member of the Board of Education with a catalogue [a 98-page mimeographed book] compiled by the high school staff concerning curriculum, etc." While the minutes correctly show that the book was a total school effort, Mr. Golden, assistant high school principal, was cited as the author, and Joyce gave him verbal credit for the work.

Joyce followed his presentation by recommending Golden for promotion to high school principal without presenting any other names to the board. Golden had a Master of Science degree from Southern State College. He had limited experience in school administration. Dyke moved acceptance of Joyce's recommendation and Farley seconed. The motion lost with Prentice, Usher, Lindzey, and Master voting against. This is followed by the following editorial comment in the minutes.

> Several members expressed the idea that they were not voting against Mr. Golden but rather against the practice of presenting only one name for consideration. They requested that several people, after applications are screened by the President and school administration, be requested to appear before the board so that the board may decide which of the candidates they feel should be employed. The board requested that Mr. Joyce request Mr. Golden make application for the position. The Board suggested that, in the future, any person employed as an assistant should be cognizant of the fact that, should their immediate supervisor vacate his position, they will not, necessarily, succeed him.[50]

Joyce had successfully won this battle more than twenty-five years earlier. The reader will recall that Chod was appointed principal over the objection of some board members. At that time the president of the board had resigned. With considerable pride Joyce had told Prentice that he had not taken the job as superintendent until the board had agreed to approve his recommendations for professional positions. For twenty-five years it appeared that Joyce had had his way. To fight

---

[50] *Ibid.*, June 19, 1962.

this fight again was like taking a step twenty-five years into the past, and this time he lost the fight. Whether or not one agrees with Joyce's behavior, one tends to sympathize with him.

After Principal Brook's death and before the June meeting, several residents had contacted Prentice to ask if he would consider becoming high school principal. He indicated that he had not given it any thought but did not think he was interested. The group also contacted Usher, Lindzey, and Master. Some of the people were at the June 19th meeting and asked to be recognized. Lindzey moved that ten minutes be provided to hear the delegation. Farley seconded and the motion passed unanimously.

Following their petition that Prentice be selected as the new principal, the minutes record, "After much discussion from the floor and the board, Mr. Prentice stated that under no circumstances would he become a candidate for the senior high principalship of this district."[51]

During the following month Prentice worked with Joyce in screening numerous applications for the position of principal. These individuals were selected as candidates for the board to interview at the July meeting.

On July 17, 1962, the board met to interview the selected candidates. Joyce indicated that Golden had submitted his resignation as assistant principal and the board unanimously accepted the resignation. The board agreed to conduct the interviews of the candidates in open session. The minutes fail to indicate that Superintendent Joyce and both assistant superintendents were present during the interviews. Following the interviews the board adjourned to executive session to discuss the candidates and make a decision. Again Joyce and the assistant superintendents were present and participated. (This fact was clarified in a correction to the minutes of July 17th that was initiated by Prentice at the July 26th meeting.) After some discussion Joyce and the board agreed on a candidate who had nearly completed his doctorate at a well-known out-of-state university. The minutes indicate that the board desired ". . . to hire Mr. O'Neil with the strong recommendation that he continue work on his doctorate."[52] Again it took an amendment to the minutes to establish the fact that the board's action came only "after consultation with the superintendent and his indication that Mr. O'Neil was his choice for high school principal."[53]

---

51 *Ibid.*
52 *Ibid.,* July 17, 1962.
53 *Ibid.,* July 26, 1962.

On July 19th an article appeared on the second page of the metropolitan morning daily stating that Mr. Golden had charged Prentice with unprofessional conduct and with eliminating him from the principalship because Prentice himself wanted the job. When the paper contacted Joyce for verification, Joyce refused to comment in spite of the fact that the minutes had already carried Prentice's statement that under no circumstances would he be a candidate.[54]

This letter was followed five days later by a letter written by Master to the editor of the same paper. In this letter Master attempted to counter the charge of unprofessional conduct:

> Nothing could be further from the truth. . . . Mr. Prentice is not seeking nor has he ever sought the position in question . . . his professional and ethical conduct are above reproach.[55]

Prentice's attorney called Golden and indicated that legal action would be instituted if Golden did not retract his statement. Golden claimed that he had not initiated the statement (although he would not say who did) and that he had claimed that Prentice's action *may* have been unprofessional. He further stated that he now believed that Prentice had not acted unprofessionally and agreed to write letters to the newspaper and the board stating that fact. The paper never published Golden's retraction, but Golden's letter was entered into the minutes of the August 14th meeting.[56] At this same time a letter from Joyce was also read stating that he had refused to make any public comment about the affair because he had felt it better for the school district if he remained silent.

Superintendent Joyce's Resignation

The motives of a man are difficult to determine. When Prentice ran for the Robertsdale School Board, he avoided the appearance of running in order to fire Joyce. He invited Joyce to the meeting that launched Prentice's candidacy. Throughout his first year as board member, he consistently opposed Joyce's method of operation but continued to supply Joyce with information that Prentice hoped would bring about change. Prentice never proposed that Joyce should be relieved of his superintendency.

---

[54] *Midwest Morning Star,* July 19, 1962.
[55] *Ibid.,* July 26, 1962.
[56] "Official Minutes . . . ," August 14, 1962.

During the next year Prentice continued to attempt to secure change without removing Joyce. Farley was more opposed to Joyce than he was to Prentice when he was first elected. Likewise, Usher opposed Joyce's administration long before he was elected to the board, nor was Wilke one of Joyce's supporters. As president, Prentice could have mobilized a 4–2 vote against Joyce.

The majority of school superintendents are performing a valuable service to their communities and school boards. Too often good superintendents are fired by narrowly oriented and vindictive school boards. For this reason superintendents, good and bad, have built up a system that tends to protect them.

Most school superintendents operate on a three-year contract. Contracts are usually extended each year. A board must fail to renew the superintendent's contract for three years before they can remove him. Other alternatives are open to a school board. The board can "retire" the superintendent, or they can "buy" his contract, or they can move him to the side (allowing him to keep the title) and hire an assistant to take over the important functions of the office. A board must be quite tenacious to remove a superintendent, even a poor superintendent. In addition, the superintendent has two years (after the first failure to have his contract renewed) to get men elected to the board who support him. Perhaps Prentice was not as "moral" as he was practical.

During his first two years in office Prentice had considerable provocation for not wanting Joyce to continue as superintendent. On the first Midmeadows vote Joyce refused to consider the data Prentice had collected on the Midmeadows pupil population. Regarding the school calendar, Joyce refused to modify his position even though it violated state law. He refused to provide code numbers for bills or teacher qualifications. He refused for a period of a year to supply agenda prior to meetings, and it took three months for Prentice to get to see the teachers' handbook. It was more than a year before Prentice was allowed to see a policy manual. Joyce also battled Prentice about the teacher salary committee and long range plans for the district.

It should be noted that the usual refusal by a superintendent is in the form of failing to comply rather than overt refusal. Thus, there is no provable insubordination, only the frustration of the school board member. The implication here is not that the majority of school superintendents operate in this way, but those who do oppose the will of the board often use this method of "vetoing" the board's decision.

During the time when Prentice was president of the board, Joyce almost completely removed himself from the usual leadership function of the superintendent. He failed to take any part in the tax elections of 1961, he refused to assist or take a stand in the annexation of Midmeadows (1962), and he refused to formulate organizational plans for the expansion of Robertsdale. After eighteen months, when Prentice had presented an organizational plan, Joyce publicly accused Prentice of unprofessional conduct.

Several other items may be recalled that brought the retention of Joyce as superintendent into question. His handling of the bills, his recommendation of an additional $1000 for his secretary just a few months before their marriage, and his refusal to adhere to policy and remove her after their marriage have already been recounted.

From his initial campaign, Prentice had contended that most board members served longer than they should and that he would not run for a second term. Thus, Prentice was a "lame duck" president with but seven months to serve. He now committed himself to the accomplishment of two tasks before the seven months expired. One was the annexation of Midmeadows. The second was the "retirement" of Superintendent Joyce.

Joyce's employment situation was as follows. In spite of the agreement not to bring up the subject of Joyce's contract renewal, during the last part of the March 9, 1961 meeting Scott moved that Joyce's contract be extended. Both Prentice and Clubb voted against the motion. (Prentice later voted yes in an effort to prevent board dissent.)

The March 3, 1961 meeting was just one month before the school board election. This was the usual time for the incumbent board to extend the superintendent's contract on the chance that an incumbent might lose. Any insurgents would arrive on the board to find that they must wait three years to do anything about the superintendent's contract and the superintendent would have two years to get his board back. Unfortunately this practice protects good and bad superintendents alike.

The 1961–62 board had not taken any action to extend Joyce's contract. At least three members—Prentice, Usher, and Farley—could have been counted on to vote against such a proposal. Prentice thought he could have mobilized enough support to include Wilke, thus pushing Joyce to the side. Still Joyce had two years to go on his present contract when Lindzey and Master came on the board. He would still have one year to serve after Prentice left the board. Prentice now began a campaign to secure Joyce's official resignation.

Prentice let it be known that Joyce would receive no contract extension and that there was considerable thrust to remove him prior to the end of his present contract. Prentice, however, indicated that he felt he could secure an agreement not to move against Joyce before the end of his present contract and, in addition, hire him as a consultant to the board for two years at his present salary. Such an agreement would depend upon Joyce's submitting his resignation at the termination of his present contract. The early resignation would provide time to hire an executive assistant superintendent to work with him during his last year and time for the board to conduct a full year's search for a new superintendent. As Joyce was sixty and had one year to go on his existing contract, the additional two years would bring Joyce within the legal retirement age (without financial penalty). For this action Prentice had the clear support of Lindzey, Master, Usher, and perhaps Farley.

Prentice did not trust Joyce to carry out a verbal resignation nor hire his successor. Therefore, it was agreed that Joyce submit his resignation in writing effective one and a half years hence, indicating the necessity of lead time in order to procure a suitable replacement. Further, it was agreed that Midwest University would be employed to study the organization and make recommendations to the board regarding the executive assistant superintendent who was to be employed.

On October 25th, these goals were accomplished. Joyce submitted a letter indicating his intention to retire at the termination of his present contract. The board then directed that a study be initiated under the direction of Midwest University.[57] After studying the district, the university was to submit a list of candidates for administrative posts. The bell was tolling the end of Joyce's reign. Midmeadows had voted in favor of annexation. Robertsdale was within weeks of completing that merger. On November 13, 1962 the evening that the Robertsdale board accepted the Midmeadows annexation, Prentice submitted his resignation as he had indicated he would. This said in part:

> It has been public knowledge for some time that I did not intend to run again for a seat on this board. As I have stated, my reason for this decision was based on my firm belief that no man should serve for such a length of time as to appear indispensable or gain too much power. Since the annexation of Midmeadows dissolves their board and since such annexation, I believe, can be more harmoniously accomplished if that group is represented on the Robertsdale board, I am willing to step aside to allow one of the members of the Midmeadows board a place on this board.
>
> It is with the firm conviction that no man is indispensable and that our school district, which now includes Midmeadows, has many dedicated, honest, and intelligent men who can and will

---

[57] *Ibid.*, October 25, 1962.

serve with distinction on the board, that I offer my resignation as
president and member of the Robertsdale School Board, effective
November 15, 1962.[58]

One can ask if the "resignation" action against a superintendent
who had served for over twenty-five years was justified. Prentice had
acted only after Joyce had accused him in a board meeting of unprofessional conduct because Prentice had submitted tentative plans for
organizational expansion. Although Prentice had been asking Joyce to
do this for more than two years and Joyce had not complied, Joyce
still felt the board should stay out of "administrative matters." This is a
central tenant in the myth system of all superintendents. Joyce believed it! The question remains how long and under what circumstances a school board believes it.

After two and a half years of trying to get things done without
removing Joyce, a new high school principal was to be hired. The
board had asked Joyce to present the names of several candidates.
Joyce had refused and the board rejected Joyce's candidate, asking
Prentice to screen additional candidates. This resulted in newspaper
publicity that was upsetting to Prentice. Joyce refused to publicly
support Prentice just as he had refused to publicly support the 1961
tax levy and the annexation of Midmeadows. At this point, Prentice
decided to act.

Was Prentice acting in a vindictive manner or was he acting because
a final straw had broken the camel's back? Who can really know? Not
even Prentice! In Robertsdale, as in other school districts where these
authors have gotten experience, it seems that many school boards
continue for long periods of time with superintendents who fail to
respond to their legislative bodies. The myth says that superintendents
are in a very precarious position, being fired at the whim of any board.
In actual practice, it is not always easy to get rid of a superintendent,
even an incompetent superintendent. School boards are composed of
lay persons and generally neither has the time nor the skill to evaluate
their chief executive officer. Most boards, therefore, fall into one of
two categories. They either fail to evaluate and take action, or they do
a bad job of it, often losing good superintendents.

ANALYSIS: THE PRESIDENTIAL YEARS

So far most of the hypotheses generated from the model originally
presented in Chapter 4 have been used to better understand the

---

[58] *Ibid.,* November 13, 1962.

Robertsdale case. This section of the case has further substantiated most of the hypotheses but has failed to deal with Hypothesis 12. This will be done in the next chapter. Here the main concern is with Hypothesis 11, which deals with the conflict between the new leadership and the old superintendent. The title of this chapter provides the analysis for this section of the case. With apologies to Daniel, it spells out three steps in the political process of local school districts. Given the changes in the social system of the community, *Mene*—the people have measured the superintendent's administration of the schools and set about to change it by defeating an incumbent board member. Given the superintendent's resistance to the changes initiated by the new board member (and here is the focus of the chapter), *Tekel*—the superintendent is evaluated and found incapable of providing the leadership for change desired by the new power group. Finally, given the power to remove the superintendent, *Peres*—even with the ouster of the superintendent, the instability of the district remains, dividing the power between the insurgents and the old guard, who war with one another for control until a new steady state is established. This is the focus in Chapter 8.

The first word of the prophesy completes the course for old superintendents. The people ". . . have numbered thy kingdom and finished it." *And finished it!* The fight is over, and only he and the board, including Prentice in the Robertsdale case, do not know it. Once the conditions exist that allow an incumbent to be defeated, there is so little likelihood that the system can be self-correcting that one can safely predict the result—superintendent turnover.[59] In Robertsdale it took Prentice some time to come to the conclusion and longer to effect the change. Four major issues wove in and out through the fabric of social events to bring about this result: the tax election of 1961, the insurance program, the Midmeadows annexation, and the board election of 1962.

The Tax Election of 1961

For a year Prentice attempted to instigate procedures to allow the schools to better communicate with the electorate. He had urged that the tax reduction during the summer of 1960 be given extensive coverage so that people might understand the tax increase Prentice foresaw for 1961. Under Joyce's leadership, nothing was done. There

---

[59] Some exceptions exist and are discussed later in this chapter.

was virtually no publicity about the tax reduction and almost none prior to the tax election of 1961. In spite of continuing motions passed by the board, nothing was done to communicate more frequently or more adequately with the public. The tactic is one still recommended by some professors of educational administration—keep things quiet and hope. The problem is that, while the superintendent and the board can remain quiet, they can in no way be assured that other groups opposed to the issue will also keep quiet.

In Robertsdale's 1961 election a candidate was running on an efficiency platform who had the active support of the Democratic Club. It is strange how fickle party politics can be. The Republicans or their disinherited ultraconservative third cousins usually appear in this guise in educational politics.

In spite of what the superintendent did or did not do, it was not a quiet election. Furthermore, it was the anti-school or at least anti-tax people who were stimulated to vote. Thus, the tax failed to receive a majority vote and had to be proposed twice more before it passed. During these considerations, Joyce never made a recommendation to the total board. It is likely that he made suggestions to Dyke and the old guard, but he did nothing he was not specifically directed to do in order to pass the tax. Just days out of the hospital, Prentice bore the brunt of a long and bitter struggle to pass a tax to support quality education in the district.

To some extent the tax referendum of 1961 drew the elements of the old guard and the insurgents closer together. While the old guard is usually not for large expenditures or rapid curriculum change, it usually is for education. In Robertsdale both segments saw Farley and his opposition to the tax as opposition to education. This may well have been a misconception, but it probably served to unite the two factions against Farley. What the experience did not do was raise Prentice's evaluation of Joyce and his leadership ability.

Finally, the political process that passed the levy on the third try, although not the focus of the book, is worth considering. The tactics the political party used to elect Farley, and probably to help defeat the tax, were also used by the pro-tax people. Handbills were distributed, newspapers were used to stimulate pro-voters and place anti-voters in cross-pressure, the radio was utilized, telephone canvasses were instituted, voter lists and poll watchers were used, and newsletters were sent by the schools. The tax passed on the third try.

In the first referendum the yes vote did not number differently from other referenda when the tax had passed. But the additional no votes had overwhelmed the yes voters. In the second referendum the yes votes increased one and a half times and the no vote decreased, but again the levy failed. The yes vote increased significantly in the third submission, the no vote showed only a slight increase, and the levy passed. This suggests that the general notions about school referenda might be incorrect. The simple increase in votes that resulted in defeats, as Carter suggests,[60] does not appear to be a factor here. It was the very action of keeping quiet in the hope that the vote would stay low which allowed the no voters to overwhelm the yes voters, who were in an actual majority. The reasoning went like this:

1) There is a stability in any school district in the voting behavior of the electorate in school referenda.
2) This stable pattern consistently passes the referenda.
3) Due to the nature of the politics of education, the first up-swing of votes upsetting this stability will result in referendum defeat.
4) The vast majority of this first increase will represent no voters, probably all the no voters in the district.
5) When the same tax is finally passed through subsequent submissions, the total vote will increase even further. This increase will almost totally be represented by yes voters.

Spinner[61] tested these notions in New York State and found them valid. Again the case study produced a fruitful hypothesis which when tested in another geographic locale was found to be correct. Additional studies concerning the parallels between voter behavior in partisan elections and school elections warranted. Based on such studies, it is likely that the notion that political theory is irrelevant to educational politics will be further invalidated.

The Insurance Program

The second issue that helped convince Prentice that progress could not be made in Robertsdale until Joyce left the superintendency was the matter of the district's insurance program. Joyce had always functioned, prior to Prentice's election, as business manager as well as

---

60 Richard F. Carter, *Voters and Their Schools,* (Stanford, California: Stanford University Press, 1960).
61 Arnold Spinner, "The Effects of the Extent of Voter Participation Upon Election Outcomes in School Budget Elections in New York State 1957-1966" (Unpublished Ph.D. dissertation, New York University, 1967).

superintendent of schools. At the time of Prentice's election, one of the major issues before the board was the matter of long overdue unprocessed bills. Joyce's secretary, later to become his wife, knew more about these business affairs than Joyce did. As evidence of this, Joyce had to call her after their marriage to straighten out the matter of contracts for noncertified personnel that he had handled incorrectly.

Along with other business matters, Joyce had handled the insurance matters of the district for many years. During the period of switching the business affairs to Frank, the newly employed assistant superintendent for business, Joyce recommended some changes in the insurance procedures that he felt might result in a savings to the district. The board asked him to investigate the matter and suggested a lay committee might be of assistance to him. Between the period of September 8, 1960, when the issue first appears in the board minutes, and the election of April, 1961, several verbal reports were given to the board but no changes or apparent progress toward change occurred.

Following the election of Farley and Usher, a board committee was appointed that included these two men and assistant superintendent Frank. Both board members had a special interest in the insurance program. Farley apparently had some political debts to pay. Prior to his election, Usher had shown interest in the lay committee, which was never formed. Between April and August a study of the insurance policies was made, and the board voted to place the insurance on a bid basis upon a recommendation from the committee.

Apparently the insurance business was patterned after the politics of the district. While the district bought more than $3,000,000 worth of insurance, all but $96,000 of that business was placed with four agents. These agents happened to be the same ones whom Dyke and Joyce used personally. One should not infer that anything dishonest is involved. There is no evidence of dishonesty. As one respondent in the case expressed it, "It's just a matter of friendship." All the agents were long-time residents of the district. In an effort to change the situation the board proposed and appointed a lay committee to study the problem and make recommendations. Again there were different motives apparent in the voting patterns of board members on this issue. Often Usher, Prentice, and Wilke voted with Farley. These votes favored changes in the policy regarding insurance. However, there was clear evidence that Farley wanted to give a large portion of the insurance business to one of his political party friends, whatever else he may have wished. Usher, Dyke, Prentice, and perhaps Wilke had no intention of doing that. Four members united for change against

Scott and Dyke who preferred the same general policy the district had been using. After the decision to change had been made, Prentice, Usher, and Wilke voted with Dyke and Scott against Farley to prevent what they considered a political payoff.

As of April 5, 1962, nineteen months after the issue had arisen, no change in actual insurance coverage had been made. A board committee had studied the insurance problems of the district and reported. A lay committee was formulating recommendations for change based on the report of the board committee. Two policy changes had occurred that were to effect changes in the district's insurance coverage: (1) the district's insurance would be placed on a bid basis, and (2) mutual companies could bid.

Following the April, 1961 election, Prentice had two additional votes he could count on—Lindzey's and Master's. By mid-July the lay committee had completed its report and the board had accepted it. Scott was no longer on the board, having chosen not to run for reelection. It was too late when Dyke recognized that he and Farley had been end-played on the insurance issue. Neither would get what they wanted. Farley could not get increased business for his party allies and Dyke was not going to prevent a change that would cost his friends the insurance they were now writing. On July 19th Farley moved the adoption of a policy that eliminated brokers outside the district but allowed agents within the district not holding broker's licenses to bid. Dyke seconded the motion. Master proposed an amendment requiring all bidders to have a broker's license and Lindzey seconded the amendment. Both the amendment and the amended motion passed with Farley and Dyke voting against both. Both men had lost. Dyke's friends could or would not bid against other brokers. Farley's friend was not a licensed broker. Without Scott's vote they could not stop the action.

In early October new insurance was written for the district and the old policies were cancelled. The fight had taken two years and saved the district $20,000 over the three- to five-year coverage provided by the new package. Farley, who admitted he lost his fight, still took credit for changing the insurance program claiming, "I started the insurance kick." He gave no credit to the lay committee and said, "It slows down board action on fundamentals."[62] The lay committee had certainly slowed Farley down. His friend not only got no more insurance but lost the $80,000 she had written for the district previously.

---

[62] Interview with Mr. Farley during the selection of an executive assistant early in 1963.

The bitterness between Prentice and Farley grew even greater. Board meetings were growing longer and occasionally unpleasant. Prentice and others on the board were beginning to ask again the question Dyke had posed at Prentice's second meeting as a board member: "If we can't take the superintendent's recommendation, I don't see why we have him here." Two years earlier Joyce had suggested a minor insurance change. For twenty-four months the board waited, formed a board committee, a lay committee, debated, investigated, and finally saved the district $20,000. During this time Joyce did nothing. Unable to act with the new power group, unwilling to act against his friends in the old group, he sat on the sidelines. The board began to ask, "Why do we have him here?"

There is another side to the story, however. After the tax referendum Prentice decided to institute change and apparently had the support to do it. When he moved, it was in the direction he believed correct. The $20,000 saved over three years on the insurance program was less than one-tenth of the budget. Was it worth all that trouble? Could that one-tenth of one per cent have bought Farley and in turn educational gain for the district? A good politician asks such questions. Prentice did not. He thought of himself as a statesman who would not compromise. He knew what was right and he moved to do it. If a train is coming down the track and you can't join it—get off the track. That is exactly what Joyce did. Such a move presents a problem to the old superintendent who cannot emotionally join the new power group. Unwilling to either confront or cooperate with the new group, he steps aside by failing to do either. Once he removes himself from the advisement function, it is only a matter of time until the board recognizes that fact and makes it official.

Based on the above analysis, there are three roles a superintendent may choose when confronted by incumbent defeat: (1) he may assess the power shift and decide to join it, (2) he may assess the power shift and decide to oppose it, and (3) he may remove himself from the situation by not recommending anything and let the board fight it out. If he chooses option 1, he bets on the new shift. If the superintendent is very capable, he may shift his recommendations just enough to co-opt the new member and then wait. If the new power wins again, he can shift again. Thus, he reduces his chance of making a wrong choice. But in reality it is difficult for a superintendent to change his allegiance from the group and the policies that have served him for fifteen or twenty years. Choice 2 and 3 are then open to him. Option 2 may provide a win for both the superintendent and the old guard group. But if he does not win quickly, if the new group is

powerful enough to survive that attack, then the superintendent loses
quickly and surely. Since most superintendents are conservative in
nature, they will choose option 3. It may even appear to be option 1
for a short time, but it is not. Unfortunately for the superintendent this
action is almost sure to cost him his job. By removing himself from the
contest, he supports no one and no policy. He himself chooses not to
be superintendent and over a period of time everyone notices that fact
and it becomes official. Such reasoning may account for the deviant
case in the studies of superintendent turnover reported in Chapter 8.

The Midmeadows Annexation

This issue lasted throughout Prentice's tenure as a board member.
From the first meeting Prentice attended, he supported annexation and
worked to accomplish it. Ever since that first meeting the old guard
with Joyce's cooperation fought against the annexation and often used
information so incorrect as to appear deliberately dishonest. The old
guard board members and Joyce publicly supported the idea of annexation but consistently opposed it with their votes and actions.
There is little need to review this issue extensively. Joyce's role was
not different from his role in the insurance issue except that his action
in supplying necessary information to the board was much more overt.
He supplied information and recommendations during the early stages,
but the information was incorrect and the recommendations precon-
ceived. Finally, at least in public, he stepped back and let the board
fight out the issue. In this issue Joyce and the old guard were acting
against the general educational recommendations of county, state, and
national educators; thus, the inaction and subversion was even more
distasteful to Prentice. In the last analysis it was Prentice and the new
majority of the board who had to carry the load and take action without the support, help, or cooperation of Joyce. The superintendent was
useless, or even worse—an obstruction to the majority wishes of the
board.

The Board Election of 1962

No direct influence of Joyce could be seen in the 1962 election.
Prentice increased his power with the election of the two candidates
whom he had "selected." Still Joyce failed to modify his behavior.
Perhaps it was already too late, but Prentice does not recall it that

way. The insurance issue was not settled, nor was the issue of the Midmeadows annexation. There was still time for Joyce to demonstrate that he would support the changes desired by the new power group. He refused to act, moving further and further out of the picture. Since the campaign of April, 1960, five of the six board members had been replaced, three by incumbent defeat. Three of these replacements were clearly Prentice men; another was an insurgent. The fifth man, Farley, liked Joyce even less than the insurgents. Only Dyke remained as a supporter of Joyce and the old guard. Even Belshazzar could have read the handwriting on the wall, but Joyce could not.

Perhaps concepts from learning theory can account for Joyce's failure to modify his behavior. Twenty-five years before, Joyce had gone against the recommendation of powerful segments of the community by recommending Chod as principal. He quickly modified his behavior, however, and built strong linkages into the religious and business sectors of the community. These had served him well for more than twenty years. As with all individual human behavior, learning proceeded due to consistent reinforcement by primary reinforcers. But over the years the reinforcers became linked with secondary reinforcers, sometimes many times removed from the primary reinforcers. In addition, the reinforcement schedule became one of variable ratio. A man is not reinforced for every response. He forgets how many rewards are required before a reinforcement is forthcoming. Many secondary rewards are available that are at least as reinforcing as the original primary reward. Some of these, like a pat on the back, or the friendship of old acquaintances, occur almost by chance and are linked with some overt response. They are not intended as reinforcers to action but are taken as such, many times unconsciously, by the actor. Thus, it is difficult to teach old dogs new tricks. This is another way of saying that once a response is learned, linked to many secondary reinforcers that occur easily and by chance in human behavior, and the reinforcement schedule has been one of variable ratio, the response is difficult to extinguish. If only school teachers understood this fact, education would take a giant step forward.

The Selection of a New Principal

It was much too late when Joyce decided to get back on the track and meet the train head-on. Early in the summer of 1962 he accused Prentice of acting unprofessionally by submitting some plans for the reorganization of the district. Later that summer Joyce refused to respond to the board's request to consider several names for the principalship of the high school. Joyce presented one name, that of an insider, and the board turned him down. They again instructed that several names be submitted to them and this time directed that Prentice be involved in the screening of the candidates' papers.

During the process there was a movement among residents of Bluffview and Elm Grove to get Prentice to accept the principalship. If Prentice considered such a move, he did not do so for long. At a board meeting following a petition from a community group that Prentice be offered the principalship, Prentice publicly stated that he was not, nor would he ever be, a candidate for that position.

Joyce now moved to comply with the board's request. He and Prentice screened papers and on July 17th the board interviewed the candidates whom Joyce and Prentice presented and hired the one whom Joyce recommended following the interviews.

This did not settle the issue, however. Golden, the insider that Joyce had previously recommended and the board had not accepted, accused Prentice of unprofessional conduct in an article in the metropolitan daily newspaper. While there is no evidence that Joyce had any part in the accusation, the words "unprofessional conduct" rang familiar in Prentice's ears. Further, Golden stated that he did not initiate the article but refused to indicate who did. He retracted the statement attributed to him. When Joyce was asked about the situation, he had "no comment." Joyce said he thought it best for the district if he remained silent. Occasionally one can damn with faint praise, occasionally with but one word. Often one can damn by remaining silent and Joyce chose to act thus. He finally took the course of head-on collision and lost. As hypothesized earlier, his demise was not long in coming.

Superintendent Joyce's Resignation

Following the events analyzed above, Prentice was ready to move against Joyce. Acting informally, he secured the support of Master, Lindzey, and Usher. Utilizing his resignation or the lack of it as a threat, he convinced Farley to insist on Joyce's resignation. (The annexation of Midmeadows was also a stated condition.) It is probable that Farley was in favor of Joyce's resigning ever since his first day on the board, and Prentice's resignation merely sweetened the pot. Finally, faced with sure defeat, Dyke saw that this was preferable to overt board action against Joyce. Probably by this time even Joyce had heard from Daniel. By the use of the same method, Prentice secured an agreement and a contract stating that Midwest University would be involved in the selection of the executive assistant to assist Joyce during his last year as superintendent.

It is likely that both Dyke and Joyce held some hope that, after Prentice had resigned and during Joyce's last year, the board would ask Joyce to reconsider. Often a man in office resigns with the hope that he will be asked to reconsider. This would place him in the position of stating conditions and getting a new vote of confidence. Such action is at best a last ditch effort and one not likely to succeed. The resignation often evokes some sympathy and a momentary increase in support. In the face of the circumstances that create the situation, it is not likely to save the day for the deposed leader, however. Joyce was allowed to resign but he did have a hand in the selection of the new superintendent. Thus, what Joyce did accomplish was to make uncertain the power that removed him and prevent the establishment of a new steady state. Robertsdale was still divided between two power groups and still unable to establish a satisfactory compromise.

The Hypotheses

Hypothesis 10 is aptly demonstrated by the events recounted in this chapter. Increasingly the focus of conflict centered upon Prentice, leader of the new power group, and Superintendent Joyce, if not leader at least the symbol of the old power group. Finally, "the irresistible force met the unmoveable object," and the object, the superintendent of more than twenty-five years, was removed.

INCUMBENT DEFEAT AND SUPERINTENDENT TURNOVER

A chain of events illustrated in Robertsdale and seen in numerous studies involving school boards has been suggested and incorporated into the series of hypotheses offered in Chapter 4. The defeat of a school board incumbent is one of its most dramatic and significant links, as Prentice's election and subsequent career on the Robertsdale School Board served to illustrate. If it can be demonstrated that other communities experience significant social and economic changes which lead to incumbent defeat, it becomes clear that incumbent defeat is seldom a result of social changes in the school district. Rather, incumbent defeat is an indicator of public demand to modify the policy-making center of the schools, including their policies, programs, and personnel practices.

The Robertsdale case further indicates that incumbent defeat leads to a change of district leadership in a relatively short time. It was as if the new social forces, held back by a relatively closed political system, did not stop with representation on the Robertsdale board once they tasted victory. Instead, these forces pushed to acquire leadership of the schools. During this process and as a direct result of it, Superintendent Joyce's contest with Prentice developed and revealed his former political power and leadership of the board. This conflict ended predictably in Joyce's becoming a turnover statistic. His age, long tenure, the nearness of his retirement, and Prentice's committment to the norms of the profession of educational administration combined to make Joyce's removal from the superintendency appear to be an insurgent reform.

The question raised by these events is stated in the hypothesis offered earlier: *Incumbent defeat leads to superintendent turnover.* How generalizable are the Robertsdale events? If they can be generalized, if evidence from other school districts supports this as a conclusion, then involuntary superintendent turnover becomes another dramatic and significant link in the chain of hypotheses resulting in a theory of school district politics.

A series of studies suggested in part by work done on the turnover of city managers provides some of the answers about how generalizable the meaning of the Robertsdale story may be. The roles of city managers and those of superintendents have similar backgrounds. The image of each of these officers and the development of their training programs are almost as similar as their traditional ideologies concerning their respective offices. Both maintain the posture of the nonpolitical servant of the board. In fact, Gladys M. Kammerer and her colleagues concluded that "[city] manager tenure and turnover are positively related to power exchanges."[63] Contrary to their nonpolitical professional images, city managers "tend to play major policy roles in the making of the principal decisions of the city and, therefore, they tend to incur political hazards."[64] Their conclusions resulted from studies of 107 council-manager cities. Parallel research in schools revealed the same results. Thus, not only is it possible to extend the generalizations gleaned from Robertsdale, but in doing so, a bridge

    [63] Gladys M. Kammerer, *et al., The Urban Political Community* (Boston: Houghton Mifflin Company, 1963), p. 192.
    [64] Gladys M. Kammerer, *et al., City Managers in Politics* (Gainesville, Fla.: University of Florida Press, 1962), p. 83.

of research links the political realities of the involuntary turnover of the city manager to the involuntary turnover of the school superintendent.

A group of studies were conducted in southern California which took the defeat of an incumbent school board member as their point of departure.[65] They were concerned with the application of Kammerer's conclusions to the school superintendency. The study involved the analysis of 117 school districts in four adjacent counties over a ten-year history of school district elections. A total of 2,651 elections and 215 cases of turnovers were found. Here there were enough cases to test the hypotheses previously generalized in Robertsdale. The difference between the amount of superintendent turnover in incumbent defeat districts and superintendent turnover in districts where no defeat had occurred was significant at the .001 level. Further evidence supporting the Robertsdale generalizations was provided when eighty-seven of the districts were examined to determine how politically stable they were. These districts were divided into two groups, those with high political stability and those undergoing political change, like Robertsdale. These were examined for incumbent defeat. A difference significant at the .001 level was found which tied district political instability to defeat of an incumbent school board member. Yet there are many reasons for turnover. Some turnover is not political and is, indeed, voluntary on the part of the superintendent. Walden separated the cases of voluntary turnover from eighty-eight cases of involuntary turnover and related this distinction to information on incumbent defeat. Incumbent defeat and involuntary turnover of the superintendent went hand in hand at the .01 level. Finally, Walden noted that it was not necessary for a majority of the board to experience incumbent defeat. One such defeat was sufficient and predicted involuntary superintendent turnover. Walden concluded that superintendent's careers, like other political figures, "must meet the challenge of the political marketplace. . . . Schoolmen must understand that in a very real sense at each school board election there is a silent candidate whose name does not appear on the ballot. It is the superintendent of schools."[66]

---

[65] "Change and Local District Politics," in *Politics in Education*, Laurence Iannaccone (New York: The Center for Applied Research in Education, Inc., 1967), pp. 82-98.

[66] John C. Walden, "School Board Changes and Involuntary Superintendent Turnover" (Unpublished Ph.D. dissertation, The Claremont Graduate School, Claremont, California, 1966).

8

The Successor Superintendent

Following Prentice's resignation there was a brief struggle for power on the board. Both Lindzey and Master
wanted to be president of the board. Both men called Prentice and expressed this desire. Prentice probably could have
"delivered" the vote of the new member from Midmeadows
to either man. Usher, who also wanted to be president, told
Prentice that he thought he had earned the position and
only wanted to be president until the next election when he
would support either Lindzey or Master. Farley was clearly
going to favor Usher as opposed to one of Prentice's men.
Dyke could not be counted on by either group.

Either Lindzey or Master could have been elected if
they could have agreed, but they could not. Prentice suggested a compromise. Both would support Usher, and in
turn, at the next election Usher would support whomever
the two of them suggested as president. Thus, Usher was
elected president following the appointment of the former
Midmeadows board member who replaced Prentice.

Midwest University completed its study in February,
1963 and recommended a list of ten candidates from which
the board might pick the new executive assistant superintendent. They recommended that the new man serve in the

executive assistant position and that a search begin for a new superintendent to replace Joyce when his resignation became effective in July, 1964. These actions were planned when Prentice resigned. In the meantime, Prentice had resigned and taken a position in another state, and it was clear that he would not be influential in the April, 1963 election.

OVERTURN, OVERTURN, OVERTURN IT[1]

As the election of 1963 approached, the parents' organization, CARE, again became active. Attempting to follow the pattern established by Prentice in 1962, they screened the candidates, selected two to support and held neighborhood coffees to introduce the men they had selected. The president of the junior high school P.T.A. was also president of CARE. Mr. Circle, the resident from Bluffview whom Prentice had talked out of running the year before, decided to run. Dyke was running for reelection and so was the Midmeadows member who had been appointed to fill Prentice's unexpired term. Sail, Usher's friend who was defeated in 1962, and the husband of the CARE president also ran for election.

There is an interesting belief which is held by school board members and candidates. This myth is that it is hard to get citizens to run for school board membership. Yet defeated candidates run again and again. Even defeated incumbents who have served on boards for long periods prior to their defeat run again after their defeat. So the myth changes, sometimes influenced by superintendents supported by incumbents. It says, "It is hard to get *good* men to run." This statement omits the possibility that those people running for the first time might be good men, especially those who defeat incumbents.

Can any man believe that he is the only one in the school district who is capable of serving on the school board? Or are there other motivations for his candidacy? Will a man tell you that he is so egocentric as to believe that no one else can handle his job, or that he loves the power and prestige of running a multimillion dollar organization? Will he say that he wants to "get" the superintendent, or that he wants to protect the superintendent, or that he doesn't like the way *his* children have been treated, or that he aspires to higher political office and is testing his wings? Can one even admit to himself that as a teacher he wants to bargin, not at the negotiation table, but all year

---

[1] "I will overturn, overturn, overturn it; and it shall be no more, until he come whose right it is." Ezekiel 21:27.

round at the board table? Except for strong reasons such as these, how can one explain the persistent efforts of some men to be school board members? Altruism seems to these authors to be a naive explanation for a man's repeated candidacy for school board membership.

The CARE organization chose to support the Midmeadows candidate and the husband of their president, a resident of Bluffview. Circle could not be disuaded from running this time. In fact, he was insulted when CARE chose not to lend him support, and he worked harder because of this. All candidates spoke at the "Meet the Candidates" nights at the P.T.A.'s. The husband of the CARE president ran on a platform described by one resident as, "I don't know much about the school or have much time to devote—but my wife does know and does have time." And so she did. She was a dedicated worker for better schools in Robertsdale. Perhaps her husband would have made a good board member. But what he said in campaigning sold his wife, not himself. The typical comment after his speech was "Why doesn't his wife run?" After looking at the election results, this is an even better question. Both of the CARE candidates lost, and Dyke and Circle won. To some extent the community lost faith in a group that would pick such an obvious insider. Even worse for CARE, the school board decided that the 1962 election was a freak and CARE, once well on its way to replacing the "old guard" as the effective power in school district elections, almost completely collapsed. As of the 1967 election, it had never again "selected" candidates.

Shortly before the 1963 election, Master resigned from the board to accept a position in another state. He was replaced by a resident from the old Lakeside area, an area which strongly supported Dyke. Following the election, Usher was again elected president of the board. Usher voted for Lindzey after the 1963 and 1964 elections, but due to Master's resignation, the best Lindzey could do, even with his own vote and Usher's vote, was to tie for presidency. Usher was still board president before the 1968 election, a long time for a man who only wanted the job for six months.

In the 1964 election Sail, Usher's friend, ran again and lost. A resident of Elm Grove defeated Farley, and Usher was reelected. It looked as if the new coalition was on the move again. Following the 1964 reorganization and his second failure to be elected president, Lindzey resigned and moved from the district. He was replaced by a Bluffview resident who also represented the insurgent group.

If one counts Circle (who defeated a CARE candidate and resented that group) as aligned with the Dyke group, then in 1964 the board was split 3–3 between insurgents and old guard: Dyke, Master's replacement, and Circle from the old guard, and Usher, Lindzey's replacement, and the Elm Grove resident the insurgent group.

Both of the candidates who replaced Master and Lindzey, one an old guard and one an insurgent, ran for their first full term in 1965 and were elected. Farley and Sail ran again but both failed to win. The 1965 election failed to change the balance on the board. In 1966 Dyke and Circle ran for reelection. After serving on the board for fifteen years, Dyke was defeated by a Bluffview resident and the balance of power swung toward the insurgents. Shortly after his reelection Circle was transferred out of state and resigned. He was replaced by a medical doctor from Elm Grove. The insurgent group of the board now held a distinct advantage.

It should be noted that during the years 1962–66, Usher had been registering a more conservative voting pattern than he had in his first two years as a board member. Toward the end of his sixth year as board member and fourth year as board president, Usher could not be called an insurgent. This movement toward conservatism appears to be normal behavior as school board members serve over a period of years.

In 1967 Usher again ran for reelection and won. The Elm Grove candidate who had defeated Farley for reelection ran. Dyke and another candidate also ran. The Dyke defeat of the Elm Grove incumbent again shifted the composition of the board, this time toward the old guard of the district, and demonstrated that a conservative candidate still appealed to many Robertsdale voters. Shortly after this election, the Bluffview candidate who had defeated Dyke the year before resigned from the board because he had transferred from the district. Instead of appointing the Elm Grove incumbent who had lost but a few months earlier to Dyke (2078 to 2343), the board appointed Tally. Tally was the former president of the Republican Club and high school P.T.A. who had refused to allow Prentice to speak at the high school P.T.A. meeting in 1960. Thus, the board was again divided 3–3 between the conservative and insurgent factions, if Usher is considered an insurgent.

Several questions come to mind. Ever since Prentice's resignation, which took place five months before an election, four other Robertsdale board members had submitted their resignations. Each of these resignations came shortly after an election. The most common time to move one's home is at the close of school and most companies attempt to provide their men with this convenience. How likely is it that none of the four men knew before April that they were to move in June? Yet they waited until after the election to resign. An earlier resignation announcement would have provided the opportunity for the voters to elect someone else, instead of requiring the board to appoint someone to fill the vacancy. Given the unlikely chance that none of the four men knew prior to the April election that they would resign within a few months of the election, what did the remaining board members do about men to fill the vacant seat? It would have been possible to appoint the candidate who had run third in the April election.[2] Or had they chosen, a special election could have been held. In no case did the board take either of these options. They appointed someone else based on their own "wisdom."

Of the five board members who resigned during the period of this case, the authors have some idea of the motives of only one. Prentice knew he would resign because he was leaving the state about a month prior to his resignation and four months before he left the district. While his offer to resign in favor of a Midmeadows board member was known, the fact that he was planning to leave the district shortly thereafter was a carefully guarded secret. Thus, Prentice's resignation and his pending departure was used to further his desire to annex Midmeadows, a political goal. Although Prentice had said he would not run for reelection, few believed him—least of all his opponents. Therefore lacking the knowledge that Prentice was leaving and given the statement that he would resign when annexation took place *and when Joyce had submitted his resignation,* Prentice's opponents could see a *quid pro quo.* If Prentice played politics with his resignation, why not the other men? It appears that the Robertsdale School Board did not really trust the voters. The fact is that a very few individuals control the politics of education, even in periods of change.

The Ghost of Superintendents Past

As indicated earlier, Joyce did submit his resignation and Midwest University recommended a list of ten candidates from which the board could pick an executive assistant to work with Joyce until his resignation became effective. Due to the lack of time, the university recommended that another search be made for Joyce's replacement. Joyce himself submitted the name of a candidate who was known to have been "let out" in a neighboring district. With the support of Dyke, Usher, and Farley, this man was appointed instead of a man from the

---

[2] In Robertsdale all candidates run at large. The two with the highest number of votes are elected.

list of university recommended candidates. During the ensuing year, the new executive assistant carefully played his role. He never crossed Joyce. (This behavior was not intended nor desired when the role was originally recommended.) He cultivated the favor of Usher, the new board president, as well as Dyke. Together with these men and Circle, who had defeated the CARE candidates in April, 1963, the executive assistant had three votes for the superintendent's position in June, 1964. Two other board members favored assistant superintendent Frank who wanted the job. Lindzey was holding out for the selection of someone from outside the district.

Prentice returned to Midwest for a Christmas vacation and Lindzey related the story and the division of the board. Prentice recommended that Lindzey switch his support to Frank at the last minute and agreed to call Usher who had followed Prentice's lead when Prentice had been board president. He explained to Usher that Frank was a reasonable alternative between the new executive assistant superintendent and an outsider. Prentice said that he knew the new executive assistant had been fired from his former superintendency and that he felt that Robertsdale was buying another Joyce. He further said that he felt he could get Lindzey to vote for Frank but not for the new executive assistant and that would deadlock the board. Usher agreed to think about it. When the vote was taken, Usher was still in favor of the executive assistant and Farley had switched from Frank to the executive assistant. Joyce had picked his successor as of June, 1964.

Joyce's victory was remarkable, though damaging and costly to Robertsdale. He managed to get the old guard to pass over ten men recommended by Midwest University's consultants and select a superintendent who had been an involuntary turnover statistic only a short time before. Both Joyce and the university consultants knew this fact. Joyce's man had assiduously but unsuccessfully sought a self-initiated personal interview on the recommendation of his friends to gain the consultant team's support. Faced with the inevitability of nonrenewal of his contract, Joyce could have made no better choice than he did in selecting his successor.

Prentice had learned another lesson. In politics when you are out—stay out. He had no influence with the voters after his resignation and, therefore, none with Usher. Further, it is likely that word got to Farley that Prentice was supporting Frank and that would have weighed heavily against Farley voting for Frank. Prentice never again suggested anything to the Robertsdale board.

As agreed, Joyce was kept as a consultant to the Robertsdale board. Undoubtedly, this caused confusion about who was running the district. In the words of one administrator, "Joyce continued to pick up his check for two more years, coming in about two days a week."[3]

As the former executive assistant lived out his first two years as superintendent of Robertsdale, the board became more and more disenchanted with him. Perhaps of more import, the entire administrative staff felt him inadequate and took many opportunities to express this feeling to individual board members. In July, 1966 Frank became the new superintendent, but the old executive assistant still had enough support to move into the consultant position vacated by Joyce. Thus, Prentice's recommendation of December, 1963 was implemented in July, 1966 but without his interference. However, the Robertsdale board had made the same mistake again. The ghost of superintendents past still stalked the school buildings of Robertsdale.

Summary of Case Hypothesis

Hypothesis 11, developed from Prentice's experience on the Robertsdale School Board, was confirmed by events following his resignation. Robertsdale had not regained its steady state. The electorate moved from the election of an insurgent to the election of an old guard member. Dyke was defeated as an incumbent, but the following year, running without incumbent status, he defeated an insurgent incumbent. Political strength continued to swing back and forth with the help of some critical appointments by the board. One cause of this instability was the social mobility that first brought Prentice into the Robertsdale district and, less than three years after his election, removed him from the district. By the end of 1967 four other school board members who had not served before 1962 resigned during their terms of office. Of the five men, including Prentice, four were insurgents and the fifth, Circle, might have been if he had been elected under different circumstances. All but one, Lindzey, resigned because their jobs took them away from the district. In Lindzey's case, the fact that he failed to become board president probably interacted with his upward mobility and his wife's desire for a larger home in a more prestigious neighborhood and school district. Thus, the mobility of upper-middle class families with growing incomes, job responsibility, and educational aspirations for their children not only created an instability that resulted in Prentice's victory over an incumbent board member and Joyce's early departure as superintendent but also main-

---

[3] Interview with a Robertsdale school administrator, July, 1967.

tained an instability that prevented the power structure from reaching a new steady state during much of a decade. So it goes too often across the nation. As Cunningham has said, ". . . school districts wait patiently on death or retirement to permit them to effect needed policy changes."[4]

It remained to be seen whether Frank could give Robertsdale the stability and new thrust it needed. He had much of the specialist skills Prentice had supplied. With the support of the P.T.A.'s and the teachers' association, and while holding the office Prentice never could count on as a power resource, it seemed as if Robertsdale's overturning might end. Frank may have been the leader the system had been prepared for.

THE STRANGER AND HIS MANDATE

Not all districts witness the ebb and flow of old guard and insurgent power for as long as Robertsdale did. Most resolve their future sooner. Following some of the clues given in *Executive Succession and Organizational Change,*[5] Robert M. Freeborn reasoned that if the objective of incumbent defeat was organizational change in the school district, and since superintendent turnover followed this, the successor superintendent would be committed to change.[6] Such a man is a stranger to the local district's organization—an alien expert. So Carlson's research indicated, but would boards behave as if they understood this? If they would, the reason for incumbent defeat would also be more surely established.

Carlson was concerned with the distinction between "career-bound" and "place-bound" successor superintendents and the differential effect of each upon the organization. These have sometimes been referred to as "outsiders" and "insiders." Generally these terms are interchangeable, for the outsider can hardly be place-bound, and the insider who does not move is obviously satisfied with his place. The terms are not synonymous, however. It is possible that in spite of one's desires he

---

[4] Luvern L. Cunningham, "Community Power: Implications for Education," *The Politics of Education in the Local Community,* eds. Robert S. Chahill and Stephen P. Hencley (Danville, Ill.: The Interstate Printers & Publishers, Inc., 1964), p. 48.

[5] Richard O. Carlson, *Executive Succession and Organizational Change* (Chicago: Midwest Administration Center, 1961).

[6] Robert M. Freeborn, "School Board Change and the Succession Pattern of Superintendents" (Unpublished Ph.D. dissertation, The Claremont Graduate School, Claremont, California, 1966).

may be forced to leave a situation or place. If his orientation or motivation is place-bound, he will also be place-bound in his new situation. If we use "outsider" to mean "career-bound," then this newcomer from outside the organization is not an outsider, nor will he behave like one. For Carlson the place-bound person is one who first likes the community and wants to stay there. He has a history in the organization; he knows the organization and how it operates. The outsider, on the other hand, may like the community but he would be happy in any number of places. The organization may be attractive but for him there are others which are also attractive. Thus, while it is possible for a successor from inside the organization to be career-bound and for an outsider to be primarily place-bound, it is not very probable.

Insider successors to the superintendency are not likely to be change-oriented. In fact, their investments are likely to be in the *status quo* of the organization whose career ladder they have successfully negotiated to become insider successors. The outsider has no such investment. If anything, as a career-bound stranger to the particular district, interested in recognition of his professional achievement from his colleagues, he is likely to initiate changes so as to achieve visibility. Career-bound superintendents and change-oriented boards seem likely to find one another if they try.

Faced with superintendent turnover, Carlson says, "School boards will tend to elect insiders to the superintendency only when the judgment has been made that the schools are being properly administered."[7] In contrast, they will seek the outsider, the stranger to the organization, when they judge it is time for a change. "School boards give outsiders, but not insiders, a mandate to act in regard to organizational development and the necessary support."[8] Why should an old guard board, satisfied with things the way they are, provide the mandate or funds for change?

Building upon Carlson's work, Freeborn tested the hypothesis that boards without recent incumbent defeats—faced with the problem of succession—would select insiders, while boards experiencing incumbent defeat would within three years of that event select outsiders as successors to the present superintendent. The hypothesis was supported at the .001 level of confidence using the history of 117 districts over a period of a decade. Several deviant cases were studied in depth and contribute to the understanding of incumbent defeat in the local politics of education.

---

[7] Carlson, *Executive Succession and Organizational Change*, pp. 69-70.
[8] *Ibid.*, p. 70.

In the deviant cases superintendent turnover does not follow incumbent defeat under the following conditions: (1) The particular defeat observed is the last of several such defeats, being the last step of a complete turnover of a school board; further, this completely new board has already hired a new superintendent. In such a case the last phase of incumbent defeat follows rather than precedes superintendent turnover. (2) The old superintendent shifts his behavior to conform with the requirements of the new board. This is only a technical exception; it seldom occurs, but when it does, there are usually two or three incumbents defeated in a single year. Thus, the "handwriting on the wall" is clear and unmistakable. (3) There are highly visible violations of community values involved in the defeat of the incumbent board member; e.g., criminal conviction, provable immorality, and so forth. (4) The insurgent group does not continue to obtain the support of the voters and the superintendent successfully fights the new movement. This is a combination of (*a*) lack of insurgent strength and (*b*) increased old guard strength supported and led by the old superintendent. In these cases the insurgents often give up the struggle and resign before the end of their terms in office.[9]

Thus, Freeborn's examination of deviant cases in which incumbent defeat did not result in the turnover of the superintendent reinforces the theoretical explanation of the school superintendent's political role.

A second type of case which deviates from the succession hypotheses which Freeborn tested involves those outsiders who are appointed without a prior defeat of an incumbent school board member. The conditions under which this second type occurs are as follows: (1) An old board employs outside consultants to help select a superintendent; an outsider is then hired and no incumbent defeat occurs. (2) There is no insider (in a very small district) to replace the predecessor superintendent; in such a case old boards select outsiders. (3) The old board, with no incumbent defeat, turns outside to avoid an inside fight. This case is rarer than many school administrations would have one believe. Evidently, the sacred politics of the old guard usually provides a means of resolving such "in-family" fights without asking for outside help. These few instances appear as technical exceptions, exceptions to the conceptual system. They are cases in which boards with incumbent defeat choose an insider to succeed the superintendent. When these boards turn to an inside administrator, such a person has usually been in the district less than four years and is career-bound rather than place-bound.

---

[9] Freeborn, "School Board Change . . . ," pp. 152-55.

ORGANIZATIONAL CHANGE: CARRYING OUT THE MANDATE

The selection of an outsider superintendent is no guarantee that organizational change or the adoption of educational innovations will be accomplished. However, it increases the probability of such results more than most superintendents would like to believe and much more than they would like their school boards to believe. The evidence concerning the chain of events which leads from a community's socio-economic change (through political action involving the defeat of an incumbent school board member) to superintendent turnover with outside succession has particular meaning not only for politics but also for programs in education. There is a small body of research concerned with the impact upon school districts of succession through an outside superintendent. This illuminating research indicates the steps which outside successors usually take, suggests other possible steps, and offers some educated guesses concerning the effect of these political changes on schools if not on pupils.

Three general areas of change are found to result from the outside succession pattern in the superintendency. These provide sufficient reason to reexamine some of the work related to changes in pupil behavior and productivity. The three aspects of the school changed by outside succession are (1) its administative structure and regulations, (2) its personnel and recruitment practices, and (3) its adoption of curriculum innovations. Carlson's work indicates that organizational response to outside succession helps to explain the impact of such succession.

Succession in the chief school officer's role is a disruptive event whether the successor comes from inside or outside the particular school or organization. The amount of ceremony and ritual surrounding the succession of chief officers in societies from the most primitive to the most civilized testifies to the tension generated by the occasion. It may loosen the customary bonds of organization, authority, and communication, modify the importance of precedent and organizational memory, and upset the organization's system of power and decision making. Almost certainly it rearranges the career lines of subordinate administrators, giving new advantages to some and placing others at a disadvantage. The successor pattern is potentially fraught with unanticipated consequences. Each of these outcomes is often aggravated by outside as opposed to inside succession. This evidence suggests that the impact of succession upon the organization, its readjustments to the successor, and his effect upon the organization are likely to be greatest during a relatively brief period at the beginning of the new regime. As the months and years pass, the organization is likely to internalize changes and adapt itself to the new chief officer. Resistance to the new regime often develops after the early stages of change. Hence, the immediate period after succession is likely to be a time of great organizational change.

Bureaucratization and Rule Making

Perhaps the first manifestation of the outsider's administration is the preoccupation with rule making and organizational revision. Such organizational change results in an increase in the degree of bureaucratization of the school. This does not mean more red tape; it could mean less. The changes tend to rationalize the organizational structures, offices, and functions. The new rule changes tend to make the organizational behavior and old policy statements more rational. Various reasons have been offered for this early pattern of behavior exhibited by the new chief officer. Carlson suggests, "Rule-making serves at least three needs of successors: the impression of being busily engaged in vital organizational matters, establishment of identity, and the means of knowing who's who and system's readiness for change."[10]

Less sophisticated explanations may suffice. (1) These are easy things to do. The new man can do them without much cooperation except from the board. The more rational the changes are, the more difficult opposing them will be. (2) His ignorance of the organization and its vested interests and history allows him to operate logically. But the outsider's lack of organizational memory is a severe handicap to the new superintendent. He is continuously faced with established traditions and informal agreements among organizational members. These embarrass him and make his ignorance of the organization's ways obvious to others. These sources of frustration can be eliminated quickly by the outside man through formal rule making. From that point on, he and the old-timers in the organization operate on even terms.

Administrative Personnel

The board gives the outside successor stronger support and more resources with which to work than they do the inside successor. The school board which results from incumbent defeat and which is led

---

[10] Carlson, *Executive Succession and Organizational Change,* p. 26.

by insurgents understands their man's need for loyalty in the organization. One of his tasks, which distinguishes him from the inside successor, is to gain support from beneath. Given his mandate and
resources, an expansion of the administrative staff usually takes place.
At this point he faces a choice not too different from that which the
board faced earlier. Where will he go to find subordinate administrators who will lend loyal support and commitment to change? His best
chance is to follow the board's previous decision and go to outside
sources for personnel. When he must turn inside, he gains support
best by promoting able younger people who may not have been in the
old line of probable promotion.

The process becomes cumulative, especially when there are a number of offices to fill. The more the outside successor turns outside for
appointments, the more likely it is that upwardly mobile, place-bound
junior administrators will become career-bound. As these administrators move to positions in other districts, additional openings become
available. Thus, the process of tapping new sources of personnel may
involve the recruitment of classroom teachers. This brings the community change first seen in incumbent defeat into the classroom.

Adoption of Educational Innovation

It appears that the chief administrator's role is the key to the
school district's rate of adoption of educational innovation.[11] Similarly,
the superintendent's tendency to adopt innovations is related to (1)
his amount of formal education, (2) his social linkages with peer
superintendents, (3) the amount of his participation in professional
meetings, (4) his prestige in the profession among peers, and (5) the
extent to which he depends on local sources for advice and information.[12]

The tie between adoption of innovations and incumbent defeat
becomes tighter when the mandate given the outside successor is taken
into consideration. James A. Reynolds investigated the differential
influence of personal characteristics, training, and previous position on
the rate of adoption of superintendents. He found that outside rather
than inside succession was the only significant variable in those sample

[11] Henry M. Brickell, *Organizing New York State for Change* (Albany, New
York: State Education Department, 1961).

[12] Carlson, *Executive Succession and Organizational Change*, pp. 49-66.

cases he studied.[13] Behind this fact stands the evidence reported in this work ranging from midwestern Robertsdale to the California Southwest and New York State. Of primary importance is the mandate rooted in the changed community's educational demands.

THE POLITICS OF LOCAL SCHOOL DISTRICTS—A SUMMARY

The myth that education and politics exists apart from each other has been repeatedly challenged in recent years. Local school board elections clearly violate this myth. The politics of local school districts is heavily influenced by the absence of two-party machinery and tends to minimize the search for consensus. Even insurgent groups, as in Robertsdale, hesitate to open as much as they might the selection process of board members. The control of nominations limiting available information and the manipulation of board decision making are the handmaidens of avoidance of open political conflict in school districts. The tendency toward closed system politics in education appears to extend beyond the sacred rural community into the suburban secular society. It cuts across monopolistic power structures and pluralistic, multicentered systems alike.

The lack of adequate legal specification of the school superintendent's responsibilities and privileges has played a part in producing the profession's political type. He emerges as the servant who manipulates his board, selects his masters, and educates them to their responsibilities. But any governing system has a tendency toward developing its own equilibrium. Those which come closest to eliminating effective dissent and avoiding public controversy come nearest to the maintenance of the *status quo*. One price paid for this stability is the tendency toward the self-perpetuation of leadership groups at the expense of the goal achievement of the social organization. Another price is found in the widening gap between the particular organization and its larger social universe. This gap widens more rapidly when the social composition of that universe undergoes rapid change. The Robertsdale School District illustrated this condition as it moved along the road toward defeat of incumbent school board members. That road appears to be more frequented now than in the past. The

---

13 James A. Reynolds, "Innovation Related to Administrative Tenure, Succession and Orientation: A Study of the Adoption of New Practices by School Systems" (Unpublished Ed.D. dissertation, Washington University, St. Louis, 1965).

Robertsdale story is a special warning to the superintendent of tomorrow, for the roots of social change and mobility continue to grow. Ironically, it appears that the very success of the superintendent in achieving stability and a high degree of control over his school system places him on the road to incumbent defeat.

The model or set of hypotheses offered in Chapter 4 serves to predict patterns of events. It is a practical model intended to assist the participants and practitioners involved in the art of local school politics. This model emerged from work done over a number of years. It developed from the relevant literature in the social sciences and the Prentice diary. It has been strengthened by later case data and verificational studies in two different geographic regions, each region different from the area in which the case study was done. This provides a model and, to a limited extent, a theory of local school district politics. The model specifies indicators of social and political change within the school district. It further specifies that within the sacred politics of public education, school boards cannot permit the new, insurgent political demands to be resolved due to a lack of conflict resolution structures and ethos. Such a condition results in a "closed" policy-making system that moves further and further from its changing community. Such a situation is finally resolved at the polls when the insurgent out-group becomes the in-group through incumbent defeat. Incumbent defeat precedes conflict on the board and is foreshadowed by an increase of non-unanimous votes. This conflict in the modern district inevitably centers on the leader of the insurgents and the superintendent who interacts with the old guard to preserve the *status quo*. Involuntary turnover of the superintendent then follows, with the advent of an organizational outsider as the successor.

Interestingly, superintendents who lose more than one incumbent old guard member in the first such election seem to adjust to the handwriting on the wall better than do those superintendents who only lose one at a time. The more dramatic the event, the better it is understood. But it is seldom that a series of events displays such sharp breaks from one period to the next. Instead, each moment slides into the next, coloring it and giving it shape. Robertsdale's board displayed such a flow of events as Prentice's alien role changed and the struggle between past and future deepened. Joyce's fate was sealed as the internal realignment of the board took place and with it the necessary readjustment of the board to its district. Nor is Robertsdale an unusual district with a deviant story.

Regardless of the nature of superintendent turnover, if it takes place soon after incumbent defeat and the redirection of a school board, it is predictable that the new superintendent will be an outsider, an individual who has not held a position in the school district or been employed in an administrative position only one or two years prior to the old superintendent's departure. What begins in a school district's social and economic history as a rapid increase in the social composition of the district's population is translated from political activities centering upon the election of school board members to a change of superintendents. Things are quite different when the departure of a superintendent and the selection of a successor takes place without the political shift indicated by incumbent defeat. In these latter instances, the successor is most often an insider, one already holding an administrative position inside the district for three or more years.

The significance of this pattern and the meaning of outside succession for the educational program turns primarily upon the nature of the mandate given the new superintendent by the school board which hires him. Typically, the outside successor's work follows a predictable pattern of organizational change. This includes the increased rationalization of the organization and its rules. It turns to new sources of supply for its personnel. It accelerates the rate of adoption of educational innovation.

Perhaps the chain of events seems too long. The cost of change in schools appears to be too great. The children for whose education the process of incumbent defeat begins are often out of school before it ends! The realistic alternatives available to voters within the present local district pattern appear too few in number. There should be a better way—both for the public citizen and his children and the superintendent and his administration. But these are the ground rules for now. Those who wish to play the roles of the American school district —the board member, the P.T.A. leader, or the school superintendent— might better know these rules than not.

Index

Educational administration (*see also*
    Superintendents):
    historical roots, 57
Educational innovation, 230-233
Eliot, Thomas H., 17
Elliot, Charles, 58
*Executive Succession and Organization-
    al Change,* 225

Freeborn, Robert M., 225, 227

Government:
    chartered cities, 9
    counties, 9
    eighteenth century, 9
    federal system, 8
    local, 4, 5, 9
    nineteenth century, 9
    state constitutions, 7
    taxation, 16
    towns, 9
    villages, 9
Griffiths, Daniel E., 19, 21, 13, 60

Handwriting on the wall, 175, 176,
    227, 232
Harris, William T., 58
Hawaii, 8
Hencley, Stephen P., 225
Hoffer, Eric, 32
Homans, George C., 138
Hunter, Floyd, 36, 45

Iannaccone, Laurence, 19, 22, 27, 28,
    54, 57
Illinois, 23
"The Iron Law of Oligarchy," 69

Jefferson School District:
    Committee for Selection of School
        Board Nominees, 61
    Committee of the Whole, 20, 63, 65,
        66
    class values, 61
    closed meetings, 21
    formal decision-making organization,
        19
    monolithic political type, 61
    open meetings, 21
    religions, 64
    sacred community pattern, 60-62
    semi-autonomous governing, 60
    semi-formal mediating organizations,
        19

Kammerer, Gladys M., 41, 216
Kerr, Norman D., 68
Kimball, Solon T., 57
Kimbrough, Ralph B., 40, 42, 43, 50, 53
Kirkendall, Richard S., 2, 96-103

Learning:
    nineteenth century rote, 15
    pupil-centered, 15
Levittown, N.Y., 25
Long Island, 25
Los Angeles, 34
Louisiana, 14
Lower-middle class, 90, 91
Lutz, Frank W., 22

Macrosystem, 86, 87
Maloney, Joseph F., 25
Martin, Roscoe C., 67
Masters, Nicholas A., 17
Maxwell, William, 58
Merton, Robert K., 54
Michels, Robert, 69
Michigan, 6
Middle class, 91
Midwest University, 222, 223
Minar, David W., 68
Mobility:
    social, 7
    geographical, 7, 52
Moreno, J. L., 13
Mosca, Gaetano, 46
Muns, Arthur C., 24
McCarthy era, 24
McClellan, James E., 57

National Education Association, 58
    National Council of, 58
National Education Journal, 82
Nebraska, 23
Negro urban centers, 95
New England, 10, 13
    town meeting, 57
New Haven, 46-50
    appointment of school board mem-
        bers, 48
    Citizen Action Commission, 48
    control by closed elite, 48
    influence of public officials, 49
    Mayor Lee, 47, 48
    pluralistic power pattern, 45
    political leadership, 46
    separation of politics and education,
        48
    specialist leadership, 49
    superintendent of schools, 48